ECONOMIC REFORMS IN THE SOVIET UNION AND EASTERN EUROPE SINCE THE 1960s

Also by Jan Adam

WAGE, PRICE AND TAXATION POLICY IN CZECHOSLOVAKIA, 1948–1970
*WAGE CONTROL AND INFLATION IN THE SOVIET BLOC COUNTRIES
*EMPLOYMENT AND WAGE POLICIES IN POLAND, CZECHOSLOVAKIA AND HUNGARY SINCE 1950
*EMPLOYMENT POLICIES IN THE SOVIET UNION AND EASTERN EUROPE (*editor*)

*Also published by Macmillan

Economic Reforms in the Soviet Union and Eastern Europe since the 1960s

Jan Adam

Professor of Economics
University of Calgary

MACMILLAN
PRESS

First published 1989

Published by
THE MACMILLAN PRESS LTD
Houndmills, Basingstoke, Hampshire RG21 2XS
and London
Companies and representatives
throughout the world

Printed in Hong Kong

British Library Cataloguing in Publication Data
Adam, Jan
Economic reforms in the Soviet Union and
Eastern Europe since the 1960s.
1. Europe. Eastern Europe. Economic
policies, 1960–1985
I. Title
338.947
ISBN 0–333–38947–6

To the memory of my sisters and brothers

Contents

viii

List of Tables

Acknowledgements

I would first like to thank the Social Sciences and Humanities Research Council of Canada, Ottawa, for the extended research grant which enabled me to work on this study.

I am obliged to those who read parts of the original drafts and whose comments enabled me to improve the final version of this book. I would like to pay special tribute to professors L. Antal, M. Bornstein, W. Brus, H. Flakierski, O. Gadó, K. Mizsei and W. B. Sztyber. I greatly benefited from consultations with scholars in the field. I especially obliged to professors L. Antal, T. Bauer, W. Brus, R. Bugaj, R. I. Gábor, W. Herer, S. Jakubowicz, C. Józefiak, Gy. Kövári, T. Kowalik, W. Krencik, D. Ledworowski, J. Lipiński, J. Mujzel,, R. Nyers, G. Révész, K. Ryc, T. Sárközi, A. Sipos, A. K. Soós, L. Szamuely, M. Swiecicki, M. Tardos, J. Timár, J. Trzeciakowski, F. Vissi, J. Winiecki and U. Wojciechowska, and general manager I. Martos. Of course, the sole responsibility for the views expressed in the book, or any remaining errors, is mine.

Most of the material for this book was collected in libraries and institutes in Europe. My thanks are due to the libraries and their workers: to the Weltwirtschaft Institut in Kiel, Radio Free Europe in Munich, Osteuropa Institut in Munich, Bundesinstitut for Ostwissenschaftliche and Internationale Studien in Cologne, Economic Institute of the Hungarian Academy of Sciences, and the Institute for Comparative Economic Studies in Vienna.

I also wish to record my appreciation for the help contributed by my research assistants: Mmes L. Kivisild, K. Lukasziewicz, S. Gruszczynska, J. Ádler-Vértes, and Mr. P. Slezák in collecting, processing and evaluating materials. Special thanks go to Mrs B. Blackman for the care and patience with which she improved the English of my typescript. To Mrs S. Langan and Mrs M. Samuels I am obliged for their care in typing several drafts of the study. To my wife Zuzana, who encouraged me in my work and helped me to collect and process materials, I am very much indebted.

A tiny part of the material in the book was published earlier in a modified form in two articles: 'The recent Polish economic reform and its results', *Osteuropa Wirtschaft,* no. 4, 1986, and 'The Hungarian economic reform of the 1980s', *Soviet Studies,* no. 4, 1987. I wish to thank the editors of the journals for allowing me to use the material in these articles in this book.

JAN ADAM

List of Abbreviations

For Countries

CSSR	Czechoslovakia
GDR	German Democratic Republic
USSR	Soviet Union

For Journals and Papers

FaU	*Finance a úvěr* (Czechoslovak)
HN	*Hospodářské noviny*
PE	*Politická ekonomie*
PH	*Plánované hospodářství*
SHN	Supplement to *Hospodářské noviny*
F	*Figyelő* (Hungarian)
KSz	*Közgazdasági Szemle*
Nsz	*Népszabadság*
PSz	*Pénzügyi Szemle*
TSz	*Társadalmi Szemle*
BK	*Bank a Kredyt* (Polish)
GP	*Gospodarka Planowa*
TL	*Trybuna Ludu*
ZG	*Życie Gospodarcze*
EG	*Ekonomicheskaia gazeta* (Soviet)
PKh	*Planovoe khoziaistvo*
P	*Pravda*
VE	*Voprosy ekonomiki*
SEG	Supplement to *Ekonomicheskaia gazeta*
GBL	*Gesetzblatt* (East German)
WW	*Wirtschaftswissenschaft*

For National Statistical Yearbooks

Nkh	*Narodnoe khoziaistvo SSSR* (USSR)
RS	*Rocznik Statystyczny* (Polish)
SE	*Statisztikai Évkönyv* (Hungarian)
SEV	*Statisticheskii ezhegodnik stran - chlenov soveta ekonomicheskoi vzaimopomoshchi* (CMEA)
SR	*Statistická ročenka* (CSSR)

For Miscellaneous Matters

CMEA	Council for Mutual Economic Assistance
EM	Economic Mechanism
FTC	Foreign Trade Corporation
NEM	New Economic Mechanism
PA	Production Association (USSR)
PEU	Production Economic Unit (Czechoslovakia)
WOG	Large Economic Organisation (Poland)

Introduction

CMEA countries are now going through the third wave of reforms, the first having been in the 1950s and the second in the 1960s. This book is devoted to the last two waves. This is not to say that the 1950s were not important for the development of the systems of management of the economy. Their importance lies not so much in the changes themselves – as is known, in all the countries the changes made did not transgress the traditional centralised system–as in their by-products, namely the experience gained, and the cracks in the Stalinist political economy caused by the debates before and during the 'reforms'. It was a formative period for future reforms and reformers, and stimulated some notable studies which played an important role in the second wave of reforms. W. Brus's book (1964) deserves special attention.

The reforms of the 1960s in Hungary and Czechoslovakia meant a breakthrough in the efforts to reform the traditional, centralised system of management. In the 1980s, the breach is being widened in Hungary. Poland is also engaged in a reform, along similar lines to Hungary. Recently Gorbachev pledged to institute a 'radical reform': from what we know about Soviet intentions, it is doubtful whether it will be radical in the near future. The fact that the Soviets are engaged in a reform at all is remarkable.

The focus of the book is primarily on an examination of changes in the systems of management of the economy (which can be called with some imprecision 'the economic mechanism'), brought about by the last two waves of reforms in the most important CMEA countries, – USSR, Poland, Czechoslovakia and Hungary – in so far as they refer to the state sector in industry (agriculture is beyond the scope of this study), and the impact of these changes on the existing systems of management. More concretely, the book examines the goals of the reforms (including all the attempts to improve the systems of management; hereafter, in this introduction, the term 'reform' is understood in this way), their structure and consistency and their impact on the development of the systems of management. The purpose of this study is also to discover the problems socialist countries face in their effort to reform the system of management of the economy.

I have given a great deal of thought to the question of how to present the reforms. This can be done in essentially two ways: each building block, for instance prices, taxation, wage regulation, can be discussed separately or the reforms can be treated, using a cross-section approach (market equilibrium, allocation of resources). The first approach has the advantage of giving the reader a good insight into how individual building blocks have been affected by a reform. However, it hides the danger that the global picture will not be clear enough. The second approach has the advantage of giving a general picture, but at the expense of more specific details about the operation of the individual building blocks and, in the final analysis, about the working of the whole system. I have opted for a compromise. The first chapter on the centralised system of management and to a lesser degree the second and the seventh, which are comparative chapters, are based on the second approach. The country chapters are structured according to the first approach; however, they are supplemented by a summary which provides a global view of the reforms.

This book is thus a study of the systems of management resulting from economic reforms. Problems, both economic (economic growth, productivity growth, welfare of the population, etc.) and political, are discussed only to the extent needed for an understanding of the rise of the reforms and their working, and so only few statistical figures are provided.

For reasons of space and also because of the language barrier, which would have forced me to rely on secondary sources, I have omitted Bulgaria and Romania. Though I know German well, I have left the examination of the 'reform' in the German Democratic Republic to my friend and colleague, Dr H. K. Betz. For practical reasons the chapter on the GDR in this book is an appendix, a self-contained study, not integrated with other chapters.

As with my two former books (1979, 1984), this one is of a historico-economico-comparative nature. It not only discusses the history of the reforms in individual countries and their specialties, but also points out their common and contrasting features. To this end Parts II and III have an introductory chapter. I have had some trouble finding a correct proportion between the joint chapters and the country chapters. I had to bear in mind three requirements: to avoid repetition, to save space and also to make the country chapters as self-contained as possible. As usual in such cases, I ended up with a compromise. Therefore the reader who is interested only in one or two countries is advised to read the joint chapters first and only then the chapters of his choice.

The book consists of three parts and a conclusion. In Part I, I discuss briefly the classification of systems of management and the traditional, centralised system of management as it existed in the early 1950s in the USSR. The purpose of this part, which consists of only one chapter, is to help readers better understand the systemic problems faced by the four countries and the significance of the reforms of the 1960s and 1980s. The chapter has also a very practical purpose: it absolves me from continuously explaining how certain new systemic changes are related to the centralised system. I hope to have the reader's cooperation here.

Part II deals with the reforms of the 1960s. It consists of five chapters; the first, as already indicated, is devoted to common and contrasting features of the reforms in the four countries. A brief economic and political background is also given. The remaining four chapters are devoted to the reforms in the four countries. The structure of the country chapters in this part is more or less the same. I follow the official Hungarian structuring of the system of management in three parts: planning system, regulation system and organisational system. Each chapter ends with a summary in which I try to evaluate the reforms from a systemic viewpoint, their effectiveness and, in most cases, their impact on the economy.

Part III deals with the reforms of the 1980s. It also consists of five chapters (and the mentioned appendix) and is structured in the same way as Part II.

Some definitions of terms used in this study are required. First, the term 'reform' must be clarified. As is known, there is no uniform definition of the term. Many economists use the term loosely; almost every change in the system of management or in its subsystems (building blocks) is called a reform. Many call the periodical price revision, though it is without any systemic significance, a price reform. At the other end of the spectrum there are many economists who reserve the term 'reform' for changes which mean a significant departure from the existing system, e.g. an abandonment of the centralised system. In using the word 'reform' they are already evaluating the significance of the changes. For practical reasons I will follow a middle course between the two approaches. I may designate changes aiming at improving the system of management as reform (mainly if the discussion refers to changes in all four countries as a whole), though strictly speaking they do not qualify for the term. I will, however, not omit to characterise every 'reform' from a systemic viewpoint (see Chapter 1).

There is a very thinly drawn line between economic policy changes and systemic changes, that is changes in the management system; in some cases the two coalesce to the extent that it is difficult to identify which is which. This is because both are the work of the government, the political leaders in power. Systemic changes – on a general level – are changes aimed at altering the institutional framework within which economic units as well as the authorities are to work. It could be said that they are economic policy changes on a more general level, whereas economic policy changes are usually, or more precisely should be, changes within the institutional framework and as such could be called economic policy changes in the narrow sense. When talking about economic policy here I always have in mind policy in the narrow sense. Needless to say, the system of management can only be effective if the economic policy is in tune with it.

In this study, I distinguish norms and normatives. By norms I understand primarily a technical relationship (norms of labour intensity) or a relationship between a certain performance and reward (performance norms, work norms). Normatives (or economic normatives) set the proportions in which money variables (revenue, net income, profit) are distributed between the state and enterprises and within enterprises.

The terms fiscal, monetary and money are not used uniformly in the literature. In my book the terms fiscal and monetary policies are used in the same way as in the West; fiscal policy stands for regulation of taxation and government expenditures, whereas 'monetary' refers to regulation of the money supply, credit and the interest rate. Both are used as instruments for influencing economic activities in a certain direction. 'Money' is used for operations where real money is applied (such as money rewards and the use of money instead of payments in kind).

The terms central planners and central authorities are used interchangeably and refer to the ruling bodies of the Communist Party as well as the government with its agencies.

JAN ADAM

Calgary

Part 1

The Traditional
Soviet System

1 The Centralised System of Management

1.1 CLASSIFYING SYSTEMS OF MANAGEMENT

The Soviet system of management was slavishly applied in all the countries of the Soviet bloc for only a relatively short period. The 1956 uprising in Hungary and riots in Poland and the resolution of the following meeting of representatives of the Communist Parties, which called on the leadership of the Parties to respect domestic conditions when applying common principles to the building of socialism, brought about change in the situation. Already, in the first wave of reforms in the second half of the 1950s, some countries had deviated somewhat from the Soviet model. (The Polish reformers wanted to abandon the Soviet model altogether, but they did not succeed.) In the second wave of the reforms the divergency in the systems became much broader. The 1966 Czechoslovak and the 1968 Hungarian reforms meant a break with the Soviet traditional system. The third wave of reforms in the 1980s is widening the gap. As a result of three decades of development the Soviet bloc has more than one system of management of the economy; of course, the number of systems depends on the nature of the system of classification used.

Before the classification of the systems is discussed, it will be useful to clarify some terms. All the European countries of CMEA maintain that they have a socialist economic system or socialist mode of production. The different management systems are regarded as socialist, an integral part of the socialist economic system. Officially the object of reforms is not the socialist economic system. Instead, the reforms refer to the economic mechanism, as the Hungarians called it in 1968, and the USSR and Czechoslovakia recently, or mode of functioning of the economy, as the Poles usually talk about it, or the planned guidance system, as the Soviets referred to the 1965 reform, or the planned management system, as the Czechoslovaks called the 1966 reform, or system of management of the economy as the Hungarians termed their changes in 1984.

From the foregoing, it is clear that at least two different terms are used in connection with reforms: economic mechanism and system of management.[1] The question is: what is their meaning and what is their relationship?

Soviet and East European economists define economic mechanism (EM) as a concrete manifestation of socialist production relations. When it comes to defining the content of EM, differences appear. The authors of a three-volume work on the Soviet economic system include in EM the planning of economic and social development as a central link, the structure of management of the economy including participation of workers, the use of economic levers and incentives to influence the agents of production, the forms of organisation of the economy and the politico-legal forms by which the EM functions (Kapustin *et al.*, 1984, vol. 3, pp. 43–4). L. Antal (1985a, p. 40), the well-known Hungarian reformer, also includes in the economic mechanism elements which are characteristic of a more decentralised system, such as horizontal intra-enterprise relations, the market, power relations, the role of social organisations (this means primarily Communist Party), etc.

Some believe that there is no difference between EM and system of management; others believe that the system of management is an integral part of EM (*Istoriia . . .*, 1980, vol.7, p. 87; Sibirev 1984, p. 4). One would expect that a book on the economic mechanism of socialist countries, written by a collective of Soviet and East European (Czechoslovak, East German, Hungarian and Bulgarian) authors, would take a clear-cut position *vis-à-vis* the relationship of EM and the system of management. However, they confine themselves to the statement that the system of management is based on EM (*A szocialista országok. . .*1984, p. 37). According to Antal (1985a, p. 41) the system of management is a narrower term than EM and includes only the areas which the government can consciously influence–planning, regulation and organisation.

In its communiqué on the April 1984 meeting, in which the decision was taken to accelerate the economic reform, the central committee of the Hungarian Socialist Labour Party (Communist Party) indirectly defined the system of management of the economy[2] as being concerned with planning, economic regulation, and the organisational and institutional system (*Nsz*, 1984, 19 April). The official Hungarian definition will be used as a departure point for my analysis of the economic reforms.

In his classic book, W. Brus (1964) distinguishes two EMs (he uses the term 'model of functioning of the socialist economy') or, for simplicity, two systems of management, centralised and decentralised – or as Brus prefers to call them, centralistic and decentralistic. In brief, it can be stated that the difference between the two EMs, according to Brus, is in who is making decisions in enterprises. In the centralised system, the centre makes not only fundamental macroeconomic decisions but also microeconomic decisions referring to enterprises. In the decentralised system, enterprises themselves make decisions about what to produce, how to produce, to whom to sell products, where to buy inputs, how much to pay in wages and salaries, all within centrally set rules, how to divide up the profit after taxation, how much of it to use for investment, and so on. In brief, enterprises themselves determine the aims and methods of production. The decisions of enterprises are guided by profitability as determined by market forces. This should ensure that enterprises behave rationally. Even in a decentralised system the centre continues making decisions about the distribution of national income and direction of investment. These direct decisions, combined with indirect decisions, aim at creating a framework within which enterprises make their own independent choices, guided by the profit motive. The market mechanism in Brus' model is not a spontaneous but a regulated one; 'it fulfills the function of instrument by the aid of which the activity of enterprises is adjusted to the macro-social priorities (preference) expressed in the plan' (p. 193). Monetary regulators (in the decentralised system money plays an active role) are used to achieve the goals which in a centralised system are attained by assigned targets (Brus, 1964, pp. 86–7, 184–93). These are, in a nutshell, Brus' views; my exposition being brief cannot, of course, capture the niceties of his classification of models.

The 1968 Hungarian reform was very much influenced by reform attempts in 1957 as well as by the pre-1964 Yugoslav model, even though the Hungarians do not like to admit it. At the same time, Brus' decentralised model was also in the minds of the Hungarian reformers when they designed their reform.

However, Brus' decentralised model was rather the product of intellectual contemplation influenced by literature (mostly by Lange's model) and probably also by the Yugoslav model. At any rate, it was not a model produced from a generalisation of an existing management system in the Soviet bloc. The 1968 Hungarian reform and its erosion in the early 1970s prompted a great debate in Hungary about the state of the management system and the ways to reform it. A by-product of this debate is also a new classification of systems presented by Antal (1985a). According to him, it is necessary to distinguish two systems apart from the centralised system – indirect and decentralised. The 1968 Hungarian reform is characterised by him as an indirect system. The decentralised system is more of an objective or aim (or maybe only a dream) which some reformers would like to achieve. If we accept that the indirect system characterises the Hungarian reform, then its description does not need to contain uncertainties. The situation is different with a system, such as the decentralised system, which has not yet been tested in practice.

The following characterisation of the two systems is mainly based on Antal's book, though T. Nagy is allegedly the mastermind of the classification. In neither system are targets assigned to enterprise from the centre. In both systems maximisation of profit is to be the guide for the decision making. For this purpose, the government is supposed to create an environment which exerts pressure on enterprises to behave efficiently. On the other hand, enterprises are to enjoy autonomy.

In the indirect system, planning still plays a leading role as a coordinating mechanism, and the market mechanism is a regulated one. Decisions about investment of macroeconomic importance are still made in the centre. In the indirect system, the soft budget constraint is retained for several reasons. Prices are not market clearing prices; they are influenced very much by government preferences. The monopoly position of suppliers has not been broken enough and replaced by competition, one important reason being that the hierarchical structure still survives. The financial instruments are not applied to all economic units equally; they are selective. Subsidies and tax breaks, which are applied initially in order to allow enterprises to adjust to the new rules of the game, are becoming a permanent institution which is growing in impact. Bargaining between central planners and enterprises about output targets in a centralised system is replaced by bargaining about regulators, subsidies, tax breaks and about what is in short supply (in Hungary, foreign exchange). The profit motive is also weakened by cutting the direct link between growth of wages and profit. In the indirect system the growth of wages is linked to performance, usually expressed in terms of a net output indicator with the help of a normative. In a strict, centralised system, as the Soviet system was before 1965, normatives have only a corrective function.

In the decentralised system, the role of planning is substantially reduced in favour of a self-regulating market. The latter is not really a market socialism; the state still intervenes in the economy not for the purpose of making the self-regulating system work, but in order to apply certain structural ideas in the economy and to cope with fluctuations in economic growth. The government intervenes in the economy with the help of monetary and fiscal tools which are as much as possible uniform. Prices, especially in the competitive sphere, are mostly market prices. The hierarchical structure of the organisation of the economy is dismantled (Antal, 1985a, pp. 134–7). It is a pity that the author does not elaborate on the role of planning in such a system.

I will use Brus' and Antal's classification for evaluating reforms. Taking their classification and other literature as a basis, in my opinion the most important elements of a centralised system which must be dropped in order to be able to talk about an abandonment of the centralised system and thus about a far-reaching reform, are: the abolition of the assignment of plan targets to enterprises and connected with it the rationing of inputs from above, dismantlement of the hierarchical structure which serves centralised planning for the handing down of targets through the chain of management, making the price formation guide flexible and eliminating price circuits separation at least partially, and elimination of the linkage of the growth of the wage bill and bonus fund to plan targets, and their regulation by indirect methods, taxes. In the 1968 Hungarian reform the first two conditions were fulfilled with some qualification, but the last three – as will be shown – were only partly fulfilled.

1.2 THE TRADITIONAL SOVIET MODEL OF MANAGEMENT OF THE ECONOMY

Introduction

The Soviet system of management came into being in the 1930s. Its rise was not a matter of a one time decision. It was the result of a relatively long process of 'trial and error'; mainly the organisation of the economy and, within it, industry especially underwent many changes. By the middle of the decade, the Soviet system of management was more or less complete. The system which arose in the 1930s is usually called a centralised or administrative system. In the West it was called a command system for a long time.

The system of management which arose in the 1930s cannot be properly understood in isolation from the political system which came into being at that time, namely the dictatorial system established by Stalin. Monopolisation of political power cannot be fully complete if it is not coupled with economic power. Strict control over the economy becomes an important precondition for stabilising political power. In a system based on collective ownership of the means of production, this can be quite easily achieved by turning collective ownership into state ownership. In this way, the state acquires a position in the economy which enables it not only to control the activities of economic units but also, as sole employer, to control people as producers.

The system of management thus was shaped by the needs of the dictatorial system. The strict centralisation of the system of management was the counterpart of the strict centralisation of political power. A coalescence of the two powers came about in which the political was dominant. This situation has survived up to now with some small modifications.

In shaping the system of management the strategy of economic development also had a paramount role. The main objective of the strategy was to achieve industrialisation, with great stress on heavy industry, in the shortest time possible. This required high growth rates, which, in practice, meant high investment ratios and high growth rates in employment. Such a strategy of economic development could not have been achieved by market forces; these would have pushed the economy in a direction not desired by the Soviet leaders. The experience with the implementation of the first five-year plan, the need to cope with new and newly emerging imbalances, low rates in productivity, inflation, etc., also influenced the designing of the different elements of the management system. The labour force available for the implementation of the ambitious industrialisation plans did not have the required skills; there was especially a shortage of trained managers which was worsened by the purge of 'bourgeois' specialists (Dyker, 1985, p. 9). In light of the important goals to be attained, it seemed reasonable to use the scarce resources of managerial talents primarily in the centre and to manage enterprises by orders.

Marx' belief that the economy of the future state would be run as a marketless economy (Brus, 1985b) backed up the push to centralisation. The Soviet leaders who waged the revolution and carried out profound social changes under the banner of Marxism could be pleased that the system of management was in line with Marxism (as they understood it) without compromising the objectives of the strategy of economic development.

What I am going to discuss briefly is the system of management as it existed in the early 1950s (which was the mature system of the 1930s), but not in all its details. I will discuss rather a model. I will start out with the planning system which is the fundamental component of the Soviet system. Then the regulation system, whose main goal is to ensure that the plan targets are fulfilled, will be discussed. This will be followed by a review of the organisational system. Finally, I will examine the advantages and shortcomings of the system of management.

Planning System

The planning system in a centralised system fulfills most functions which the market mechanism fulfills in a market economy. The state economic plan (more precisely the annual plan) coordinates the economic activity of enterprises of different sectors of the economy, takes care of the distribution of producer and consumer goods and concerns itself with equilibrium in the macro- and microsphere. Finally, its role is to ensure price stability, full employment and proper wage differentials.

In the centralised system, the market mechanism has a very limited role to play in the first economy.[3] Since freedom of choice of jobs exists the market mechanism fulfills a certain function in the distribution of labour. The role of the market – in the sense of what can be bought and sold for money – is much larger. Consumers are free in this system to use their money as they wish. (They are, however, not allowed to turn it into capital.)

All important macroeconomic decisions are made by the central planners and incorporated into the plans. The planners determine the targets for the distribution of national income between consumption and accumulation as well as for the distribution of the consumption fund into personal and collective consumption, and for the distribution of investment funds between the productive and non-productive spheres, and between sectors of the economy. The growth rate of incomes of individual socioeconomic groups and of incomes in individual sectors of the economy, as well as the distribution of collective consumption, are planned. As a result of all these decisions, the rate of growth of the economy and the growth rate of individual sectors are to a great degree determined.

In their macroeconomic decisions, the central planners are guided by the so-called chief goals which they regard as crucial in light of the existing possibilities and needs of the economy, of course, as they see them, and political and state security considerations. All the other goals are subordinated to these chief goals (cf. Brus, 1964, p. 90).

Production targets for the whole economy are disaggregated

through the channels of management down to enterprises. Consequently, microeconomic decisions rest also in the hands of the authorities. The plan of an enterprise in terms of the size of output, profit, productivity and other indicators is nothing other than part of a plan of the supervisory body, and, in turn the plan of the supervisory body is equal to all the plans of enterprises which are subordinated to it. Each enterprise has a certain role in the structure of the national economy; it is supposed to produce certain products and not others. It is not allowed to diversify its production without the permission of the planners. A switch to products other than those sanctioned by the plan may upset the planned structure of production. There is no role for competition in such a system.

Technological progress is also planned, and the concern for it rests primarily in the hands of centralised research and development institutes, the rationale being that in a socialist country there is no room for technological secrecy. Enterprises are assigned targets for development of technology.

To enable them to produce the assigned targets, enterprises, when they are established, get fixed assets, which are the property of the state, and working capital. If the planners believe that new capital is needed, it will be allocated to enterprises. Producer goods are also allocated to enterprises; there is no market for producer goods. The planners also determine the size of the work force and wages to be paid and they help enterprises to get the needed labour.

To make sure that the demand for inputs resulting from the planned size of production (including exports) is in balance with the available or possible supply (imports also considered), one of the most important methods for working out the plan is material balancing. Demand for produced goods in physical units is balanced with supply in the same measurement units.

The planners also carry out manpower balancing, but this cannot be of as much value to individual enterprises as material balancing. If material inputs are balanced, plans fulfilled and the authorities responsible for material technical supply do their job properly, then judging simply on the basis of the model, one would expect that the producer goods would find their way to enterprises where they are needed. The situation with manpower resources is different; even if freedom of choice of jobs is eliminated, people cannot be treated like producer goods. In direct allocation of labour the authorities cannot entirely ignore personal problems, mainly those related to health. In addition, planning for professional workers must be done four or five years ahead of the need, which is difficult.

The system of balancing as a method of planning also includes financial balancing; its role is to ensure a physical flow of resources according to the plan and to help maintain market equilibrium.

If there is no market for producer goods and producer goods are allocated to enterprises in the sense that a supplier is assigned to them, it is clear that horizontal links (between suppliers and buyers) are determined from above. In the centralised model, the same is true of consumer goods; enterprises producing consumer goods must sell them to certain wholesalers, and retailers usually buy certain consumer goods from certain wholesalers. Only the consumer is completely free to satisfy his needs where he wants to, provided there is no rationing of consumer goods. Rationing of consumer goods is not an integral part of the model; there is freedom of choice of consumer goods, and the consumer is free to use his purchasing power as and where he wishes. The only constraint is the availability of goods.

Resources are not allocated on the basis of price fluctuations and profit expectations, but on the basis of the plan. Enterprises are obliged to surrender the so-called remainder of profit to the state budget, and the same is true about the amortisation fund. The central planners distribute funds for investment purposes according to the objectives of the plan and not according to performance. In practice, this means that enterprises which produce huge amounts of profit may not be allocated funds for investment, whereas enterprises, which do not make a profit or even end up with losses, may receive investment funds. What is worse is that central distribution of investment is governed very little by efficiency criteria and is much influenced by political considerations. Enterprises need not repay the funds or even pay interest on them. The funds represent budgetary grants.

Foreign trade is also planned. In planning, imports are the point of departure. Their purpose is to overcome bottlenecks in the economy, ensure new technology which is of great importance to the objectives of the plan but cannot be produced at home for lack of know-how, and goods which cannot be produced at home for geographical reasons. Exports are primarily intended as repayments for imports. To strengthen the control over foreign trade, domestic enterprises are not allowed to trade directly with foreign firms. This activity is reserved for special enterprises, so-called foreign trade corporations, which are managed by the ministry of foreign trade.

Market equilibrium on the national scale is planned by balancing the total purchasing power (minus expected savings) with the value of the supply of consumer goods plus services. For this purpose, the global wage bill as well as total non-wage incomes are planned for each year.

Since the global wage bill is the sum paid out during the year in enterprises and organisations, the wage bill as well as the work force of enterprises are planned too. The market disequilibria, to which the economy in a centralised system is exposed, result not so much from deficiencies in macro-equilibria planning, as from the planning of micro-equilibria which present the planners with insurmountable problems.

It has already been mentioned that the market mechanism is of little consequence in the Soviet system. However, market categories, commodity market (money) relations as the Soviet economists call them, still exist, but they play a passive role. Prices are naturally not the result of market forces; they are planned by the authorities. When new retail prices are set, their level is planned with the objective of clearing the market. Once they are set, they remain stable for a long time; they do not react to changes in demand and supply. Changes are only made if great disparities arise. Needless to say, such a system, in substance anti-inflationary, produces shortages and a black market.

Wholesale prices perform more of an accounting function; they are used primarily as a yardstick of plan fulfilment. They are used only rarely to influence the decision making of enterprises about choices of inputs. Their calculation is made on the basis of a cost plus profit formula. Wholesale prices are rigid too; they change only after long intervals.

Agricultural procurement prices (at which collective farmers sell their products to procurement agencies) are also set by the central planners. In contrast to wholesale prices for non-agricultural products, procurement prices are one of the few factors which determine the incomes of collective farmers. In the state sector, wages of workers are not dependent on the performance of the enterprise in which they work. Incomes of collective farmers depend on the performance of the farm of which they are members. With regard to incomes as well as the financing of investment, collective farms are treated as genuine cooperatives. Otherwise they are subordinated to the planning system more or less like the rest of the economy.

Bank credit is planned and extended for certain purposes. The interest rate is also set by planners; it is not viewed as a price for the use of credit and it influences very little the extension of credit, not to say investment decisions, which are the prerogative of the centre. Custom tariffs have a passive role; they do not regulate imports, which are regulated by the plan. Custom tariffs are primarily used as a bargaining tool in trade negotiations with other countries and as a source of income.

Economic efficiency is assumed to be achieved by the planning activity itself in the sense that all resources, including human, are used, and by making the plan targets taut. The stress is on macroeconomic efficiency which means that the microeconomic can in many cases be sacrificed. This does not mean that microeconomic efficiency is completely neglected. It is to be achieved by the planning of technical coefficients, norms of labour intensity of products and performance norms for piece workers. Last, but not least, the regulation system is supposed to play an important role in efforts to increase the level of economic efficiency.

Finally, physical planning is of a paramount importance. Material balancing is only one of the components of physical planning, but a very important one. The assignment of targets in physical units, norms of labour intensity and technical coefficients are also part of physical planning.

The Regulation System

The regulation system's function is to make sure that the plans are implemented and, as much as possible, at minimum cost. To this end, direct methods are supplemented by incentives and disincentives. Of course, if the premise assumed by the planners about identity of interests between state and enterprises reflected reality, no regulative system in the form it exists would be needed. At any rate, money incentives would not be needed. The regulation system, as a result of its function, must be intertwined with the planning system. In some areas, they coalesce to the extent that it is difficult to draw a line between the two.

The term 'regulative' or 'regulation' is broad and encompasses two functions: regulative in the narrow sense and stimulative. The first is concerned with the growth of variables within the limits of the plan (e.g. wages, prices, costs, etc.) and the second is geared to an encouragement of the growth of productivity. It is obvious that the two functions are interrelated to the extent that it is difficult in some cases to draw a distinctive line between them, but at the same time they may conflict. For example, the stimulative function can be more effective the more wages grow if all other factors remain the same. Increases in wages beyond a certain point may be in conflict with the regulative function, since they may generate inflation.

The most important component of the regulation system is the *khozraschet* principle, that is, accountability. This principle makes enterprises into autonomous financial units which are expected to arrange their activities in such a way that they can cover incurred costs by receipts from the sale of products and make a planned profit. The *khozraschet* principle also means that enterprises are liable for their activities. It is expected that this principle can induce enterprises not only to fulfil targets assigned to them but at a minimal cost in resources, including human. In this sense, it has to fulfil both functions, regulative and stimulative. Needless to say, the principle does not make enterprises economically autonomous units. Enterprises cannot decide about the scope of their activities and methods of operation. Not only this, they must obey the orders of superior bodies even if these mean losses to them.

The *khozraschet* principle is backed up by a whole system of incentives. Enterprises are not only assigned output targets, but are also promised material rewards for the fulfilment and overfulfilment of targets. The setting of targets is not a one-sided act of the central planners (or lower level of management); it is more the result of bargaining between the latter and the enterprise managers. For obvious reasons enterprise managers are interested in being given soft targets and an allocation of maximum material inputs and labour. To this end they try to understate the output capacity of 'their' enterprises and conceal their reserves. Their behaviour is also motivated by their desire to combat uncertainty caused by shortages, and, even more, because they know that the central planners have opposite interests. Knowing the tactics of enterprises and driven by ambitious plans, the central planners resort to a simple rule: they try to impose on enterprises taut plans by increasing the targets by a certain percentage (the ratchet principle) each year above the level achieved in the previous year. The planned level of the previous year becomes, as a result, more or less irrelevant for planning purposes. Planning from the level achieved in the previous year somehow becomes one of the characteristic features of a centralised system. Needless to say, the outcome of bargaining about targets is not only a matter of the persuasive power of arguments based on facts, but also of personal and power relations (cf. Nove, 1983, pp. 78–9).

The targets are expressed in, and their fulfilment is measured by, indicators, of which the most important are those that have an effect on the size of the wage bill and bonuses. The size of the actual wage bill is determined by the main output indicator, whether it is gross value of output or commodity production. If output targets are fulfilled, the actual wage bill is equal to the planned; if output targets are overfulfilled additional funds are allocated to the wage bill. The allocation is made on the basis of a normative (called an adjustment coefficient) which here has only a corrective function.[4]

The central planners control not only the wage bill, but also the wage rates, which are the most important component of earnings of employees, and the size of the work force. The wage rates set from above are binding on enterprises and change only at long intervals. The control of wage rates is supposed to contribute to the control of wage growth as well as wage differentiation.

Bonuses for non-managers began to play an important role after the 1965 reform. Only little of the Directorial fund (later enterprise fund) established in 1936, whose size was dependent on the fulfilment and overfulfilment of the profit target, could be used for bonuses (*Istoriia* . . . , 1978, vol. IV, p. 61; Sielunin, 1971, pp. 102–3).[5]

Enterprises are also induced to fulfil targets by conditions, generated by the system of management, in which enterprises can fully concentrate their attention on achieving output targets. In the centralised system, domestic production in the state sector as well as in the cooperative sector is separated from consumption and from foreign markets. Signals from consumers and foreign markets have no direct effect on production. This is achieved by the mutual separation of different price circuits. Wholesale prices are separated from retail prices in the sense that the former can rise without affecting the latter. Increases in wholesale prices are carried out at the expense of the turnover tax which is mostly a residual difference between retail prices, minus the retail profit margin, and wholesale prices.

The separation of wholesale and retail prices would not make the separation of production and consumption complete if the fulfilment of plan targets were not measured in constant wholesale prices. Because this is so, the only thing enterprises should be concerned with is the fulfilment of the plan. Consumers' preferences do not affect their well being. No objection could be raised to such an arrangement if the plan expressed adequately the possibilities of the economy and the preferences of consumers. The problem is that this is not the case. This separation has, of course, another important motivation, to shield the consumers from inflation without really depriving the planners of the possibility of changing wholesale prices when they see fit.

The separation of domestic prices from foreign market prices follows aims similar to those of the separation of wholesale and retail prices. It also shelters domestic producers (enterprises) from world market pressure, including imported inflation. Domestic producers sell their products earmarked for foreign markets to foreign trade corporations at domestic prices, and possible losses are financed from a special budgetary fund, and possible profits are channelled into this fund. Imported products are sold to domestic producers at prices equivalent to domestic prices. Exchange rate plays a passive role entirely.

The State Bank, which fulfils the twin roles of a central bank and a credit rationing institution, exerts an important supervisory function. It monitors the fulfilment of the plan and checks on the withdrawal of funds for wage purposes. To this end, enterprises are obliged to conduct all their financial operations through the bank branch in their location. In addition, enterprises are not allowed to extend loans to each other.

In fighting inflation the central planners do not rely on price rigidity alone. They try to avoid a situation which may generate pressure; for this reason, the policy of price rigidity is backed up by planning and regulative measures. One is the strict regulation of the growth of average wages, or more precisely, the wage bill. The policy rule that wage increases should lag behind labour productivity is, of course, also helpful. Another is the balancing of incomes with the value of goods and services available. Last, but not least, is the separation of price circuits.

In contrast to price stability, full employment, the other commitment, is rather the result of the concept of economic development and, of course, the result of ambitious economic growth. Planning has also contributed to it in the sense that planning is tuned to the needs of employment.

Organisational System

The function of the organisation system is to serve the planning system which, as a result, determines it. This does not mean that the organisational system has no impact on the planning system. Once it is established, the organisational system has a quasi life of its own and may influence the whole management system. It should be borne in mind that an organisation can function only if it is 'manned' by people and the interests of all the people need not be in accord with the interests of the economy.

Obviously, in a management system where all important decisions are made by central planners and output targets are assigned to enterprises, organisation structure must be moulded in a way that eases the handing down of assignments and the control of their implementation. Considering all this, it is clear that the organisation structure of the economy, especially its most important sector, industry, can be nothing other than a hierarchical system in the form of a pyramid. And indeed, this is how the economy in a centralised system is organised.

The organisation structure, as it existed until Khrushchev's reorganisation in 1957 and as it exists with certain modifications even now, can be characterised as a branch type management. In industry, this means that it (industry) is divided into many branches, and one or more branches are managed by a ministry (branch ministry). The branch ministries through their sectoral departments (*glavki*) and functional departments manage enterprises in all their important activities. Disregarding the ministries, one can argue that, in the past in most cases, a two-stage management existed: *glavki* and enterprises – the basic unit of industry.[6]

This organisation structure did not come about all at once. The Soviet economy underwent many organisational changes in 1926–32 till the mentioned system was established. For example, *glavki* were instituted in 1926 and later abolished, to reappear in 1932. But their role increased in 1936 when they were given, in addition to planning and management functions, supply and marketing functions (see *Istoriia* . . . , 1977, vol. III, p. 50, and 1978, vol. IV, pp. 37–8; Nove, 1982, pp. 213–6).

In the Soviet system, management of enterprises rests on the principle of one-man management. This principle was already adopted in 1929 and has survived until now. Formally, the top manager of an enterprise is in sole charge. In practice, it is different since the top manager in his decision making has to reckon with the right of the Party organisation to control the economic activities of enterprises.

1.3 EVALUATION OF THE CENTRALISED SYSTEM

This evaluation covers the centralised system as it existed at the beginning of the 1950s; in other words, changes, which were later introduced with the aim of curing some of the shortcomings of the system, are disregarded here. Since the advantages and above all the disadvantages of the system are widely known,[7] I will record them rather than try to give a deep analysis of the reasons for their rise.

A centralised system has the advantage of enabling quick

mobilisation of resources for certain priority projects. Who knows whether the Soviet Union would have achieved such progress in its industrialisation effort in such a short time without that system? One can go even further and ask whether the USSR could have become the second largest industrial power without that system?

Being a supply (resource) constrained system it has a tendency to full employment of resources, including human ones. (See p. 18). Finally, this system is arranged in such a way that open inflation can easily be held within defined limits, provided the authorities are willing to accept the costs involved.

The disadvantages of the system could be summarised in brief in the following way; it is inefficient, hampers innovation, generates shortages and leads to frequent market disequilibria. A system based on annual planning with relatively detailed targets cannot be effective for the simple reason that it is almost impossible to work out a plan which would correctly reflect the needs and possibilities of the economy and the preferences of consumers. Let us assume for the sake of argument that the planners somehow manage to work out a perfect annual plan which meets all the criteria mentioned above. If the plan is to remain perfect it must be an open plan; it must be possible to subject it to changes, as the economy deviates from the anticipated assumptions, including changes in the relationship of supply and demand. But there are many difficulties which inhibit the carrying out of such changes.

The reworking of an annual plan may be a very laborious and time-consuming job, especially if a reworking of material balances is involved. In addition, it takes some time before information about changes which have arisen passes through all the channels of the hierarchical structure and arrives at the appropriate office. In the meantime, the information may no longer be true, since new changes have occurred. Obviously, one could argue that modern computer technology could master all these difficulties. Let us assume that such an argument is fully valid. The computers cannot, however, force enterprises to make a truthful reporting if this is contrary to their interests – a frequent phenomenon.

The centralised system with its incentives is designed in a way to allow enterprises to concentrate their attention fully on the fulfilment of output targets without being distracted by other duties. Such an arrangement would be logical if the assigned targets reflected the needs and possibilities of the economy and the preferences of consumers. Because this is not the case, there is therefore a conflict between what is produced and what is required by the market, and disequilibria in the microsphere must necessarily arise, all the more that prices are rigid.[8]

The centralised system stimulates waste for various reasons. The fulfilment of the plan is measured by success indicators which, in a centralised system, tend to be quantitative and gross. Indicators, especially quantitative ones, lend themselves to abuse, and as the Soviet experience shows, managers utilise all the loopholes possible in the system in order to fulfil the plan regardless of social cost and quality of products. The logic of the system of success indicators is that their number necessarily grows. Their large number impedes the initiative of enterprises with negative consequences for innovation.

In every system, especially a centrally planned economy, rational prices are needed in order to be able to make rational economic calculations which are crucial for an optimal allocation of resources. Prices, which are determined by the authorities and reflect to a great degree their preferences and which, in addition, lack flexibility, and on top of this price circuits, each of which can move independently of others, obviously cannot fulfil such a role.

Centralisation of decisions about investment activities, especially the financing of investment projects from the state budget, must necessarily be a source of waste. If enterprises are not liable for the investment projects, why should they be concerned with their efficiency?

The separation of domestic markets from world markets frees enterprises from world market pressure and thus from pressure to increase productivity and efficiency.

The centralised system, mainly in its three features – lack of market for inputs, separation of domestic markets from world markets and a hierarchically organised economy – puts enterprises in their capacity as suppliers in a monopolistic position which enables them to impose products of low quality on their partners, the buyers. Combined with soft budget constraint, the system shares in the responsibility for enterprise indifference to innovation.

I have mentioned briefly only some of the disadvantages. Now I would like to analyse in greater detail one of the disadvantages which has recently received more attention than in the past, that is the generation of shortages.

J. Kornai (1983, pp. 22–3) is rightly credited with developing a theory of shortages under socialism. In his view, shortages are caused by two factors, both of a systemic nature. One is what he calls a quantitative drive and has to do with the authorities' push for increases in production. In the centralised system, this occurs through attempts to impose taut plans on enterprises. In non-centralised systems, the insatiable demand is generated by the soft budget constraint (by the firm's ability to spend more than it earns). The expansion drive, which can be generated by the taut central investment plans, is the second factor. Labour shortages and full employment are also the result of this process. Kornai explicitly states that full employment 'is not brought about by specific economic policy measures aimed at increasing employment' (p. 29).

Since, in the socialist system, demand is insatiable, the only constraint on increases in production is supply of resources. Therefore, the socialist system in its traditional form is a resource constrained system.

I have only two comments about Kornai's conclusions. In my opinion, his two factors do not have the same impact. In a centralised system, if the second factor is in force, the first one is necessarily activated after a certain time. This is all the more worth stressing since, in the Soviet economy, the ambitious and obsessive plans for economic growth have been instrumental in bringing about this resource constrained system. It is also my view that he underestimates the role of economic policy in achieving full employment. He is correct in saying that the system sooner or later brings about full employment. However, without specific measures, the economies of certain countries and in certain periods would have been marked by unemployment.

Part II

Economic Reforms of the 1960s

2 Common and Constrasting Features of the Reforms of the 1960s

2.1 INTRODUCTION

An optimistic mood bordering on a feeling of omnipotence prevailed in the leading circles of the Soviet bloc countries in the late 1950s. The great political tensions in 1956, generated by the riots in Poland and the uprising in Hungary, had abated; even the wounds in directly affected countries were slowly healing. Economic growth continued to be high and the standard of living registered some improvements (see Table 2.1). Fuelled by ambition and excessive optimistic hopes of rapid economic development, Khrushchev challenged the USA to a competition in the economic sphere; he promised to overtake the USA in output per capita in 15–20 years. For this and other reasons the USSR embarked on an ambitious seven-year plan in 1959; its purpose was to 'achieve a leap in the construction of the material-technical basis of communism and ensure victory to the USSR in a peaceful economic competition with capitalist countries'. This was to be reached through the preferential growth of heavy industry equipped with new technology (*Istoriia . . .* , 1980, vol. VI, p. 229). Needless to say, East European countries rushed to the help of the USSR. They embarked on a new investment drive in 1959, and the new five-year plans for 1961–65 were designed in the spirit of the new effort.

The economic situation soon changed. In the early 1960s the countries under review (except Poland) experienced a slow down in economic growth (the worst being in Czechoslovakia) which was reflected in a substantial decline in the growth rates of real wages, especially in the smaller countries,[1] at a time when the governments were eager to avoid such a situation. In addition, the smaller countries encountered problems in sustaining external equilibrium. The minor institutional changes introduced there in the second half of the 1950s did not produce the expected results. They were also confronted with social-political factors, though in each country in a different way. Calls

Table 2.1 Selected performance indicators for 1956-75[a] (annual growth rates in per cent)

	USSR				Poland				CSSR				Hungary			
	1956-60	1961-65	1966-70	1971-75	1956-60	1961-65	1966-70	1971-75	1956-60	1961-65	1966-70	1971-75	1956-60	1961-65	1966-70	1971-75
1. National income produced	9.2	6.5	7.3	6.3	6.2	6.5	6.0	9.8	7.0	2.0	6.9	5.7	6.0	4.1	6.8	6.2
2. Industrial production, gross	10.4	8.6	8.5	7.4	8.6	9.7	8.4	10.5	10.0	4.6	6.0	5.9	7.5	7.7	6.2	6.4
3. Agricultural production, gross	6.0	2.3	3.9	2.5	2.8	3.7	1.8	3.7	1.3	-0.6	4.6	2.2	0.3	1.1	2.8	4.6
4. Employment in the economy	4.4	4.4	3.9	2.5	1.7	1.6	2.3	1.8	0.3	1.2	1.5	0.5	1.1	-0.4	1.4	0.4
5. Investment in the economy		5.4	7.3	6.7	6.7	9.0	8.1	17.5	13.1	1.9	7.2	8.2	8.2	8.6	7.7	7.7
6. Social labour productivity[b]		6.1	6.8	4.5		4.6	4.0	8.1	7.7	1.6	5.1	4.6	5.1	4.5	5.2	6.3
7. Capital productivity[c]		-2.9	-0.7	-2.1	2.4	1.7	-0.1	-3.2	2.2	-2.8	2.3	0.0	1.9	-0.8	1.2	-0.4
8. Balance of trade[d] [da]	-0.2	+0.3	+1.8	+0.0	+1.5	-1.5	-0.6	-3.5	+1.5	+0.8	+0.3	-0.4		-1.0	-0.2	-1.2
9. Terms of trade[e]						+0.3	+0.2	+0.5	+0.6	0.0	-0.6	-2.0		-0.2		-3.8
10. Personal consumption per capita[f]	2.8	3.6	5.8	4.4		3.5	4.3	7.5	5.5	2.2	5.2	4.2	2.8	2.9	5.4	4.3
11. Real wages		2.5	4.5	3.3		1.5	2.1	7.2	4.5	1.2	3.6	3.3	8.0	1.7	3.4	3.3

Notes: [a]These are official figures based on constant prices; [b]refers to national income per employee in the material sphere; [c]plus indicates the average annual rate at which national income growth outstrips the growth of fixed assets in the material sphere. Minus means the opposite; [d]plus means that exports exceed imports at an average annual rate in per cent. Minus means the opposite; [da]Soviet figures in the first three columns refer to 1960, 1965 and 1970, respectively; [e]plus means that export prices grew faster than import prices at average annual rate in per cent. Minus means the opposite; [f]figures for the Soviet Union refer to real incomes per capita.

Sources: USSR – Nkhs and SEVs; Poland – Rss; CSSR – SRs and Historická . . . 1985; Hungary – SEs.

for reform resurged; their purpose was, to express it briefly, to create an environment for putting the economies on an intensive path instead of the extensive one on which they found themselves. Of course apart from common economic difficulties, each country had it own particular problems.

USSR

In the USSR the fulfillment of the seven-year plan encountered difficulties. Industry did not grow at the expected rate, one reason being a decline in the growth rate of productivity. Putting new capacities into operation lost speed and new technology was slow to come. The situation was the worst in agriculture. The seven-year plan envisaged a 70 per cent increase in gross agricultural production; the actual increase was 15 per cent. Needless to say, the planned growth rate for national income could not be met (Pécsi, 1984, p. 40; Ciepielewski, 1977, pp. 88–9).

Whether the difficulties which emerged in the economy were the main reason why Khrushchev allowed economists to engage in a debate about the system of management is unclear. Probably there were important political considerations too.[2] The debate started with E. Liberman's proposal published in *Pravda* (1962, 2 September), but was soon snuffed out – surely at the initiative of the Party, perhaps also at the request of conservative economists – and not rekindled until late 1963. During Khrushchev's tenure nothing serious came of the debate except some experiments with direct links between buyers and sellers in some enterprises (Zaleski, 1966, p. 122). What is known as the 1965 economic reform was instituted by the new leadership under Brezhnev and Kosygin, which was committed to undoing certain 'reforms' carried out by Khrushchev, such as the territorial system of management, structural changes in the provincial and district committees of the Party, etc. (see Mlýnář, 1983, pp. 28–47). Khrushchev's reforms were motivated primarily by political considerations and they antagonised many Party and government functionaries. The people affected joined a growing opposition to Khrushchev in the highest circles of the Party, which engineered his ouster, and they naturally expected compensation from the new leadership. No wonder that the new leadership annulled most of Khrushchev's reforms, especially when it itself felt that some of the reforms, mainly in the Party sphere, undermined the Party's leading role (Hazard, 1966). This was also the opportune time for an economic reform, for solving some of the pressing problems such as slowing economic growth, declining economic efficiency, and poor quality and design of products; Khrushchev could be blamed for the shortcomings in the economy, and the new leadership could take credit for the reform.

Poland

Some minor systemic changes, carried out in the second half of the 1950s (extension of the rights of enterprises in, among others, investment decisions, increased role of financial indicators, and linkages of bonuses to profit), introduced some flexibility in the Polish management system (see Brus, 1985a, pp. 101–4). This, combined with changes in agricultural policy and reduction in investment outlays, helped to renew market equilibrium. In the period mentioned, Poland experienced high growth rates in wages, primarily in 1956–57 in order to manage the political crisis, which were not eroded by price increases in the following years.

In 1959 Poland embarked on what the Polish economists call the second phase of industrialisation which ended in 1970. The five-year plans for 1961–65 and 1966–70 were adjusted to this objective; they envisaged a faster development of the raw material base and intensification of agriculture and foreign trade. The ambitious plans were backed up by the need to create a growing number of jobs for the rapidly increasing working age population resulting from the post-war 'baby boom' (Böröczy, 1984, pp. 120–5; Golebiowski, 1977, pp. 124–5).

The economy grew relatively fast, but it was marked by great disproportions (e.g. consumer goods industries lagged behind in growth) and therefore the Polish leaders resorted to an austerity policy. In 1961–70 real wages grew at the lowest rate in the CMEA, on the average by 1.8 per cent, at a rate which 'does not exceed computational error' (Brus, 1983, p. 29). Such a rate cannot guarantee all segments of the population a rise in the standard of living (if increases in employment are disregarded).

During the 1960s the Polish leaders did not attempt to carry out any major systemic changes in the management system. The changes made during this period were confined on the whole to attempts to improve the incentive system without really transforming the administrative system. The reform prepared for 1971 with great fanfare also focused primarily on the incentive system.[3] After the riots of December 1970, which were a reaction to the announcement of upcoming huge increases in consumer prices, aimed at coping with increasing market disequilibrium, the reform was scrapped (see Adam, 1979, pp. 27–32). The new leadership under Gierek promised, *inter alia*, a new economic reform (see Chapter 6).

Czechoslovakia

In 1958–60 the Czechoslovak economy grew relatively fast, one reason being that many investment projects started in the early 1950s came on stream in 1958. In 1959 Czechoslovakia started a new investment wave of a much smaller magnitude, of course, than at the beginning of the 1950s, and in 1961 it embarked on an ambitious five-year plan projected as a technical–material base for the transition to communism. To this end the old concept of economic development, with great stress on heavy industry, was to be continued at a much higher pace. It soon turned out that the plan was beyond the reach of Czechoslovakia and it was scrapped. The situation was compounded by the collapse of trade with China and a poor performance in agriculture which brought about difficulties in the supply of foodstuffs. Czechoslovakia was engulfed in a recession; it was the only country of the four under review where national income declined absolutely. Among the provisions which the government undertook in order to cope with the new situation, the annulment of the 1958 'reform' figured prominently (see Goldman and Kouba, 1967, pp. 34–59; Bernášek, 1969).

The new economic situation gradually sparked a great debate about the system of management. In their helplessness the Party leaders reluctantly agreed to listen to professional economists, political scientists and writers. Their reluctance was understandable; they knew very well that the debate would spill over into the political arena and provide ammunition for the political opposition. What was worse, they were afraid that it would again touch off demands for the revision of the 1952 show trials, which indeed happened. The debate in 1963–65 brought the government under tremendous pressure to reform the management system; debates in other countries, mainly the preparations in the USSR for a reform, markedly helped the reformers' cause, at least in the beginning.

The negative experience of the 1958 reform[4] played an important part in the determination of the reformers to push the reform of the 1960s beyond the framework of the centralised system (hereafter far-reaching reform).

Hungary

Soon after the suppression of the uprising in Hungary (November 1956), a team of economists from various ministries came up with quite a radical reform proposal which envisaged *inter alia* a substantial expansion of the autonomy of enterprises (abolition of the assignment of output targets to enterprises), and a considerable role for market forces and also for workers' councils existing at that time. The new proposal[5] became the basis of the 1968 reform. With the dismantlement of the workers' councils, which had become the spokesman for the opposition to the new regime, the proposal was abandoned. Very soon, a new proposal, in which workers' councils no longer figured, was worked out (see Varga, 1957), but this again was vetoed by the Party bureaucracy. At that time many economists and Party officials believed that the ills of the economy could be cured by minor systemic and organisational changes. The relatively fast political and economic consolidation seemed to back up these views.

It did not take very long for the opponents of the reform to be proved wrong. The old diseases of the economy reappeared, this time on a larger scale. Hungary had again to wrestle with imbalances, resulting primarily from foreign trade. Indebtedness to the West grew fast, not because of a deterioration in the terms of trade, but simply because the Hungarian economy was not able to produce enough commodities in the parameters demanded for Western markets. The situation was compounded by the fact that exports of machinery to CMEA countries, which were not as easy as the architects of industrialisation assumed, often required exports from the West (Berend, 1983, pp. 417–26).

It became clear that these problems could not be solved without an adjustment in the structure of the economy and an improvement in economic efficiency. And these required a change in the system of management, and therefore calls for reform reappeared. It is interesting that the political leadership itself, without great prompting, decided to embark on quite a far-reaching economic reform. The fear of political consequences if the economic situation deteriorated was an important factor which induced the leadership to act. The 1956 events left some deep imprints on the thinking of the political authorities. A second factor was a shuffle in the highest body of the Party (which had almost nothing to do with the economic problems) that substantially strengthened the reform-oriented group in the body.

2.2 REASONS FOR DIFFERENCES IN THE ECONOMIC REFORMS OF THE 1960s

Pressures for economic reform varied in extent in each country. The USSR was, no doubt, under less political and economic pressure than the other countries. The USSR did not experience such a great slowdown in economic growth as the CSSR and Hungary. In addition, it was, and is less dependent on foreign trade. For this reason, it did not want to take the risks involved in a far-reaching reform which must be combined with some political changes. At least there is a need for a halt to the excessive meddling of the Party in the affairs of the economy, mainly enterprises, otherwise economic reform is necessarily doomed to erosion. Such political changes, however, may generate dissatisfaction in the ranks of the Party bureaucracy with possible adverse consequences for the highest party leadership.

Party leaders were afraid of a far-reaching reform for other reasons too. They were afraid that a widening of the authority of managers might stimulate trade unions to demand more rights or even the establishment of workers' councils.

In the Soviet leaders' considerations about reform, international power interests also played an important role. The decentralisation of decision making in the economy may strengthen centrifugal forces in a multinational country like the Soviet Union. It may fuel smouldering nationalism and generate demands for ethnic autonomy. Such a development may weaken the Soviet Union in the superpower race. Needless to say, the USSR has always tried hard to avoid such a situation. There is no doubt that one of the reasons for the Soviet invasion of Czechoslovakia was fear of the possible effects of the Czechoslovak reform on the Ukraine. As is known, the Prague Spring promised to turn Czechoslovakia into a genuine federal state. At that time the Soviets were probably also afraid of the negative impact of a far-reaching reform on CMEA and thus on the cohesiveness of the socialist camp. It was believed that introduction of elements of the market mechanism to the USSR might trigger far-reaching reforms in other CMEA countries with the result that economic cooperation between socialist countries would be weakened.[6]

Were Hungary and Czechoslovakia, which embarked on far-reaching reforms, not afraid that the Soviets might oppose their action? The Hungarians made it clear from the beginning that the reform was first intended to be confined strictly to economic matters; there were some hints that some political changes might be a matter for discussion later, but it was clear that no substantive political changes were on the cards. The Hungarian leaders and reformers were much more cautious than the Czechoslovaks. In Hungary, in addition, there was no great danger that, once the reform was under way, the leaders would come under pressure – as happened in Czechoslovakia – to institute political reforms also. First, the Hungarian reform was instituted from above without considerable pressure from below, and therefore the leaders' room for manoeuvering was quite extensive. Second, in the post-revolutionary period after 1956 a climate of liberalisation set in. One of the most hated men of 1956, János Kádár, who allied himself with the Soviets against the revolution, was the architect of this liberalisation. Kádár has proved to be a very shrewd politician. Understanding well the psyche of a nation under siege, he knew what was necessary in order to be forgiven and to gain the trust of the Hungarians. The political relaxations he instituted (travelling abroad, allowing Hungarian refugees to return home or come for a visit) were regarded by many as the maximum achievable at that time, considering the geographical location of Hungary. And the Hungarians reciprocated Kádár's deeds with trust. In the late 1960s, the Hungarians saw in the economic reform introduced in 1968 the culmination of the process of liberalisation and not a step to further political liberalisation.

The Czechoslovak reformers overestimated Soviet tolerance. There were several reasons for this. The Czechoslovak reform resulted from a push from below to which the political leadership agreed with great reluctance. And therefore the manoeuvering space of Czechoslovakia's political leadership was much more limited than that of Hungary. The Hungarian experience of 1956 was not without an effect on the thinking of the Czechoslovak reformers; however, they assumed that the international situation was different in the 1960s than in 1956. The attempts to reform the Soviet system and, later, the refusal of the Soviet leadership to help A. Novotný to maintain his position as First Secretary of the Party boosted the confidence of the reformers. The change in leadership – the coming to power of a new man, A. Dubček, who was well disposed to reform – created an atmosphere of excitement and radicalisation which was enhanced by Soviet threats: these were all phenomena which reduced soundness of judgement.

In the case of Poland the question can be asked: why did Poland opt for only a much more limited reform than the other two smaller countries? The answer lies mainly in the political sphere. Gomulka came to power partly with the help of intellectuals, but very soon managed to antagonise them by his authoritarian methods. As a result he was afraid that a reform might strengthen the movement to democratisation. He was also afraid that the frail coalition, which he put together after 1956, would collapse under the pressures brought about by a far-reaching reform. After the occupation of Czechoslovakia in 1968 the favourable international atmosphere for far-reaching reforms disappeared (Bielasiak, 1983; Kowalik, 1986), a development which was surely not regretted by Gierek's leadership.

2.3 COMMON AND CONTRASTING FEATURES OF THE REFORMS OF THE 1960s

First, let me make it clear that the reformers, especially in the smaller countries, did not regard the economic reforms in themselves as a panacea for economic ills. They saw in the reforms an instrument for creating an environment which would engender favourable conditions for curing the ills of the economy. It was clear to them that, without tackling such substantive problems as the restructuring of the economy, a renewal of economic equilibrium and a change in the strategy of economic growth, the economic reform was doomed.[7] A reformed system of management can only be successful if it is combined with an economic policy responsive to the needs of the economy. Of special importance was and is the restructuring of the economy along the lines of domestic and foreign demand. And this is not a simple problem. All the smaller countries have a huge heavy industry, inherited from the 1950s, which is material and energy intensive and mostly inefficient. A scaling down of heavy industry is opposed by powerful forces because of vested interests.

In Chapter 1 I explained how the centralised system deals with such important problems as allocation of resources, technical progress and market equilibrium, and also how it ensures full employment and price stability, goals to which a socialist system, especially the traditional one, is committed. The question may be asked: have the reforms brought about a change in all this?

As to the USSR, the answer is no, with one exception. Efforts were intensified to stimulate technical progress in the form of new and better quality products, primarily by price mark-ups and additional allocations to the bonus fund, but with no great success.

It was only natural that, if market forces in the smaller countries were to be given more scope as promised, prices would have had to play –

and really did play – a somewhat greater role in allocation of resources, stimulation of technical progress (which was also aided by an extension of the rights of enterprises in investment activity and financing) and maintenance or restoration of market equilibrium.

The rigid price stability policy characteristic of the Soviet Union could not be sustained in a more decentralised system for known reasons. In addition, more flexible prices were also needed to cope with the great price distortions, inherited with the take-over of the traditional price formation system. And, indeed, all three smaller countries tried mostly in a planned way to adjust prices to costs and demand, and to pass on to consumers at least part of the increased costs due to increased agricultural procurement prices and world market prices. Czechoslovakia and Hungary in particular were careful not to let inflation rates exceed a politically tolerable limit. This was also one of the reasons why the countries approached with such circumspection the renewal of the linkage of domestic and foreign market prices.

Full employment remained a sacrosanct commitment on which the legitimacy claim of the regime was largely based, and no changes were made in the methods used to attain it.

In this context let me touch on wage differentials, a problem which was not discussed in Chapter 1. The centralised system produced narrow wage differentials which may dampen the initiative and entrepreneurship, including interest in innovation, needed for the promotion of economic efficiency, and for the working of market forces. Therefore, the smaller countries committed themselves to a widening of wage differentials, a commitment which, mainly for political reasons, they did not honour (see Adam, 1984).

Planning System

It would be no exaggeration to state that most economists in the CMEA countries (in one country more and in others less) came to the conclusion that the centralised system had not succeeded, that steering the economy in great detail from one centre had failed to make enterprises strive for economic efficiency; on the contrary, it encouraged waste, discouraged innovations and produced shortages. Only in Hungary and Czechoslovakia, and to a much lesser degree in Poland, did a situation develop which allowed a far-reaching reform. No doubt the Soviets also wanted to make planning more effective and enterprise activities more efficient and oriented to the needs of consumers, but were not willing to go beyond the centralised framework. As a result, the reform was confined – to put it with some simplification – to improvement in methods of planning, reduction in the number of indicators and a new incentive system.

In the smaller countries (to a much lesser degree in Poland), the view prevailed that a remedy for the problems could be found only in a system in which planning is supplemented by the market mechanism, thus creating an environment in which enterprises would have to produce what the market required. In such an arrangement there can be, of course, no place for binding targets and allocation of inputs from the centre. This does not mean that the reformers wanted to expose enterprises to spontaneous market forces. At that stage, what most reformers wanted was a market regulated by the plan; they believed that society should determine its priorities in a planned way, that the market could be useful if it was regulated from the viewpoint of socialist principles (full employment, reasonable price stability, more equal distribution of income), all the more because some problems could not be solved by the market alone. The plan was not supposed to be simply the model of the future market (Kouba, 1968, pp, 222–31).

The plan was thus to remain the main coordinating mechanism; what was to change was the way the plan was drafted and primarily how the objectives of the plan were to be achieved. In the new system of management, enterprises were to be to a great degree autonomous units, pursuing their own interests. The objectives of the plans should not be imposed on enterprises; the central planners should create an environment equipped with incentives and disincentives, in which the objectives of the plan – of course, substantially reduced compared to the past since much of the supply could be left entirely to market forces – would be followed willingly because they were in the interest of enterprises. They would behave rationally because their possible expansion and the well-being of their employees would depend on the extent to which they were able to realise their products on the market. And the market demand would be to a great degree influences by the objectives of the plan, mainly in investment.

The reforms in smaller countries thus intended to bring about a redivision of decision making between the centre and enterprises by allocating to each the sphere of decision making which is close to its interests and which it knows best, namely to the centre the macrosphere and enterprises the microsphere. Such a solution should allow the benefits of both central planning, confined primarily to the macrosphere, and the market mechanism, applied to the decision making of enterprises, to be combined. In Chapters 4–6 this model, whose second part was only partially implemented, will be discussed in greater detail and it will be shown why it could not work as expected.

Regulation System

The regulation system in the Soviet system where directive planning was retained could not be the same as in the management systems of the smaller countries where the market was to play an important role and therefore plan targets and allocations of inputs (both with exceptions of different extents in individual countries) ceased to be assigned. In the Soviet system the reform supplemented direct methods with indirect, whereas in the smaller countries indirect methods were to play the decisive role, and direct methods were to be used where indirect could not fulfil the objectives of the plan. In the Soviet system the increased role of money incentives, linked, of course, to plan targets, together with some other changes (use of profit and sales as indicators, increased role of normatives, charge on assets, reduction of the number indicators) aimed at giving enterprises more choices and in this way making them more interested in market demand and economic efficiency.

In the smaller countries the role of incentives increased and normatives played a role even in Hungary, but neither of them was linked to plan targets. The economies were to be managed increasingly by indirect methods: by money incentives, fiscal tools (taxes, subsidies) and to a lesser extent by monetary tools (credit, interest rate). Profit and gross income were to become important incentives and guides to decision making. Of course, they could not be as powerful incentives as under capitalism, since, under the existing socialist conditions, managers and other employees were primarily interested in maximising earnings. Money started to play an active role in areas where it had not before. Its role, however, was still restricted by various administrative regulations which were justified partly by ideology. On the whole, regulators used in the market economy were slowly, though with various limitations, infiltrating the regulation system.

The authorities in Hungary and in Czechoslovakia promised to apply the regulators as much as possible uniformly. As could be expected, they did not manage to honour their promise. On the one hand, the conditions in different economic units varied considerably.

On the other hand, the authorities were reluctant to allow even poorly working enterprises to get into a deep financial crisis. Very soon the door was opened for a new kind of bargaining; instead of being over plan targets, characteristic of a centralised system, the object of bargaining became regulators including everything which might affect the performance of enterprises.

At that stage of economic thinking, the authorities in the smaller countries were not prepared to give up evaluation of enterprises' performance as a means, *inter alia*, of exerting pressure on enterprises to achieve higher economic efficiency. The three countries opted for different solutions in their selection of an evaluation indicator which, by its nature, was to become for enterprises an object of maximisation and thus an incentive and guide to rational decision making. Czechoslovakia opted for gross income (only in a small percentage of enterprises was profit used), Hungary for profit and Poland for output added (which is similar to gross income) with managerial bonuses, however, linked to profit.

In the three countries, the debate about gross income versus profit revolved mainly around the question: how would the two indicators influence wage bill determination? Those who were in favour of allowing enterprises to determine the wage bill argued for gross income. In Czechoslovakia, interestingly enough, it was mostly the economists who had fought for maximum decentralisation who favoured gross income, while their opponents preferred profit. The former argued that the adoption of profit as an indicator and a basis for taxation would not allow the old praxis of assigning the wage bill to enterprises to be abandoned which they very much desired (Šik, 1964; Kodet, 1966; Sokol, 1966). What they probably had in mind could be explained briefly by the words of J. Pajestka (1973), who argued in the Polish debate against profit that, under socialism, the managers are not a sufficiently strong social power to be able to resist pressure from the personnel for wage increases. In other words, if managers were to be given the right to determine wages without any constraint being put on profit, they might be induced to pay excessive wages and thus reduce the amount of profit.

Some Hungarian economists objected to gross income, believing that enterprises should not be allowed to determine how much of gross income should be used for wages since their decisions might be at the expense of investment (M. Timár, 1973, pp. 56–7); others believed that application of gross income would lead to great wage differentials and undermine the principle of distribution according to work (see Csikós-Magy, 1965).[8]

The creation of a rational price system was perhaps the most formidable task which the central planners faced. The old price system was in so many respects different from what one would regard as a rational system: it was rigid, distorted (prices were set arbitrarily without due regard to scarcity also because wholesale prices had to promote investment and retail prices had to fulfil social functions), and the individual price circuits making up the price system were separated. To change the existing price system into a rational one would require a radical restructuring of prices which could not be achieved without great social tension.

All four countries carried out wholesale price reforms (in Hungary and Poland they were called producer price reforms) without really changing the level of retail prices. The purpose of the reforms, which brought about an increase in the level of wholesale prices and changes in their relativities, was to reflect social costs better, to accommodate the newly introduced charge on assets and the rearrangement of the incentive system and to adjust wholesale prices to the new system of regulation of enterprise incomes (smaller countries). All four countries abandoned the old price type formula, according to which profit mark-up was calculated. The USSR opted for the so-called production price type (profit calculated according to employed capital) whereas the other three countries chose the so-called two-channel type: profit calculated as a percentage of capital employed and wage bill used.

The CSSR and Hungary (and Poland to a lesser degree) also introduced some flexibility in price formation and control in order to give greater room to market forces. Price determination of certain products – primarily those produced in competitive conditions – was left to an agreement between suppliers and buyers.

The smaller countries also took the first steps to renew the linkage between individual price circuits and to eliminate irrational consumer price relativities. As is known, these countries embraced the Soviet consumer price system in the beginning of the 1950s; this meant that prices of foodstuffs and services were relatively low, whereas prices of industrial consumer goods were high. Both problems had to be solved by a reform of the turnover tax – the former (as long as it pertained to the linkage of wholesale and consumer prices) by a reconstruction of the turnover tax and the latter by the elimination of the excessive tax rate differentiation.

Considering that such far-reaching restructuring of the turnover tax would have meant great changes in composition of demand and consumer prices, and a redistribution of incomes at the expense of low income groups and pensioners, it was no wonder that a decision was taken in Czechoslovakia and Hungary to carry out the reform in stages. Taking such an approach was all the more warranted in that no free capacities in light industry existed to satisfy the shift in demand (see Šik, 1967; Adam, 1974a, pp. 186–9; Csikós-Nagy, 1969, p. 140).[9]

In the first stage, the turnover tax reform was confined to a unification of tax for similar products (within individual groups of products). The newly created rates were already a fixed percentage of wholesale or consumer prices[10] (Koudelka, Libnar and Havel, 1968; Csikós-Nagy, 1968; Cholewicka-Gozdzik, 1974, p. 174).

In the field of taxation, only in smaller countries were changes made. The reforms completed the process of introduction of a tax on profit. In addition, taxation was used for controlling wage and employment growth. However, taxation was not applied uniformly; a whole system of tax reductions and exemptions was used.

In wage-bill regulation and in determination of wages for individual workers, there was predictably no uniform approach. The Soviet reform made only minor changes, whereas the other three countries, primarily Czechoslovakia, gave enterprises greater freedom in determining the wage bill. Interestingly enough, in this area the reforms went the furthest. Apparently, the political authorities felt that wage growth could be controlled most effectively by indirect methods and that greater autonomy for enterprises would reduce the authorities' exposure to criticism in a very important area and thus achieve a decentralisation of exposure to discontent. While, in the traditional system, the actual wage-bill depended on the extent of fulfilment of plan targets regardless of the marketability of the products produced, enterprises in the reformed systems were supposed to 'earn' funds for wages. In Czechoslovakia most enterprises got the right to determine the wage bill; the growth of wages was controlled by taxes. In Hungary and Poland, wage growth was dependent on performance and a normative and, in the former, also on taxes.

In the determination of wages for individual workers, no important changes were made in any country. In Hungary, some flexibility was introduced into the system of wage rates.

All four countries made some changes in the incentive system. In the Soviet Union, this is the area where the reform went the furthest. In the Soviet Union, Poland and Hungary a special incentive fund was established and it was not only fed from but also, and this was a novelty, determined by profit (in the USSR only to a degree), whereas in Czechoslovakia there was no special incentive fund in most enterprises (enterprises were given the right to determine whether the wage bill would be used for wages or for bonuses).

In employment regulation the difference between the Soviet reform and that of the other three countries was not so large as one would expect. The extent of labour shortages had an almost greater effect than the desire for systemic consistency. The Soviet reform eliminated compulsory limits for employment at the enterprise level as did Hungary and Poland. Czechoslovakia went half-way because of huge labour shortages. All four countries expected an improvement in labour economy from wage and bonus regulation. Taxes for stimulating labour economy were used primarily by Czechoslovakia.

If planning has to be the main coordinating mechanism, its role must be felt primarily in investment, which is crucial for economic growth, the structure (and restructuring) of the economy, technical progress, and improvement in working and living conditions. And therefore, central planners, even in an indirect system, are reluctant to forego control over investment.

As already mentioned, the application of the administrative system to investment activity and financing generates waste and economic inefficiency. It encourages over-investment with all its unfavourable consequences; it leads to an extension of time needed for the completion of investment projects, and, as a result, the volume of unfinished investment projects has a tendency to increase. Under conditions of rapidly developing technology, the excessively long lead time makes many investment projects obsolete before they can be put into operation. In addition, over-investment with its consequences produces inflationary pressures.

Needless to stress, all four countries were interested in coping with the shortcomings mentioned. The Soviets tried to involve enterprises in financing investment without really losing any control over investment decisions. The other three countries opted in one or another form for the pre-1964 Yugoslav system which used regulation of investment activities as an important tool for making enterprises follow the objectives of the state plan. Enterprises were given the right to make decisions about certain investment projects and were obliged to finance them from their own resources. However, taxation of enterprises and disposal of the enterprise amortisation fund were engineered in such a way that enterprises would not have enough funds for investment and would be forced to seek interest-bearing credit from the state bank. And the bank distributed loans for investment activities according to two criteria: objectives of the plan and returns on investment. If the two criteria clashed, the first mostly prevailed. In other words, the bank did, to a great degree, the job which is done by central planners in a centralised system. As a result, the interest rate, which was supposed to play a role in regulating decentralised investment activities by influencing the returns on investment, was reduced to an ineffective tool.

In line with the investment system even the smaller countries left the mono-bank system intact. In smaller countries some of the supervisory functions of the bank (checks on withdrawal of funds for wage purposes) were eliminated as well as some of the restrictions on extension of credit. Since state enterprises became involved in all the countries in financing investment, long-term credit became available.

There was again a difference in approach to foreign trade in the Soviet reform and in the reforms in the smaller countries. The Soviet authorities did not feel a need for changes for either systemic or economic reasons. The Soviet reform, as mentioned, did not go beyond the centralised framework, and foreign trade did not play an important part in the Soviet economy. At that time, the role of new technology had not yet taken on such prominence as in the 1970s and 1980s. Therefore, the Soviets could stick to the traditional concept of foreign trade.

In the smaller countries, for systemic and economic reasons, it was regarded as essential to make enterprises feel the effects of foreign market pressure. To this end, the first steps towards a renewal of linkage between domestic and world market prices were taken; exported and imported goods were supposed to be priced at world market prices recalculated in domestic currency by a conversion ratio which was based on the cost needed to produce one unit of foreign exchange by exports. The effects of world market prices on domestic production were, however, limited (the smallest in Poland). The smaller countries shielded their economies from foreign competition and imported inflation by subjecting imports to strict licensing and by subsidising directly or indirectly imported goods. Because the conversion ratio was based on average costs, the countries had also to subsidise a great portion of exports.

Before the reforms, foreign trade was carried on the account of the state budget; the reforms shifted the risks involved in foreign trade to a great extent to foreign trade corporations and producing enterprises, some of which have received direct access to foreign markets.

Organisational System

The reforms of the 1960s did not bring any important changes in hierarchical relations, except in Poland. The concentration in industry, which was carried out by administrative methods and which preceded the reforms in Czechoslovakia and Hungary, was left intact. Only in the last stage of the reform in Czechoslovakia was there strong pressure for basing the grouping of enterprises in associations on economic principles. In both countries, vested interests impeded changes, though they were of crucial importance for the expansion of the autonomy of enterprises and the unfolding of market forces. In Poland the reform itself was based on large enterprises. In the USSR the process of concentration in industry started in earnest when the reform ended.

In the smaller countries, there was a shift in decision-making power from branch ministries, which lost influence when output targets ceased to be assigned, to functional ministries and some state agencies. The reforms in Hungary and Czechoslovakia, especially the latter, increased the role of the trade unions and also contributed to a political liberalisation; in the CSSR the decision making in enterprises was democratised to some extent.

2.4 CONCLUDING REMARKS

Only the Hungarian reform has survived; all the other reforms were short-lived. Even the Hungarian reform came to a halt in 1972–73; not only this, but Hungary experienced recentralisation in some areas and an erosion of the main principles of the reform. The watering down of the reform without its abandonment made it easier in the 1980s, when a new wave of reforms started, to return to its original principles and goals and in many areas to go beyond them.

As will be shown later, the reasons for the abandonment of the reforms together with the reform's erosion in Hungary were quite different. There was, however, a common reason if Czechoslovakia is disregarded, a deterioration in the economic situation, a factor of different weight in individual countries. In the face of the economic setback, one of the measures to cope with the new situation was to turn against the reform which was all the easier since in all the countries an opposition to reforms existed in the political leadership. One must agree with Brus (1979) that the reforms had 'low priority in the list of serious economic alternatives'.

Though the reforms of the 1960s, except the Hungarian, were short-lived and thus were not given a chance to stand the test of time, they made some impact on the management system. None of the countries returned entirely to the old system; some elements of the reform were retained. In addition, the reformers gained some experience, which is being used in the reforms of the 1980s.

Of course, of great importance is the survival of the Hungarian reform, not only because it has transformed the system from centralised to indirect, proven its viability in the face of a deterioration in terms of trade, and managed to succeed in an area where the centralised system has failed, namely, in renewing and maintaining market equilibrium, but also because it is a 'live' laboratory for reformers inside and outside the country (see Chapter 7).

3 The Soviet Economic Reform of 1965

3.1 INTRODUCTION

In 1964 the Soviets started to experiment with new methods of management, first of all in two garment enterprises and later in several hundred enterprises, almost all of which were in light industry. Experimenting enterprises were assigned only a few targets – in many only sales and profit – and some had to determine their output mix in line with orders received from buyers (Felker, 1966, pp. 82–93). It was no accident that the experiments were applied in light industry. There, planning is the most difficult, since, in order to achieve and maintain market equilibrium it is necessary to react promptly to incessantly changing demand. The failing of the planning system in light industry was reflected in shortages at a time when huge unsalable inventories existed (Katz, 1974, p. 106).

The reform itself was approved at a Central Committee meeting in September 1965 after a report by A. N. Kosygin (1966, pp. 3–46). The principles of the reform were by no means as far-reaching as the experiments indicated; enterprises in general did not receive the leeway which the experimenting units had. In addition, the later an enterprise joined the experiment, the narrower was its autonomy (Schroeder, 1968).

The reform was intended to be implemented in 1966–68. However, it started out slowly; in the first year, only 8 per cent of enterprises in terms of volume of output were converted to the new system. By the end of 1968, the number was 72 per cent. Enterprises with a good performance were first transferred to the new system (Bush, 1970). By the end of 1970, the transfer in industry was more or less completed (Katz, 1974, pp. 182–3), but it still continued in other sectors of the economy.

3.2 PLANNING SYSTEM

As already indicated above, no major changes in the planning system have been brought about by the reform. It was not the intention of the

40

central authorities to reduce the role of planning. What they really wanted was, on the one hand, to improve the methodology of planning as the coordinator of economic activities and, on the other, to improve the implementation of the plan objectives. The first goal was to be achieved, *inter alia*, by making the five-year plan the 'basic form of planning' and by breaking down the important figures of the five-year plan into annual plans. In addition, enterprises were to draw up a five-year plan apart from the annual plans, and, in this way, their plans could be fully synchronised with the national plan. In his speech, A. N. Kosygin complained that targets for the seven-year plan were not broken down into annual targets,[1] and enterprises were left in the dark about future plan targets. Finally, the planning process was to be improved by using computers and expanding the balancing methods (see Kosygin, 1966; Feiwel, 1972, pp. 275–6).

The provisions for achieving the second goal formed the focus of the reform. To spur managerial initiative the reform promised to enlarge the autonomy of enterprises directly by giving them a certain leeway in decision making about planning, incentives, employment, profit and investment, and indirectly by reducing the number of assigned targets (indicators) and by using economic levers (incentives and disincentives) for guiding enterprises to the fulfilment of plan objectives (*Istoriia . . .*, 1980, p. 88). The number of targets was reduced from the former 38–40 to nine (volume of goods to be sold, main product mix, wage bill, total profit and rate of profit, payments to and allocations from the budget, volume of centralised investment, targets for new technology and targets for materials and equipment) (Schroeder, 1971; Campbell, 1968).

At first glance the reduction in the number of indicators can be interpreted as a major change, all the more since gross value of output (which is a stimulus to waste and market disequilibrium) was no longer among the success indicators; sales and profits figured prominently instead. To put this in perspective, one must add several explanatory notes. As will be shown later, gross value of output was not fully eliminated; it was still kept as a regulator of wage-bill growth and used to calculate productivity. In addition, the ministries' targets were continuously expressed in terms of gross value of output (Katz, 1974, p. 143). Nor did the elimination of a certain target mean that enterprises could act entirely freely about it, or that the central authorities gave up control over it; enterprises were obliged to submit their plans to the superior authorities for approval. Only after this could enterprises work out their production and financial plan which no longer required approval (Sharpe, 1966, p. 300). In addition, enterprises were not free to determine what they would produce (as mentioned, main product mix was still a target) and where they would buy or sell their inputs. True, Kosygin promised to introduce a market for inputs gradually, but this promise was honoured to a negligible degree only.

3.3 REGULATION SYSTEM

As mentioned in Chapter 2, the Soviet reform supplemented direct methods by indirect, mainly by increasing the role of incentives. What is also of importance is that sales and profit became success indicators. This was, no doubt, progress, especially if one considers that the central planners put aside ideological inhibitions when agreeing to link the calculation of profitability to invested capital. However, the new success indicators could play only a limited role under conditions where enterprises enjoyed only a little autonomy, and where the profit remaining after enterprise funds had been replenished, had to be surrendered to the state budget.

The reform set rules for the order and the way in which profit should be distributed. In the traditional Soviet system, there was no place for a genuine tax on profit, set in advance, and the reform did not bring about change in this regard. The only quasi-tax introduced (called a charge) was on fixed assets and working capital, the rationale being to make enterprises more interested in the economical use of capital. The new tax was to become an important source of revenues at a time when yields from the turnover tax were declining as a result of the wholesale price revision of 1966–67.

Enterprises were obliged to use their profit first to pay the capital charge and interest on bank credit. After these payments were made, profit could be used for feeding three incentive funds. Next in order was the use of profit for the repayment of credit, expansion of working capital, and so on. The difference between the sum of produced profit and the allowable payments from profit was surrendered to the budget as the free remainder of profit (see 'Decisions' of the Central Committee of the CPSU and Council of Ministers of 4 October, 1965, hereafter 'decisions of 1965') (*Khoziaistvennaia* . . . , 1969, p. 121).

Incentive System

The reform introduced three funds: two for stimulating managers and workers, a fund for material stimulation (hereafter bonus fund) and a fund for social and cultural needs, and one for stimulating the enterprise as a whole, which we will call the development fund. All three funds were fed from profit (the development fund from other sources also) and depended fully or partly on two success indicators, so-called fund-creating indicators, sales (or total profit) and rate of profit.

The bonus fund (which was separate from the wage bill) was no longer supposed to be fixed directly by the authorities; its size was to result from the rate of increase in sales (or profit)[2] over the previous year and the achieved level in profitability, and the normative which was expressed in terms of a fraction of a percentage of the wage bill.[3] The normative varied by branches of industry and also by groups of enterprises. This 'automaticity' in fund formation aimed at boosting the initiative of enterprises in voluntarily proposing taut plans, which of course had to be approved by the authorities. The planners hoped to find in this new arrangement a cure for the reluctance of enterprises to accept taut plans and thus to reveal reserves. Why should enterprises be reluctant to change their behaviour and not accept taut plans, if they have the assurance that for every increase in sales (or profit) and for every per cent of profitability achieved, they will be given an allocation to the bonus fund? Why should the centre impose higher and higher targets every year if enterprises are willing to improve their performance out of sheer material interest?

In order to be surer that the new incentive system would act in this direction, the planners applied two further provisions, both new. The new system penalised both over-fulfilment and under-fulfilment of the plan. If an enterprise over-fulfilled both or one of the fund-forming indicators, the normative for that portion which exceeded the plan was reduced by at least 30 per cent. A roughly similar disincentive was specified for under-fulfilment of plans (Egiazarian, 1976, p. 155; *Khoziaistvennaia* . . . , 1969, p. 245; Kletskii and Risina, 1970). This provision aimed not only at encouraging enterprises, as already mentioned, to accept demanding plans, but also at discouraging them from committing themselves to unrealistic plans. The second provision involved the introduction of long-term normatives, which was meant to ensure that normatives would not change annually, and thus to help to extend the managers' time horizon in decision making.

The type of indicators chosen gives evidence not only that a new approach was being taken to incentives, but also that a certain amount of thought was being given to the idea of offsetting the adverse effects of linking wage growth to output targets. As is known, such a linkage made enterprises interested only in the fulfilment of targets and indifferent to the situation in the market. The linking of the bonus fund to sales and profitability had to make enterprises interested in market demand and quality, and also in greater economic efficiency.

Interest in demand and quality was to be strengthened by developing direct ties between producing and consuming enterprises with the help of a system of contracts. Of course, the direct ties were not supposed to replace the central distribution of important means of production; their function was only to turn the targets set from above into contracts about specific deliveries (Koldomasov, 1965).

What was also of importance was that rate of profit was assigned an important role and was defined in a new way. Usually rate of profit was defined as a ratio of profit to production costs; for the first time, it was calculated as a ratio of net profit to invested capital. Rate of profit thus defined had to induce enterprises to become more efficient by a better utilisation of capital (see Adam, 1973).

Price System

The economic reform did not bring major changes to the price system. The only provision worth noting was the industrial wholesale price 'reform' implemented in 1966–67. Even this was only a belated periodic revision of prices (the last one was in 1955). The price revision reflected the needs of the economic reform in quantitative rather than qualitative terms; it was not marked by any major systemic changes which would transgress the framework of the centralised system. The new prices continued to be a result of administrative decisions, based on the well-known formula of cost plus profit. As will be shown later, only the distribution of profit into prices was this time made differently than in the past.

The central planners put some important constraints on the wholesale price revision: it was not allowed to affect either consumer prices[4] or most input prices for agriculture in order not to upset the agricultural procurement prices (Rzheshevskii, 1971). The reform did not even have as a goal the elimination of the separation of the price circuits.

The price revision had to fulfil several goals: (1) to accommodate higher expenditure from profit; (2) to improve price relativities by reflecting more accurately costs in prices and, in this way, contribute to higher economic efficiency; (3) to create more favourable conditions for technological progress by encouraging improvement in the quality of products.

(1) Before 1965 the bulk of the bonuses came from the wage bill, which was included in the cost of production, and in small part from the so-called enterprise fund (previously the Director's fund) which could also be used for some small investment (see Sielunin, 1971). The three newly introduced funds (without entirely abolishing bonuses from the wage bill) were to be financed from profit. In addition, bank interest and a newly introduced charge on capital assets, as well as differential rent payable in some extractive branches, were also to be financed from profit. Therefore, profitability, and thus the level of prices, had to be increased in order to enable enterprises to discharge the new commitments. Finally, the desire of the authorities to make all branches profitable also worked in this direction. And, indeed, wholesale prices were increased by 8 per cent; a 15 per cent rate of profit on the average (against the 3–5 per cent in the past) was allowed. However, the resulting profitability was much higher. Needless to say, price increases and profit rate changes varied considerably by branches of industry (Schroeder, 1969; Grossman, 1977, p. 144).

(2) The price increases were quite differentiated and deliberately so in order to reduce considerably the huge inter-branch and inter-enterprise differentiation in profitability.[5] Many extracting enterprises were operating at planned losses or at very low profitability. On the other hand, machinery managed to achieve quite a high rate of profit by utilising (or more precisely abusing) the institution of 'temporary prices'. As a result of the price reform, oil prices increased by 230 per cent and coal went up 78 per cent, whereas prices of machinery and metalworking remained the same (Feiwel, 1972, p. 350; Schroeder, 1969; Gusarov, 1973, p. 231).

It would be wrong to assume that, as a result of the reform, all enterprises achieved equal terms in profitability. Profitability continued to differ (Bornstein, 1976, pp. 22–4), one reason being that many enterprises managed to pad costs. Not only this, unprofitable enterprises continued to exist, though to a much smaller extent. The principle that costs for the same products must be calculated on the basis of the average costs of enterprises with average conditions usually creates unprofitable enterprises (see also Feiwel, 1972, p. 354).

(3) In his report at the Central Committee meeting, Kosygin stated that prices must play an important role in improving quality, a problem closely linked to the pricing of new products. Specific rules pertaining to the pricing of new products did not appear until 1969. They replaced

the old rules which to some extent had decentralised the setting of prices for new products (so-called temporary prices) and in the absence of restraining forces had led to inflationary pressures. The new rules distinguished three categories of new products: substitute products, supplementary products and fundamentally new products (produced for the first time). The basis for pricing the first category was the economic gains brought by the new products, compared to the existing ones. The price was not to be too low for the producer, considering the expected profitability, or too high for the consumer, considering the parameters of the products. This meant that the saving achieved by the new price was to be split between the producer and the consumer. The start-up costs including the break-in costs of the first year of production were to be financed from a Fund for Mastering New Technology which was established in 1961. The price of the second group was determined by the technical parameters of the new products, compared to the existing group of products for which they were to be a supplement. In the third category were goods which had no Soviet analogue, and therefore their temporary prices were set by the usual formula, costs including start-up costs plus profit. The temporary prices for new products were supposed to be in force for two years and then be replaced by prices reflecting the costs of matured products. To encourage the continuing replacement of products by newer ones, some new prices were stepped prices – they were supposed to decline by steps, in line with the expected reduction in costs (see Bornstein, 1976, pp. 27–34; Feiwel, 1972, pp. 361–3; Grossman, 1977, pp. 160–4).

In the past, profit was distributed into prices according to cost of production. After long debates and hesitation, the reform adopted a formula which was labelled by some as almost a heresy since, according to Marx, it had been used under capitalism. According to the new formula, the profit margin was related to capital employed (fixed and working). The so-called price of production was applied only to whole branches or groups of products. The profit so computed was divided between individual products according to cost of production.

The central planners 'committed' another 'heresy' by replacing the formula of average costs plus profit with marginal costs plus profit in the case of many extractive products. Enterprises in better working conditions had to pay a differential rent (Grossman, 1977, p. 144; Sielunin, 1971, pp. 82–4; Bornstein, 1976, p. 22).

Neither the economic reform nor the 1969 guidelines for the

determination of prices of new products brought about flexibility in pricing. True, none of the political leaders was prepared to let prices move in response to changes in demand and supply. There were, however, indications that a mechanism was to be created in the form of normatives for the calculation of prices which would guide enterprises in making price changes for certain products. As could be expected, the authorities changed their minds (Katz, 1974, p. 168; Bornstein, 1974, p. 98).

Wage and Employment Regulation

The 1965 reform reduced the number of indicators of the labour plan from four (average wage, wage bill, number of employees and labour productivity) to one – the wage bill. As has already been stated, the central planners did not lose control of the other three indicators by the move mentioned. The other three were still planned on the macroeconomic level, and enterprises were supposed to include them in their plans. In addition, enterprises would not have gained much leeway in the matter of wages even if the other three had fully ceased to be planned; the rigid wage rate system was maintained, and this did not allow much manoeuvering. Still, more room was created for managerial decision making about wages. The elimination of the average wage indicator allowed enterprises, by juggling the classification of workers and norms, to increase the wages of some workers as long as the wage bill was not exceeded.

Once the central planners decided not to deviate from the traditional rigid price stability policy, it could be expected that no changes would be made in wage regulation. And indeed, the growth of the wage bill over the previous year was linked to an output indicator as before. Gross value of output or commodity production mostly fulfilled this role. If an enterprise fulfilled the assigned target for the output indicator, the actual wage bill equalled the planned. Overfulfilment of targets was rewarded by additional funds to the wage bill. In 1959 the normative (adjustment coefficient) was reduced below unity and ranged between 0.6–0.9 depending on the sector and branch of industry (Margulis, 1976).

The economic reform did not bring any important changes in the determination of wages for individual workers. In 1969 an adjustment of wage rate started; it was a normal periodic review of rates which did not really make them more flexible. The central authorities continued setting the wage rates which remained rigid till the next review. The only change worth noting was the reduction in the huge number of wage rate scales in order to reduce their differentiation (Shkurko, 1975; Sucharevskii, 1975, p. 249).

As mentioned, the economic reform abolished direct assignments of limits for employment. In connection with the campaign for reducing the cost of management personnel, limits for white collar workers were reintroduced. Despite the great labour shortages[6] no measures were instantly undertaken to stimulate labour economy. The central planners probably believed that enterprises would be interested in labour economy because this would enable average wages as well as bonuses to be increased, mainly if the wage bill and normatives relevant for the formation of the bonus fund did not decline for several years. If this was the case, then they underestimated the effect on enterprises' considerations about employment of the possibility of getting additional funds for the wage bill for overfulfilling the output target. Even the reduction of the normative below unity makes overfulfilment mostly an attractive goal to strive for. Usually the additional funds to the wage bill are higher than the labour costs involved in the overfulfilment. However, the intention to overfulfil may not allow a reduction in the work force or may even require the hiring of new workers and thus works against the expected labour economy. In addition, the normatives for the formation of the bonus fund changed frequently. Finally, the fact that these normatives were expressed in terms of a fraction of the wage bill did not encourage labour saving if there was no guarantee that the wage bill would remain the same even if the work force declined (see Novikov 1969).

The well-known Shchekino experiment was also based on the idea that enterprises would be interested in reducing the work force if a large portion of savings in labour costs could be used for average wage increases for the remaining workers. The experiment started in 1967 and was approved for application in other enterprises in 1969. In Shchekino, the experiment was quite successful for some time, since the combine was greatly overmanned (Bush, 1970). In other enterprises with less overmanning and where the authorities were reluctant to allow enterprises to use any considerable portion of saving for wage increases or bonuses, the experiment lost its attractiveness.

According to one writer, the Soviet experts considered introducing a tax on employment increases beyond a certain limit (Sielunin, 1971, p. 155) – a method used primarily in Czechoslovakia. It is doubtful that such a measure was introduced, but even if it had been, it could not have been of great value in the Soviet conditions of 'soft budget constraint'.

Investment Decisions and Financing

In his report, Kosygin talked quite frankly about the well-known, formidable problems which the central planners faced in investment activities. He also suggested some cures which were specified in the 'Decisions of 1965' and later elaborated in a new resolution of 1969.

The changes introduced by the reform moved primarily in two directions: they were supposed to reduce state involvement in the financing of investment by engaging enterprises in this activity (decentralised investment) and to create new incentives for construction enterprises to speed up the completion of investment projects at the lowest possible cost.

The reform distinguished between investment in construction of new enterprises and modernisation (introduction of new technology, replacement of old machines, mechanisation, etc.) of existing enterprises. Construction of new enterprises was to be financed from long-term credit (extended by the Construction Bank) provided the invested funds could be recouped within five years after the new capacity came on stream. (Where a longer period was needed for the recoupment of the investment fund, the project was to be financed from state revenues as before.) The intent was to make the newly established enterprise repay the investment (Shor, 1973, p. 216).

Financing of modernisation of existing enterprises was to come from the enterprise development funds and credit (again from the Construction Bank) repayable from the development funds. If the credit contributed to the expansion of consumer-goods production, 50 per cent of the turnover-tax yields could be used to pay off the credit (Kosygin, 1966, pp. 9–12; 22–5; *Khoziaistvennaia* . . . , 1969, pp. 132–2). Thus the real involvement of enterprises in investment was in modernisation, and only this investment could be termed decentralised or non-centralised as it was called in official documents.[7]

The rationale for this decentralisation was to give enterprises greater responsibility for investment in the hope that, if their own funds were involved, they would care more about the effectiveness of investment. There was no great fear that such investment would escape the control of the authorities. Investment in modernisation had to be included in the plans of enterprises, and these required the seal of approval. Some control was also exercised by the bank extending credit.

The development fund was fed – as already mentioned – from profit, a portion of the amortisation fund and proceeds from the sale of capital assets. The portion coming from profit depended on indicators as the other two funds did (for material stimulation and for social and cultural needs) with the difference that the normative for the indicators was expressed in terms of a fraction of a percentage of the average value of the fixed capital during the year. Enterprises were supposed to retain 30–50 per cent of the total amortisation fund; the exact percentage was apparently to depend on the amount of fixed assets and the need for their replacement. The amortisation portion made up the major share of the development fund (for 1969 it was planned at 58 per cent, whereas profit was 39 per cent) (Sielunin, 1971, p. 126; Krylov, Rothstein and Tsarev, 1966; Podshivalenko, 1969, p. 59).

It was calculated that, with the conversion of the whole industry to the new system of management, the development fund would make up 20 per cent of all industrial capital investment and represent 5.5–6 per cent of fixed assets (Feiwel, 1972, p. 392, even mentioned a figure of 11–12 per cent). In reality, it was much lower, 2–3 per cent of fixed assets. In spite of the rules some ministries withheld a portion of the amortisation fund belonging to enterprises (probably for financing centralised investment), and a portion of the development fund had to be used for construction of roads. What is perhaps even worse, enterprises could not fully use the remaining development fund (in 1964 they only used 69 per cent). Enterprises had difficulty obtaining needed machinery and equipment and finding construction enterprises which would be willing to perform the construction work, particularly if a smaller project was involved. The plan for investment for 1966–70 was too demanding; it exceeded the capacity of construction enterprises and the potential supply of materials and machinery, and centralised investment had a preferential claim on construction capacity and supply (Krylov, Rothstein and Tsarev, 1966; Rumiantsev and Filippov, 1969, p. 36; Feiwel, 1972, pp. 394, 488–90).

The central planners attached great importance to bank credit; they believed that its expansion would be a further stimulus to enterprises to be more careful in the economic calculations of cost benefits when investment decisions were made. They assumed that credit would also play an increasing role as a source of working capital (Garbuzov, 1965). However, the results deviated substantially from the expectations. Bank credit, as a source of investment financing for the modernisation of enterprises, and as a possible influence on the behaviour of enterprises, played a negligible role. For 1968 it was planned in the amount of 3.4 per cent of investment outlays for modernisation. Nor did credit as a source of financing working capital increase substantially. Due to the difficulties in spending the available development fund, enterprises on the average did not need much credit, and they could even use the development fund for working capital (Podshivalenko, 1969, p. 60; Feiwel, 1972, p. 395–7).

To stimulate construction enterprises to complete projects more rapidly, new incentives were introduced. A Resolution of 1969 called for experimenting with the financing of the construction of several new enterprises by credit obtained by the contractor. The customer was supposed to pay only upon completion of the project. If the contractor finished the project before the agreed delivery time he was to share in the resulting profit. Any savings made by the contractor belonged to him (*Khoziaistvennaia* . . ., 1969, p. 150). (See also p. 241.)

3.4 ORGANISATIONAL SYSTEM

The economic reform put an end to the territorial organisation and management of the economy, which had been introduced by Khrushchev, and was now replaced by the traditional branch principle. This meant the re-establishment of branch ministries (Kosygin mentioned twenty in his report), part of them being all-union ministries and the others union-republic ministries (with dual subordination – to the republican councils of ministries and the union republic ministry in Moscow). In the distribution of branches between the two types of ministries the reform departed from the old tradition according to which only the less important industries (consumer goods) were left to the jurisdiction of union-republic ministries. As a result of the reform, besides light industry and food branches, some branches of heavy industry were also subordinated to union-republics. J. N. Hazard (1967, pp. 75–8) saw in this a new approach to republics, a departure from Khrushchev's intentions to reduce their role. It seems that there was a good reason for such an approach. Despite its many shortcomings in a centralised planning system (it made it more difficult for the central bureaucracy to control the activities of enterprises and thus to carry out a uniform policy, it also complicated important national projects of military significance), the territorial system had the advantage of giving the small republics an important say in the management of the economy. They used their supervising role to orient enterprises more to local needs, including production of consumer goods (Kushnirsky, 1982, p. 51). The placing of branches of heavy industry under the jurisdiction of union-republic ministries was probably some kind of compensation for loss of influence. For completeness it should be added that Kosygin's announcement about granting new rights to union republics was much devalued by the concentration of the distribution of materials and equipment in the hands of the all-union ministries and by the establishment of the state committee on Material and Equipment Supply which was in charge of the realisation of supply plans (Kosygin, 1966, pp. 36–7; Kushnirsky, 1982, p. 52).

The reform was supposed to extend the autonomy of enterprises and, with it, the powers of the top managers. J. Hazard (1967, p. 78) speculates that the expansion of the authority of managers was to reverse the trend, initiated by Khrushchev, of imposing strict Party control over managers. F. Kushnirsky (1982, p. 79) maintains in substance the opposite, namely, that Party control increased with the removal of Khrushchev.

One thing is clear – the expansion of the autonomy of enterprises was short-lived. Already in 1969 the authorities had started to contemplate the creation of new associations. This idea gained a more concrete form with the establishment of industrial associations (all-union and republican). The new associations were loose organisations compared to the production associations (their members maintained independence); nevertheless they contributed to a further centralisation of management (Kushnirsky, 1982, p. 70; Laptev, 1973) (see Chapter 10).

3.5 CONCLUDING REMARKS

From the foregoing it is clear that the 1965 reform was a modest one which did not transgress the framework of the centralised system. The expansion of the authority of enterprises was miniscule, at any rate not sufficient for a significant change in the behaviour of managers. Yet the reform introduced some new elements, perhaps the most important being the introduction of profit not only as a source but also as an indicator of the size of the incentive fund, greater regard for market demand (sales became a success indicator), some strengthening of horizontal ties, and decentralised investment. However, the reform was short-lived. Some of its building blocks started to crumble when it was still expending to other areas. In 1969 productivity targets were reintroduced; what is worse, the most important element – a new approach to the formation of the bonus fund – was dropped. Starting in 1971 the bonus fund was again assigned to enterprises from above, and the fund creating indicators, sales and profit, were reduced to corrective indicators (Adam, 1980). The number of success indicators started to grow again. Decentralised investment, for reasons already mentioned, played a minimal role.

As usual, so also in this case, the reform was eroded by a combination of economic and political factors. The economy did not perform well enough to impress the opponents of the reform. It grew faster in 1966–70 than in 1961–65. Its development, however, showed some disquieting phenomena; primarily the relationship between wages and productivity in industry was not to the liking of the central planners. Nominal (and real wages) grew fast, but productivity lagged behind the target. In the period 1966–70 wage increases in industry reached an unprecedented ratio – 86 per cent of growth in labour productivity (Sucharevskii, 1975, p. 229). Many authors blamed this on the reform and the design of the new incentive system (see Moskalenko, 1971).

The reform could not live up to the expectations because it was from the beginning marked by many inconsistencies and contradictions, and the economic policy drifted not infrequently in a direction different from the reform. It introduced sales and profit as new success indicators, but on the other hand the formation of the wage bill, which was a source of inefficiencies, was not changed. Profit and profitability can be powerful incentives if the price system is rational; the price 'reform' was limited to wholesale prices, but even here, no rational prices came about.

Some branches were left with low profitability, the very branches which usually have political clout in a socialist economy (e.g. coal, ferrous metallurgy) (Rzheshevskii, 1973) and they undoubtedly pushed for changes in the bonus fund formation.

Sales as an indicator could have induced enterprises to have greater regard for the market, had the economic policy acted in tune with the reform. Continuous orientation to high growth rates, with the stress on heavy industry, strengthened the hands of suppliers. Under conditions of a sellers' market, sales as an indicator, even if combined with a system of direct ties, could not bring about change in the behaviour of suppliers. They continued to disregard market demand as to products, and their quality and design. The economic policy was also to blame for the fact that 'decentralised investment' did not amount to much.

Expressing the normatives for performance in sales (profit) and rate of profit in terms of a percentage of the wage bill – a provision motivated by the desire to avoid great differences in the bonus fund –

acted as a disincentive for productivity growth. Since managers received a larger share from the bonus fund, they were interested in a higher wage bill and increased employment at the expense of productivity.

The long-term normatives, which were supposed to play an important role in the incentive system as a whole, were largely reduced to a formality. The idea of long-term normatives makes sense if it is possible to set stable output targets for a certain period of time; if this is impossible, as the practice of the Soviet Union and other countries has shown up to now, and if plans must be changed frequently, the long-term normatives turn at best into annual normatives. In addition, the normatives were also changed in order to ensure that certain enterprises had a certain bonus fund or to curtail the bonus fund's growth (Egiazarian, 1976, pp. 259–60).

There are good reasons to believe that the introduction of the reform was not supported by all the Soviet leaders to the same extent. Some believe that Kosygin and his supporters should be credited with the introduction of the reform while Brezhnev and his supporters were sitting on the fence. When concern about low labour productivity came to the forefront, Brezhnev deserted the reform and started to rely on old methods: a tightening of labour discipline and control (Katz, 1974, pp. 183, 202).

The 1968 events in Czechoslovakia surely did not contribute to a strengthening of the reform. They frightened the leaders of East European countries, and some reversed their reform (Bulgaria, East Germany). Pressure was exercised on Hungary to halt its reform. It is not clear what impact the Czechoslovak events of 1968 had on the USSR and to what extent the new wave of conservatism, which swept the USSR and was reflected in culture and ideology, was the result of the Czechoslovak events. At any rate they delivered ammunition to the opponents of the reform. Needless to stress, those in the Soviet bureaucracy who were not excited by it, also had a share in its demise.

4 The Economic Reform in Czechoslovakia, 1966–69

4.1 INTRODUCTION

The economic reform in Czechoslovakia, in the form it existed at the beginning of 1969, was the result of a gradual development. Its progress was furthered by political events, primarily the change in political leadership and the Soviet led invasion in August 1968. These events radicalised the reformers; they naturally tried to utilise the change in political leadership for a more consistent reform and, after the occupation of Czechoslovakia, attempted to democratise the management structure, as, *inter alia*, a defence against interference in the reform. Needless to say, the economic reform made some contribution to these political events.

Three phases can be distinguished in the development of the reform. The first, 1964–66, was marked by the preparation of a reform proposal by a working group of economists and its approval by the Party bodies in 1964–65 (*Život strany*, 1965, no. 4). (The approved document referred to the upcoming changes as an improvement in planned management, implying that radical changes would not be tolerated.) With this action, the fight for the acceptance of the reform (in the beginning there was quite a lot of opposition, primarily from one part of the Party and government apparatus, from managers and from simple workers who were afraid that the reform might introduce a state of instability, Selucký, 1970, p. 74) shifted to the public arena. The year 1965 was used for drafting legislation and for trying some of the significant aspects of the reform in some important enterprises.

The second phase started with the introduction of the principles of the reform in 1966 and lasted up to the occupation of Czechoslovakia. Since the reform of the price system could not be carried out instantly, and since discussions were still going on about certain elements of the reform, many of the 1966 provisions could be regarded as preliminary. In January 1967 the price reform was carried out, and a programme to accelerate the reform was set in motion. It started to develop fully when A. Novotný was removed from his post as general secretary of the Party in January 1968 and replaced by A. Dubček. This is also the period when the Action programme of the Party was approved (*Rok*

55

. . ., 1969 pp. 103–46) and the fight for democratisation of the management structures and political life was intensified. In the CSSR more than in any other country the fight for economic reform was coupled with the fight for democratic changes in the political system (see also Brus, 1985a, p. 207).

The third phase ended with the resignation of A. Dubček and his replacement by G. Husák, who very soon started to dismantle the reform. The very rapid spread of workers' councils in enterprises was the most important addition to the reform (Kosta, 1973, p. 180).

4.2 PLANNING SYSTEM

The resolution of the Central Committee made it clear that planning remained the main coordinating mechanism.[1] The role of planning was primarily in the macroeconomic sphere; it determined the most important macroeconomic proportions, the direction of economic growth, including the distribution of investment between sectors of the economy and important investment projects. It also had to take care of the international division of labour and technical development. Finally, the plan determined the economic regulators and their application (*Život strany*, 1965, no. 4; Sokol, 1965).

The Resolution of the Party did not explicitly mention the abolition of the assignment of targets to enterprises. However, the Order in Council, which put into legislation the resolution of the Central Committee to accelerate the reform, limited assignment of output targets to 'unavoidable' cases. Exceptions from this rule were foreign trade (transitionally) and central investment, where binding targets could be set for enterprises.

The annual state plan still contained targets, though in a much reduced number, but these were supposed to be only for the information of enterprises (orientation targets) and the state authorities. Enterprises were to use this information for drafting their plans, and the state authorities for monitoring enterprise performance. If the branch ministry came to the conclusion that the real structure of production deviated substantially from the orientation targets, it could assign so-called *exceptional binding targets*. Enterprises so affected could claim compensation if wage growth or financing of investment suffered as a result. Otherwise the centre was supposed to coordinate the objectives of the state plan and enterprise plans by economic regulators. The law mentioned two kinds: long-term (in substance fiscal) taken preferably from the five-year plan, and short-term (monetary, prices, etc.) (*Život strany*, 1966, no. 6; *Sbírka zákonů*, 1966, no. 100; Feiwel, 1968, pp. 232–5; Sokol, 1965).

One would expect that, as a result of the Order in Council, the number of binding targets would decline dramatically. But this was not the case; branch directorates of productive economic units (PEUs) – associations – which had taken over to some extent before 1967 the job of the branch ministries in imposing targets on enterprises in many cases, did not change their behaviour as a result of the order. PEUs also used their power to tighten their monopoly position (Šik, 1966; Golan, 1971, pp. 64–5; Horálek *et al.*, 1968). It would be wrong to assume that the hierarchical subordination ended at the level of branch directorates. It should not be forgotten that the branch ministry had various instruments to influence the branch directorates, one being that it appointed, dismissed and evaluated the performance of the general manager.

Despite these limitations the measures could be regarded as great progress over the traditional system. The autonomy of most enterprises increased substantially. They could determine the product mix, how to produce and where to buy inputs,[2] and they also obtained much greater freedom in determining wages and employment.

Czechoslovakia was the only country of the Soviet bloc in the 1960s which introduced workers' councils. The first mention about the need of introducing self-management bodies was in the Action programme (*Rok . . .*, 1969, p. 127). In the beginning, many top reformers had objections to workers' councils; though they readily took over many elements of the Yugoslav system, this one they disliked. They were concerned that abandonment of the principle of one-man management would make the decision making more cumbersome and less professional so that economic efficiency might be affected unfavourably. Probably the fear that it would be difficult to restrain the workers' councils' pressure for wage increases also played a role. Thus, in the beginning of the reform, the managerial-technocratic ideology prevailed (Kosta, 1973, p. 191).

It is not entirely clear what brought about the tilt of the scale to the other side, but it was probably the desire to gain the support of the workers for the reform; this seemed all the more important in face of the developing conflict with the USSR. In June 1968, preliminary principles for the establishment of workers' councils were published. The final principles were supposed to be incorporated in the act on enterprises which was also to set the relationship between enterprises and the administration. Before the bill on enterprises could be passed into law, the reformers were ousted from their position of power.

The preliminary principles were a compromise between 'managerialism' and self-management; the role of the workers' councils was quite limited; it was rather advisory. Their position was conceptualised in the same way in the initial bill on enterprises (see Ernst, 1968). In 1969 many workers' councils assumed economic policy functions volitionally (Kouba, 1969).

With the publication of the preliminary principles, the establishment of workers' councils spread quickly. Very soon after the fall of Dubček, their activities came to a halt.

4.3 REGULATION SYSTEM

The Czechoslovak reform put the maximisation of gross income[3] in the centre of the regulation system (profit was used in only a small percentage of enterprises). This indicator was to be the main incentive, in the sense that wage growth and bonuses depended on it, and a guide to decision making and the basis for taxation. It was not supposed to be an indicator in the old sense; enterprises were not assigned targets for the fulfilment of gross income. The authorities regulated its growth and distribution by indirect methods, primarily by taxation.

Regulation of Gross Income of Enterprises

The reformers were determined to terminate the old practice of rewarding poorly performing enterprises at the expense of those performing well. This also shaped their approach to the taxation of enterprises. They replaced the well-known principle that the more you have, the higher your tax rate, with the idea that the more you have, the more you have for remuneration. The purpose of the structure of taxation ceased to be to mitigate income differences and instead was supposed to become an instrument of efficiency. Taxes had to show enterprises to what extent their performance was efficient and, on the other hand, to exert pressure on enterprises to increase the efficiency of their operations (Sokol, 1968).

For all these reasons, beginning in 1967 the taxes on gross income, on the wage bill and on the growth of employment were proportional and as much as possible uniform. In industry and construction the tax on gross income was 18 per cent, and on profit, where this was applied,

32 per cent. Apart from this tax, enterprises in industry and construction also paid a 6 per cent tax on assets and 2 per cent on inventories from gross income. After paying taxes, interest and a contribution to the branch directorates, enterprises were supposed to use the balance of their gross income first for the creation and replenishment of funds (reserve fund, fund for cultural and social needs, construction fund) whose size was influenced by the rules laid down for their formation, and then, from what remained, for the wage bill (in Czech: *fond pracujicich* – fund of employees).

Price System

To give the market forces their proper role in the reformed system, radical changes were needed in pricing, preferably instantly. For political as well as for economic reasons (great shortages, monopolisation) this was possible only gradually. In addition, reformers could set only limited goals in pricing, because, *inter alia*, the 1966 Party resolution called for maintaining the level of consumer prices. The main objective was to let market forces (domestic as well as world) play a role in the formation of prices and consequently in the decision making of enterprises. This objective entailed further goals: to introduce flexibility in pricing (let prices react to the changing relationship between supply and demand) and to renew the linkage between individual price circuits (primarily between wholesale and consumer prices, and domestic and world market prices).

To this end, a revision of wholesale prices, a grouping in pricing and a change in the construction of the turnover tax (see Chapter 2) were carried out. The wholesale price revision was only to be the first step in the process of making prices more rational. Its objective was to increase the general level of prices so that new taxes could be accommodated, and, at the same time, to change price relativities so they could better reflect social costs and better serve the intended incentive system. It did not intend to solve the distortions *vis-à-vis* consumer prices and world prices; this was to be the task of further changes in pricing.

The wholesale price revision was carried out in two stages: in the first, prices of group of products (in total 25 000) were recalculated. Profit was added to the production costs in accordance with the two channel price type (an invention of Hungarian economists) which meant a percentage of the capital employed (in this case 6 per cent) and a percentage of the wage bill used (25 per cent). As a result capital and labour shared in profit in a ratio of approximately ¾ to ¼, which meant that capital intensive groups of products with the same production costs were priced higher than less intensive groups. Apparently, the reformers wanted to stimulate labour savings. In the second stage, prices of individual products of each group were recalculated by distributing the profit of the group on the basis of actual costs, taking into consideration supply and demand (Typolt and Novák, 1966; Typolt, 1968; Kýn, 1975, p. 124; Kosta, 1984,. pp. 152–3).

The level of the new prices and profitability was much higher than planned (prices increased by 29 per cent against 19 per cent); enterprises apparently managed to 'sell' their padded costs to the price authorities. The inflated prices disrupted the working of some important subsystems of the reform (wage, investment financing, to mention the most important) and hampered its unfolding.

The grouping of prices, whose purpose was to reduce central control over prices in order to increase their market sensitivity, had already been introduced in 1966. It consisted, according to the Yugoslav practice, of three categories: fixed, limited and free. Naturally, the first category included basic raw materials and semi-finished products, which have a great influence on costs in processing industries, goods through the control of which it is possible more or less to control prices throughout the economy, and consumer goods, which have a crucial impact on the cost of living. Products in short supply were also included in the fixed category.

The category of free prices could be applied to products for which a competitive market existed, items with luxury finishing, novelties, and so forth. These prices were supposed to be a result of negotiations between suppliers and buyers. Limited prices, which were a result of an agreement (about an average price for a group of products within which prices for individual products could be changed freely) between the authorities and suppliers, were applied to the rest of the products (Sbírka zákonů, 1967, no. 46).

It was assumed that, with the progress of the reform, the category of free and limited prices, particularly the former, would expand at the expense of fixed prices. However, the freeing of prices progressed much more slowly than had been assumed; prices rose faster than had been envisioned, and therefore the authorities curbed their freeing up. In 1968, 23 per cent of consumer prices and 6 per cent of wholesale prices were free; for 1969 government guidelines assumed further expansion of free prices (Koudelka, Libnar and Havel, 1968; Government . . . , 1969). However, this intention could be furthered only for a short time, since, after a change in political leadership, categorisation of prices came to a halt.

Wage Regulation and Incentives

Under conditions of the elimination of binding output targets for enterprises, it was, of course, unthinkable to continue the old practice of linking wage growth to plan output targets. The central authorities even took a further step which made Czechoslovakia the first country in CMEA countries to control the wage bill growth of enterprises (this referred only to those which used gross income as a material incentive) only by taxes, though for just a short period. The reformers hoped that managers would use the newly gained leeway in decision making to bring wages more in line with performance and that thus productivity would increase. The wage bill was used for wages as well as for bonuses.

In 1966 enterprises (if not otherwise stated it is assumed that these are enterprises applying gross income) were allowed to increase average wages to a certain limit; once they exceeded it, they had to pay a progressive tax (Both, Pokorný and Voják, 1966, p. 33). In line with the new principles for acceleration of the economic reform (which included a uniform tax on gross income) a stabilisation tax was introduced in 1967. Its purpose was to regulate wage increases as well as employment for the sake of the following three aims: (1) to keep average wages in line with the state plan. To back up this policy, a government resolution stipulated that the wage-bill should not grow faster than other outlays from gross income; (2) to discourage enterprises from increasing output by an increase in employment, and (3) to have a built-in stabiliser – hence the name 'stabilisation tax' – which would keep wage differentials between the material and non-material sphere within acceptable limits. Taxes collected from increases in wages in the material sphere had to provide funds for wage increases in the non-material sphere (*Sbírka zákonů*, no. 63, 1963; Kutálek, 1966).

The formula for the stabilisation tax (T) was

$$T = \frac{30\,(W - 90\,wE)}{100 \quad 100} + \frac{r.W}{100}$$

where W is the actual wage-bill, E the number of employees, r the growth rate of employment, all three for the year for which the tax is payable, and *w* the planned average wage in the previous year. As the formula shows, the tax consisted of two divisions, and only the left division referred to wages.

This purely indirect regulation of wages did not last long. The stabilisation tax as a proportional tax was not powerful enough to restrain wage growth within the limits of the plan at a time when enterprises had much higher gross income than was assumed as a result of the wholesale price reform and the monopoly position of production economic units (PEUs). In addition, the high incomes were in branches[4] where wages were anyhow high and where it was desirable to reduce the existing intensive investment drive.

First, the government tried to remedy the situation by strengthening the stabilisation tax through linking wage increases to productivity growth by normatives differentiated by branches of industry. This provision, which was contrary to the spirit of reform, came under attack, and was soon abandoned as a result of an agreement between the government and trade unions (*Práce a mzda*, 1968, no. 11) and replaced by a progressive surtax on the first division of the stabilisation tax. Already earlier the government had introduced a new tax on profit at the rate of 45 per cent which, of course, undermined the concept of having gross income as an exclusive incentive (*Government* . . . , 1969; Kudrna, 1968).

An aim of the reform was to bolster the personnel's interest in the performance of their enterprises by making a portion of wages dependent on this performance. According to this concept, wages of individuals consisted of two parts: one, dependent on the performance of the individual, included wage rates and some additional payments, and the second, directly linked to the performance of enterprises, included bonuses for qualitative results and rewards for performance as a collective (year-end rewards). It was contemplated that, with the progress of the reform, the variable component of the wage would grow, and thus also the responsibility and interest of the enterprise personnel in the performance of the enterprise. It was assumed that, by the end of 1970, the variable component would make up 30 per cent of wages (in especially efficient enterprises, 35 per cent) (Both, Pokorný and Voják, 1966, p. 51; Tomášek, 1967, p. 31).

The reformers well knew that workers were not excited about being even partially responsible for the performance of enterprises which they could only slightly influence, and therefore, in order to placate them, a state wage guarantee amounting to 92 per cent of the previous wage was introduced (Both, Pokorný and Voják, 1966, pp. 67–8).

Incentives to improve economic efficiency had also to come from a widening of wage differentials which the Action programme (*Rok . . .* , 1969, pp. 111–12) fully supported. The widening of wage differentials was to be achieved by increasing wages in the non-material sphere, where wages on the average were low, and by using the variable components of wages for larger bonuses to managers and engineering staff (Moravec, 1967). For political reasons – not to irritate blue-collar workers – little was accomplished in this respect (see Adam 1984, pp. 206–8).

In the years 1966–69 the authorities began to make preparations for an overhaul of the tariff system, pay forms and setting of work norms including job evaluations. But no real changes (with the exception of allowing enterprises to deviate from the existing wage rates by 10 per cent) were made; the reform was scrapped before major changes could be introduced (Tomášek, 1967, p. 33; Horálek, 1966).

Employment Regulation

Since the autonomy of enterprises also depends on the extent to which they are allowed to make decisions about employment, one would assume that the pre-reform practice of imposing employment limits would be completely dropped under the new conditions. Studying the legislation pertaining to the reform, one can be strengthened in such a belief. The situation was, however, more complicated. Czechoslovakia suffered from labour shortages (of course, combined with overemployment) and therefore the authorities were reluctant to commit themselves to a complete abandonment of compulsory limits. In the initial period, limits were set for the ministries and the provincial governments, and it was left to their discretion whether they would disaggregate the limits as compulsory or only as orientation targets. On the whole, the idea prevailed that gradually, as the tightness of the labour market loosened, the administrative methods would be dropped (Formánek and Pick, 1965).

The reformers expected an improvement in labour economy from the new system of incentives and the stabilisation tax. It was hoped that enterprises would be interested in maximising of gross income (or profit) and this would encourage them to try to save labour, all the more because labour savings could provide funds for higher average wage increases. The stabilisation tax was supposed to be the stick if the carrot did not prove enticing enough. It was quite high if the regular rate was paid (there were many exemptions and reliefs); it amounted to the additional wage costs resulting from employment growth. However, under the financial conditions which developed after the price reform of 1967, this was not a great obstacle to hiring, if enterprises felt a labour shortage. The small impact of the second division of the tax was also due to the low tax credit (0.3 per cent for a 1 per cent reduction in the work force). Enterprises which could release labour only temporarily were reluctant to do so (see Bajcura, 1969, pp. 63–4).

The systemic changes alone could not cure the disease of the economy. The strategy of growth also needed to be changed (from maximum to balanced growth) and, of course, the economy had to be restructured in the direction of domestic and foreign demand. Both were formidable tasks, because they could not be achieved without liquidating inefficient and obsolete enterprises and reducing over-employment in other enterprises. The situation was all the more serious in that many inefficient enterprises had the skilled labour which was lacking in many thriving and modern enterprises (Sokol, 1965). To correct the situation meant tackling not only a sensitive economic but also a political problem which could generate conflicts. Nevertheless, the authorities undertook several provisions to ease the situation. They expanded retraining programmes for workers who had to be transferred to other jobs and also, for the first time, introduced unemployment benefits for those who might not instantly find jobs despite the help of the dismissing enterprise and the local government (Kudrna, 1967).

Investment Decisions and Financing

Because of the crucial importance of investment, this was perhaps the sphere where the disagreements between the reformers were the largest. Many of the reformers – interestingly enough, among them the most influential – believed that state control in this area should be the greatest. It is worth noting that in 1965, when the architects of the reform had already a good idea of what they wanted in various areas (see *PE* 1965, no. 4), they were able to offer no major changes in investment (Hejkal, 1965). Therefore the reform in 1966 brought only minor changes in investment regulation. In 1967, when the price revision was carried out and, in the meantime, the reformers' views clarified, quite a different system of regulation and financing of investment was introduced. In substance, the Yugoslav system of investment regulation before 1964 was adopted.

In more concrete terms, categorisation of investment, which still existed in 1966, was dropped. Strategically important investment projects in the material sphere – needless to say, in the non-material sphere (infrastructure) direct methods were maintained – were still to be evaluated and approved by the central authorities. The decision about all other investment projects rested in the hands of PEUs or enterprises.

Investment projects were financed from enterprises' own resources (that is primarily from the construction fund) and especially from bank credit. State subsidies were to be extended only in exceptional cases. The construction fund consisted of allocations from gross income (or profit), amortisation fund (on the average 27 per cent), sale of assets and other sources. The fund had also to be used for the repayment of bank credit.

The planners assumed that 60 per cent of investment costs would be financed from bank credit, 25 per cent from the construction fund and 15 per cent from the state budget. The high dependence on bank credit was intentional; it was supposed to give the State Bank the possibility of influencing investment activity.

Enterprises had to compete for bank credit by tender. In selecting the successful claimants for credit, the bank tried to reconcile two principles: commercial soundness and the objective of the plan. The commercial principle meant that enterprises were obliged to prove that their investment project fulfilled the minimal terms of efficiency (the greater the expected portion of profit in the redeemable principal the greater the chance of receiving credit) and that they would be able to pay the interest rate (6 per cent) and the tax on assets (6 per cent) and repay the principal on time. The bank was allowed to deviate somewhat from the orientation guidelines for the distribution of investment credits if the two principles clashed (Tesář, 1966; Pohl, 1966).

It soon turned out that the new system of investment regulation and financing did not produce the results the central planners expected. The share of bank credit in investment outlays was much smaller (in 1967, 22 per cent) than was assumed (Trojan and Vacovský, 1969), new criteria of efficiency did not work properly, and enterprises continued pressing for maximum investment which contributed to inflation. Many enterprises had 'excessive' revenues and viewed investment as the best instrument for protecting funds against possible government taxes; others did not care about efficiency in the belief that the new system was only of a temporary nature.

The old tendency to pursue extensive growth prevailed. When, at the end of 1966, the tender procedure was summarised, it turned out that only 22 per cent of investment funds was earmarked for reconstruction and modernisation.

The excessive number of investment projects (mostly old) in the process of construction was another obstacle to the assertion of the new system. What compounded the situation was that many projects were of no great value. Despite the stopping of many projects in progress, only 10 per cent of the investment funds remained for new projects. No wonder that, under such conditions, plans for restructuring the economy could go ahead only very slowly, all the more because powerful forces (some heavy industry branches) opposed a radical restructuring (Židlický, 1967; Reh, 1968).

To cope with the mentioned shortcomings the central planners, on the one hand, applied a restriction to bank credit and, on the other hand, started to revert to the old administrative methods. Needless to say, this policy was criticised. Some economists saw a solution to the problems in investment by giving greater room to market forces and by limiting planning (with the exception of the first sector) to the role of an analysis of future markets (Horálek *et al.*, 1968). Other economists objected to the great role of bank credit and suggested using other means for the distribution of capital (to some extent a capital market an idea which at the existing conditions had few followers) (Tesař and Petera, 1968).

Foreign Trade

In 1966 the authorities took the first steps in the dismantlement of the centralised system in foreign trade. Directive planning was eased; targets were set for PEUs in global terms and the number of specified targets was substantially reduced. Compared with other sectors of the economy, foreign trade, because of its possible effect on price stability and external equilibrium, remained under the strict control of the planners (Svoboda and Kubelka, 1965). In the following years some easing of controls was carried out, and the State Bank tried by indirect methods, such as making allocation of foreign currency for imports dependent on the import of foreign currency, to bolster exports (Šedivý, 1968). Furthermore, foreign trade corporations (FTCs) were turned into *khozraschet* units. In contrast to the previous situation when all the overhead expenses of the FTCs were financed from the state budget, they were now supposed to be financed from the corporations' own activities. Gains and losses from foreign trade operations were reflected in their gross income (Summary . . . , 1967; Pleva, 1966).

As to the alignment of foreign and domestic prices, the authorities opted for so-called price equalisation, which meant applying subsidies and taxes to the foreign price equivalent in Kcs, differentiated by branches and groups of commodities. Not until 1969 did the government stipulate a uniform adjustment coefficient (premium) to the exchange rate for the ruble trade (125 per cent) and for the dollar trade (275 per cent) combined with further premiums, primarily on the dollar (Summary . . . , 1967; *Government* . . . , 1968).

The monopoly of FTCs was to be dismantled gradually. Only a few PEUs obtained instantly the right to have direct ties with foreign firms. Apparently, the foreign trade ministry and FTCs managed to convince the authorities that dismantlement of FTCs might harm the economy. In 1968–69 some progress was achieved. The call of the Action programme of the Party for enterprises to be allowed to choose the FTC they wanted to do business with was to be partially implemented in 1969 (Valeš, 1968). If really implemented, this would have meant a breakthrough, since the monopoly of FTCs was based on the right to trade with certain products. Further weakening of the monopoly had to come with the enacting of the bill on the role of enterprises (see pp. 57–8).

Some economists also called for the introduction of the convertibility of the Czechoslovak crown. But in conditions of stagnating exports and economic disequilibrium, this proposition had little chance. For similar and other reasons imports could not be used for strengthening competition within the economy (Valeš, 1968).

4.4 ORGANISATIONAL SYSTEM

The 1965 resolution of the Central Committee of the Party, which put into motion the economic reform, did not contain any directive to weaken the hierarchical build-up. On the contrary the branch directorates of associations[5] were to continue to be a link in the state management, being the highest authority in the *khozraschet* sphere. Enterprise authority was to be determined by the branch directorates (*Život strany*, 1965, no. 4). In other words, the administrative organisation of the economy, which was an instrument of the centralised system and the source of strict monopolisation, was to remain intact.

Needless to say, economists pushed for a change (see, e.g. Kocanda, 1967; Kraus, 1968) which finally was reflected in the Action programme.[6] This established as a principle that enterprises must have the option to associate on the basis of economic interest and that branch directorates should cease to have administrative power. Not much came of these principles; they were supposed to be included in the act on enterprises which was never passed (Golan, 1973, p. 29).

The Action programme also stipulated that decision making at the central level should be democratised. Part of the democratisation process, which included an increased role for the Parliament, was the establishment of the National Economic Council in 1968 (made up also of members from outside the government) whose function was to evaluate and recommend policy decisions pertaining to important macroeconomic issues (Golan, 1973, p. 30).

Democratisation of the system of management was much helped by the changes in trade unions in 1968, especially after the invasion. The trade unions ceased to be simply a transmission belt and regained to a great extent independence from the Party. This allowed them to resume their pre-1948 function, primarily to protect the interests of the workers.

4.5   CONCLUDING REMARKS

The Czechoslovak economic reform was not given enough time for many ideas to be put into practice or to stand the test of time; it was dismantled because of pressure, primarily from outside. Nevertheless, it can be subjected to an evaluation, particularly from the viewpoint of its economic and systemic consistency, and also from the perspective of its effect on the economy.

In my opinion the reformed system of management, even in its 1969 form, that is without the realisation of many provisions which were under way, meant tremendous progress compared to the traditional Soviet system. As a result of the reform, the Czechoslovak system ceased to be a centralised system: using Brus' classification, the Czechoslovak system, like the Hungarian, came close to what he defines as a decentralised system; however, if Antal's classification is applied, both systems can be characterised as indirect. In several respects, the Czechoslovak reform went further than the Hungarian (in workers' participation in decision making, in dismantlement of the hierarchical build-up and in wage regulation), and in other respects it lagged behind the Hungarian in that there was greater government interference with enterprises, and an opting for gross income instead of profit (which in itself was not, in my opinion, a shortcoming; however, the defintion of gross income was deficient because it also included changes in inventories). On the whole, the Hungarian reformers were more realistic and practical.

The reform was not free of shortcomings and inconsistencies which were complicated by the economic policy and the disequilibria in the economy. Understandably, the reformers pushed for a quick introduction of the main building blocks of the reform, but they did not weigh sufficiently the possible consequences of each provision. It was correct to control wage and employment growth in enterprises only by taxes, but it was not prudent to do so by proportional taxes, though the objective of this move was in line with the reform. It could have been expected that enterprises would use their newly won authority for fast wage increases, all the more because restraining market forces were still weak. For the same reason the reformers had also to be concerned with possible rapid employment growth; besides, the work week was shortened by two hours. The relaxed wage and, especially, employment control, created an environment for inflationary pressures which impeded progress in freeing price formation, and this in turn hampered the assertion of market forces. In addition, the failed wholesale price reform, which brought about a much higher increase in the level of wholesale prices than had been assumed, made matters even worse. The opposition to the reform thus obtained ammunition against further decentralisation and used it.

Certain progress was achieved in linking domestic prices to foreign market prices, but this was brought about up to 1969 through a complicated system of subsidies and taxes differentiated by individual products. This, combined with a whole series of subsidies and tax reliefs outside foreign trade (Horálek *et al.*, 1968), undermined the uniformity principle and thus the potential effectiveness of the reform.

The reformers pushed hard for a dismantlement of the hierarchical build-up, but, because of resistance from the opponents of the reform, and also because they could not agree among themselves on methods and extent, the autonomy granted was to a great extent limited to associations (Discussions . . . , 1968).

In 1966–68 the economy grew relatively quickly (national income grew on the average 7 per cent) because of the rapid growth of industrial and, what was surprising, agricultural production (5 per cent on the average compared to the average of 1963–65). What was especially appreciated was the faster growth of national income than of the aggregate social product, which meant that some economy in productive consumption was achieved. Social labour productivity also grew relatively quickly. Real wages increased on the average 4.5 per cent (in 1968 the increase was 6.9 per cent) (*Historická . . .* , 1985, pp. 89, 349; Šimon and Říha, 1968).

Some credit should be given to the economic reform for this positive development. The reform had, however, also some share in the negative phenomena, primarily in market disequilibrium. It no doubt helped to remove some sources of disequilibria, but added – not surprisingly – some of its own; it is almost impossible to make the transition from a centralised system to a system in which market forces are to play an important role without creating temporary disequilibria.

The market disequilibrium had its roots partially in foreign trade. Central planners had an old ambition to produce, through export of machinery (which made up approximately 48 per cent of exports) and other commodities, enough funds to finance the import of raw materials needed for the production of machines, foodstuffs, and also new technology from the West. The ambition was only partially achieved, due to the high material content of the machinery and to a quality which was frequently below Western standards. The reformers put an additional onus on foreign trade – to finance increased imports of consumer goods in order to ease market disequilibrium and exert pressure on the domestic market – and they fared with this claim no better than with the previous one (see Šimon and Říha, 1968; Adam, 1974a, pp. 34–9).

The main direct cause of market disequilibrium was a faster growth of total incomes than of the resources available for the production of consumer goods and the immobilisation of a large amount of resources in investment by the huge number of uncompleted investment projects. It must be made clear that the rapid growth of total incomes was a result of, not only an increase in wages, but also of employment growth, its share in the increase of the total wage fund being 32 per cent. Employment grew 2.2 times faster than labour resources. In the rapid growth of average nominal wages (in 1966–68 25.2 per cent), the rate of growth in 1968, when discipline loosened very much due to the Soviet led occupation, was 10.1 per cent (*Historická . . .* , 1985, pp. 146, 350).

The market disequilibrium could have been corrected by price increases. Primarily the opponents of the reform depicted the existing inflation as a horrendous phenomenon, despite the fact that in 1968 it was 1.3 per cent, and in 1969, when it was at its highest (4 per cent), even the reformers were scared (Kadlec, Kouba and Koudelka, 1969). The fear of inflation was used for slowing down the unfolding of market forces.

5 The Hungarian Economic Reform of 1968

5.1 INTRODUCTION

As already indicated, the Hungarian reform, like the one in the USSR, was a reform from above. Decisions about the direction of the reform were taken in two stages in Party committees without pressure from below. In the first stage, the initial guidelines of the reform prepared by the committee were approved in 1965 and, in the second stage, the final version was approved by the Central Committee in 1966. The reform itself started in 1968 and was supposed to be fully developed in two years. All the important principles were, however, applied simultaneously. Thus the Hungarian reform was not preceded by experiments as the Czechoslovak was; the Hungarians opted for a 'big leap' after a three-year preparation (Portes, 1972).[1]

The Hungarian reform brought about a system of management (or, as the Hungarians call it, New Economic Mechanism (NEM) which was and is somewhere between the Soviet and the Yugoslav systems. In his speech at the Central Committee meeting which approved the reform, Nyers (1966, p. 56), who was the reform's chief architect, stated that the reform would integrate central planning and the market mechanism. The disaggregation of annual plans with the assignment of binding targets, a characteristic feature of the Soviet system, was dropped. Decisions were to be divided between the centre and enterprises in such a way that each decided about matters it had most knowledge of and in which it was most directly interested. The central bodies were to settle macro-issues, whereas enterprises would decide about micro-issues. Greater autonomy was given to enterprises in the hope that in pursuing their own interest they would simultaneously satisfy market demand. The role given to the market mechanism was smaller by far than it is in the Yugoslav system where it is supposed to be the coordinating mechanism; in Hungary this task was reserved for central planning. The function of the market mechanism was to make enterprises '. . . endeavour to use resources the most rationally and satisfy customer demand well' (Nyers, 1966, p. 58). Its role also was to objectivise plans, to check on their practicality and in this way influence the planning process (Hetényi, 1969, p. 41). Central planning and the regulatory system based on it were to determine the limits and terms of operation of the market mechanism. The role of the market was to be backed up by a strengthening of the cooperative sector and by allowing an expansion of the private sector.

5.2 PLANNING SYSTEM

According to the 1966 resolution of the Central Committee in NEM, planning was to determine the main goals of economic development and the most important macroeconomic proportions. In addition, the centre made decisions about the nature of the regulators and their application. In NEM even the objectives in the macrosphere were to be achieved primarily by economic levers (*A gazdasági* . . . , 1966, pp. 17–18; Nyers, 1966, p. 58; Friss, 1969, p. 15).

Though the state annual plans ceased to function as the coordinating mechanism of enterprise activities, they continued to be drawn up, but with a new role. They were a description of the objectives of the five-year plan, whose importance increased under new conditions, to be achieved in the year in question. Needless to say, they could not be an exact prorated portion of the five-year plan. The economy is continuously changing and the plans must adjust to it. For planning purposes, this means, on the one hand, that the five-year plan must be an open plan and, on the other, that the changes must be reflected in the annual plan. This has necessarily an effect on the regulators. On the whole, there was a tendency to make the regulators as stable as possible, and necessary changes were included in the annual plans. The plans also contained additional measures aimed at ensuring equilibrium in the economy, the most important being the state budget (Hetényi, 1969, pp. 55–6).

Enterprises were obliged to draw up their own plans, five year and annual. Unlike past plans, these were not supposed to be a portion (cut-out) of the state plan, but one which reflected the interests of the enterprises. This was also reflected in the fact that enterprises were not obliged to submit the plans for approval to higher authorities. To make the plans valid, only the directors' approval was needed.

Was there not a danger that the enterprises' plans would deviate markedly from the objectives of the state plans? No doubt such concerns were expressed, but they were rejected by referring to the known fact that even during administrative planning deviations occurred (Nyers, 1966, p. 61). It was also hoped that enterprises in their own interest would take into consideration the objectives of the state plan when drafting their own plans. It should not be forgotten that, even under the new conditions, the state plan would determine a considerable portion of investment. In addition, enterprises would have to include in their plans certain tasks determined from above (large investment projects approved by the government and export tasks resulting from interstate trade agreements). Finally, the reformers envisioned certain methods for the coordination of state and enterprise plans. The literature of the time of the reform primarily stressed exchange of information (Morva, 1969, pp. 76–9). Needless to say, enterprises needed information for their plans about the state of the five-year and annual plans and about changes in major regulators, and, on the other hand, central planners needed information about enterprises' intentions. In the course of time, some additional procedures were adopted (A. Balassa, 1979, pp. 386–410); some of them, as will be shown later, were used to limit enterprises' autonomy.

The 1968 reform expanded substantially the autonomy of enterprises. Managers of enterprises were given the right to make decisions about what to produce, how to produce and where to buy inputs, how many workers to employ and 'how to use resources for development purposes'. They were also given greater leeway in decision making about wages, prices and investment. It is important to stress that the rationing of inputs was in substance eliminated; with the exception of certain producer goods in short supply, the market was reintroduced for all other producer goods.

Despite all the measures mentioned, the autonomy of enterprises was by no means complete. The state as the owner of the means of production kept certain rights which ensured that it still had great, direct control over enterprises. (It is important, however, to stress that an effort was undertaken to define the rights of the state.) These rights, delegated to the branch ministries or local governments by conferring on them the title of the founder, included founding and liquidating enterprises, determining the sphere of activity of enterprises, appointing and dismissing directors and their deputies (with the approval of the appropriate Party body), and setting their salaries and bonuses. In addition, the founder had the right to merge enterprises into a trust. Finally, the founder was entitled to impose on enterprises certain targets in exceptional cases (for defence or for meeting certain tasks resulting from foreign trade agreements). Losses arising from such orders had to be borne by the founder (Friss, 1969, pp. 17–18).

The expansion of the autonomy of enterprises did not bring any important change in the existing minimal participation of workers in decision making. The Hungarian architects of the reform had two good reasons for not suggesting any kind of self-management. First, the Hungarian leadership was not well disposed to the idea of workers' councils as a result of the 1956–57 experience, and second, what might have been more important, they wanted to avoid the impression that the Hungarian reform was in some way a carbon copy of the Yugoslav reform.

5.3 REGULATION SYSTEM

As already mentioned in Chapter 2 profit was supposed to be the centre-piece of this regulatory system. It was to become an incentive to the promotion of economic efficiency and a guide to rational decision making. For this reason I will begin with how it was determined and distributed.

Regulation of Enterprise Incomes

Profit depends *inter alia* on producer prices and taxation. When producer prices were changed in 1968, a 25 per cent tax on wages (which could not be deducted from wages) and a 5 per cent charge on fixed and working capital (already introduced in 1964) were built into them. Of the 25 per cent, 17 per cent was earmarked for social insurance contributions (Flór and Horváth, 1972, p. 44). These taxes on factors of production were needed, not only because of the functions they were to fulfil, but also because of the declining yields from the turnover tax. In the second phase of taxation, enterprises were subject to a so-called production tax and a tax on profit. The production tax was to siphon off the huge profits realised by some sectors as a result of the price reform and also the differential rent from extractive branches (Csikós-Nagy, 1968, pp. 344–6). The profit was calculated as the difference between enterprises' revenues and their production costs. The tax on profit was graduated according to the purpose for which profit was used. In this way the central planners wanted to make sure that enterprises would not excessively feed the wage bill and the bonus fund at the expense of investment.

To make sure that the objective of the central planners was adhered to, enterprises were obliged to divide profit into two funds according to a set formula:[2] one for complementing wages (so-called sharing fund) and the second to be used for the development of enterprises, the development fund. The part earmarked for the sharing fund was taxed progressively (0–70 per cent) and the second part linearly 60 per cent. At first glance it seems that the sharing fund was treated more generously in terms of taxes; it should not, however, be forgotten that the development fund was much larger than the sharing fund. (In 1971 the former was 2.7 per cent times larger than the latter) (for more see Adam, 1974b.)

After taxes were paid, 10 per cent of the balance of both funds had to be channelled into a reserve fund on which enterprises could fall back if a turn-down in performance occurred. The 10 per cent was payable until such time as the reserve fund amounted to a sum of 8.5 per cent of wages and 1.5 per cent of the value of fixed assets combined (Sulyok, 1969, p. 172).

Price System

It was clear from the beginning that a consistent dismantling of the traditional pricing system was neither economically realistic nor politically viable at that time. Under the existing structure and organisation of industry (strong monopolisation), far-reaching changes, primarily in consumer price relativities, would have produced severe inflation and a redistribution of income, politically and socially undesirable phenomena.

Therefore the central planners set limited goals. In the first place, they wanted to make the pricing system more exposed to market forces by loosening the control of the centre over price formation and by a partial restoration of linkage between price circuits. They could introduce flexibility into pricing without great risk since they kept control over the pricing of the most important products. Four price groupings were introduced; fixed, maximum, moving between limits and free.

Fixed prices were applied to energy, some basic materials (30 per cent), agricultural products (59 per cent) and foodstuffs especially important for the cost of living (30 per cent). Producer prices for manufactured goods (78 per cent) and a wide range of domestically produced raw materials, and retail prices for consumer goods and services (23 per cent) were freed. Thus, producer goods not only ceased to be rationed (with some exceptions), but a great many of them were also freed from price control. Free prices for consumer goods were mainly applied to clothing and household goods, primarily those which tended to be luxury items; goods of mass consumption were subjected to limited prices (for more see Csikós-Nagy, 1980, pp. 52–4).

Free prices, which were supposed to result from an agreement between sellers and buyers, could not be changed freely. The president of the Material and Price Office, which is responsible for price administration, had the right to veto such changes within one month after notification about the changes intended by the enterprise was given. It was understood that the Office should use its veto right primarily in cases where the enterprise seeking price changes had a monopolistic position (Denton, 1971, p. 10). The central planners assumed that, with increasing equilibrium, it would be possible to expand free and 'limited' prices at the expense of fixed prices.

With the start of the economic reform, a revision of producer prices was effected. It pursued several objectives: to bring prices more in tune with input costs and market forces, thus bringing producer and consumer prices closer, and to renew the linkage between price circuits, to mention the most important.

New producer prices were instituted by recalculating costs and rates of profit. Before the reform, imported goods used for further production were calculated in domestic prices. In an endeavour to renew linkage between domestic and world market prices, the departure point for calculating fixed prices was mostly the weighted average of domestic and imported prices. More realistic depreciation rates were established on the basis of a global reevaluation of fixed assets. Prices were also to cover the costs to society of schooling, training and health care in the form of a tax on the wage bill. Finally, prices included a tax on fixed and working capital (B. Balassa, 1970).

On the average a 6.5 per cent profit for industry was calculated. (The rate of profit was calculated as a ratio of profit to fixed assets.)[3] In individual branches, profitability was differentiated, depending on efficiency, involvement in foreign trade, relationship of supply and demand for products, etc. The actual level of profitability was much higher (9.4 per cent); enterprises inflated costs in order to achieve more favourable rates of profit (Csikós-Nagy, 1969, pp. 141–6; 1980, pp. 47–51).

Recalculation of costs and profitability caused producer price relativities for non-agricultural products to change substantially and brought producer prices closer to consumer prices. Since the level of consumer prices changed only little, and the old, chief consumer price relativities set during the price reform of 1951 remained in substance the same, subsidisation of consumer prices had to be substantially expanded. (The unification of turnover tax rates, which was intended as a first step in turnover tax reform and thus in the renewal of linkage between producer and consumer prices, had no impact on the main consumer price relativities.)[4] The increase in producer prices also caused the turnover tax as a source of revenue to decline dramatically; this was, however, offset by higher direct taxes and social insurance contributions (Csikós-Nagy, 1969, p. 136; 1980, pp. 45–6).

The changes brought about in the price system introduced some flexibility and market sensitivity to price formation. However, hopes that, with the unfolding of the reform and the renewal of market equilibrium, it would be possible to make prices more and more sensitive to market forces did not materialise. When free prices grew faster than was assumed in some sectors for a period, the government came under pressure to tighten control over free prices,[5] all the more since this was a period when the reform was falling into disfavour. Dramatic increases in prices on world markets also worked in this direction. Again a tendency to price rigidity combined with periodic price revisions prevailed. This policy was backed up by old arguments according to which promotion of the profit motive requires price stability. Adjustments in consumer prices from above were carried out annually (Hare, 1976; Nyers and Tardos, 1978).

Wage Regulation and Incentive System

Wage regulation was probably the only important sphere where the 1968 reform started with an interim solution. Party guidelines adopted by the Central Committee meeting in May 1966 were quite specific about other important spheres, but they had little to say about wage regulation. Could the reformers not agree on wage regulation, or did they want first to size up the process of the reform before committing themselves to a certain systemic solution? Considering that the reformers were not sure how the price liberalisation would work, it is no wonder that they wanted to proceed cautiously in wage regulation.

After a three-year transitional period, in which wage increases were financed from the sharing fund and a 4 per cent ceiling on earnings (wage plus bonuses) was applied, a new system of wage regulation was introduced, which, with some modifications, was in force for twelve years. The main principles of the system were linkage of wage increases to a performance indicator measured in comparison to the previous year and a normative (which set the relationship between the increase in performance and wage increases). This was the first defence line against the excessive growth of wages; the second was taxes.

In the first phase, the Hungarians continued regulating average wages, because this is more conducive to a full employment and anti-inflation policy and allows easier control of wage differentiation. The central planners were afraid that the stimulation of profit maximisation might produce unemployment.

In 1971, gross income (profits plus wage bill) per employee became the indicator of performance in most industrial enterprises.[6] For every 1 per cent increase in gross income per employee, average basic wages could increase by 0.3 per cent. Increases in average wages were subject to taxation (50 per cent of the increased wage costs) which came from the sharing fund. The increased wage costs had to be included in the production costs, in contrast to the previous situation where they were covered from profits. Enterprises were allowed to increase wages above the limit matching increases in gross income per employee provided that they were willing to pay from the sharing fund an additional progressive tax amounting to 150 to 400 per cent of the newly incurred wage costs (Flór and Horváth, 1972, p. 104; Kónya, 1971).

The new wage regulation meant an end to the wage increase ceiling. At the same time it increased the tax burden for wage increases. This provision was offset by a more generous allocation of funds to the sharing fund (the wage multiplier was increased on the average to 3, see note 2).

The new wage regulation put an end to the Soviet system of allocating funds for wage purposes; in the new system, enterprises were supposed to earn the funds needed for wages. It was supposed to be an automatic system which would not require government interference in wage increases for productive enterprises. It took only a short time to belie this assumption; however, the creaks in the system's operation were of exogenous origin. Many large enterprises, primarily in the coal and energy industries, lagged behind in wage increases. This was partly due to their lower economic efficiency and partly to the price grouping. Their products were subject to fixed prices, and therefore increases in profit could only come from more efficient or higher output. At any rate, they were in a less advantageous position than many middle-sized enterprises. However, they had much greater political influence and they applied it. To placate the workers, the government ordered relatively large wage increases (effective in March 1973), primarily for wage earners in the affected industrial branches (*F*, 1973, nos. 4 and 5). In addition, some branches, which fared poorly under the new system, became subject to a direct assignment of the wage bill by the centre (*Műszaki Élet*, 1974, 7 June). This episode deserves attention because, according to some authors, it played an important role in the erosion of the reform.

In the determination of wages for individual workers some flexibility came about though wage rates were still set from above. A new tariff system, introduced in 1971, reclassified all manual workers and salaried employees on the basis of their skills. For manual workers six skill grades were introduced, and each grade was divided up into four groups according to working conditions. The new wage rates were set in broad spans, leaving managers the right to set the wage rates for individual workers according to their performance. They also meant a reduction of the differences in remuneration for the same work in different industrial branches (Berényi, 1974, pp. 29, 107; Kővári, 1981, p. 320).

The reformers believed that the success of the reform depended on managers and therefore made provisions for quite a large differentiation in bonuses. In order to make this differentiation more acceptable, it was combined with a reversed differentiation in wage (salary) guarantees. For the distribution of bonuses from the sharing fund, all employees of an enterprise were divided into three categories. In the first category, consisting of top managers, bonuses could amount to 80 per cent of their salaries (salary guarantee 75 per cent). Members of the second category (heads of departments, supervisors, engineers, etc.) were entitled to 50 per cent of their total salaries as a group (85 per cent salary guarantee). Blue collar workers and others who made up the third group were limited to bonuses amounting to 15 per cent of earnings as a group (100 per cent wage guarantee) (Buda and Pongrácz, 1968, pp. 83–4; Sulyok, 1969, p. 170).

This distribution of bonuses was very much resented by blue-collar workers not only for material reasons, but also because they saw in the system an act of discrimination against them. In addition, it introduced conflicts of interest as to the use of the sharing fund. Top managers were interested in using the sharing fund as much as possible for bonuses. From an increase in the amount of bonuses corresponding to 1 per cent of the wage bill, they themselves could expect an increase in salaries of 4–5 per cent, whereas blue-collar workers received only

0.7–0.8 per cent in earnings (Buda and Pongrácz, 1968, pp. 94–6). Due to political pressure the authorities abolished the mentioned distribution of bonuses. In order to retain the incomes of top managers a new bonus was introduced and designed in a way that it would not conflict with the interests of wage earners (Bánki, 1973).

The wage regulation system was quite successful in its regulative function (money wages grew in 1968–70 by an annual average of 4.8 per cent and consumer prices 0.8 per cent), but not very effective in its stimulative function, as the following subchapter shows.

Employment Regulation

The reform granted enterprises the right to determine the number of employees and their skill mix. All vestiges of restraints on labour mobility were more or less removed, at least for a short time. At the same time, local governments received the right to impose on enterprises the obligation to hire workers through exchange offices or to impose on workers compulsory placement (*A Magyar Szocialista* . . . , 1978, p. 358). The latter was used much more often than the former, but both applied only to restricted groups of enterprises and workers, and only up to 1981. The restrictions were necessary because, instead of the unemployment feared as a result of expected improvement in labour economy, which did not materialise, labour shortages started to show up.

The 4 per cent wage ceiling led to labour hoarding because it encouraged hiring workers in order to be able to increase wages for skilled workers already on the payroll. Hiring unskilled or semi-skilled workers who could be paid less than average wages reduced the average wage and enabled higher wages to be paid to some skilled workers or professionals. Even more attractive was the hiring of part-time workers who were counted as full-time for the purpose of average wage computation. In addition, newly hired workers were usually not eligible for bonuses (Balogh, 1971). According to one author, labour hoarding amounted to 100 000 workers in 1968–69 (Kónya, 1971) and most of it was apparently caused by wage regulation.[7]

The wage regulation of 1971 did not fully solve the problem though it lessened it. The linkage of wage growth to gross income per employee can act as a powerful stimulus to labour saving if the savings attained in labour costs due to a decrease in the work force are considerable and can be used for wage increases. It should be borne in mind that

increases in average wages were subject to taxation, and the transfer of
more profit to the sharing fund, in order to take care of the increased
taxation, brought about higher taxes on the sharing fund. In the final
analysis this meant that a 1 per cent saving in wage cost provided
funds to an extent that allowed only a tax payment for a fraction
of a 1 per cent average wage increase. Needless to say, such an
arrangement was not a powerful stimulus to labour saving. The
changeover in 1976 in most industrial enterprises to wage-bill
regulation linked to value added, which is in theory more conducive to
labour economy, and the easing of taxation on wage increases could
have altered the situation markedly, had the authorities not been
reluctant to allow enterprises to use labour cost savings for average
wage increases (Adam, 1979, pp. 157–63).

Investment Decisions and Financing

The reform divided decision making about investment activities
among three institutions: central authorities, enterprises and banks.
The role of the central authorities in decision making was diminished,
but not really decisively. They reserved for themselves the right to
determine the growth of the economy and its direction. In practice,
this meant that the government made decisions about major
investment projects that had great bearing on the structure of the
economy, about their technical development and, of course, about
non-productive investment which took place in cooperation with local
governments. In 1968 these investments were supposed to make up 60
per cent of total investments (Sulyok, 1969, pp. 178–9). The rest of the
investments, primarily in manufacturing, were to be determined by
enterprises; in practice, these decisions were influenced by indirect
methods and by the banks when enterprises took out credit.

Apart from non-productive investments which were financed from
the budget, all other investment projects were to be financed by
enterprises from their own resources, state loans and bank credit.
State loans were available only for the financing of major investment
projects decided upon by the central authorities. The loans were
repayable, under terms set by the centre, from the increment in the
development fund, resulting from the new investment, of the
enterprise that operated the new capacity.

Enterprise investments were financed from the development fund
(which was made up of a portion of profit allotted according to the
mentioned formula for distribution of profit (see p. 236) and of 60–65
per cent of the amortisation fund) and bank credit. Enterprises could

get medium and long-term credit. The former was usually extended for three, exceptionally five, years. Long-term credit was extended for six years.

Enterprises were supposed to compete for credit. In extending credit commercial aspects on the one hand (expected profitability of the project – minimum 7 per cent – the terms of repayment, technical level, etc.) and, on the other hand, the plan objectives were taken into consideration. Investments geared to an expansion of exports, changes in the structure of the economy, and to saving energy got preferential treatment. Such projects could get credit under more favourable conditions (lower interest rate, longer repayment period) (Sulyok, 1969, pp. 180–1).

Considering the high demand for credit the existing interest rate (7 per cent) was low and therefore could not really serve as an effective instrument for the rationing of credit (Denton, 1971, p. 13; B. Balassa, 1970). Yet it is questionable whether the central planners had any wish to attribute such an important function to the interest rate. After all, the extension of credit itself was supposed to give them a tool for influencing enterprise investment.

Enterprises' leeway in investment activities was reduced by the fact that they had to finance investment started by the state and regarded as state investment.

Decentralisation in investment decisions and financing of enterprise investment from own resources and bank credit did not heal the known diseases of investment activities. Though enterprises' decision making about investment increased (in the middle of the 1970s it amounted to 55 per cent) capital productivity did not improve. The screening of the investment projects (including the calculation of expected profitability in world market prices, which became more or less a formality) by the bank did not turn out to be an instrument of efficiency, and long-term bank credit was extended to investments preferred by the government. Investment activity grew at a greater rate than the economy could afford; because of the improper working of the reform enterprises had more funds for investment than was assumed; on top of this investment activity was marked by quite large fluctuations. The reform with its inconsistencies was only part of the problem; the main 'culprit' was the economic policy which still adhered to a great extent to the old strategy of economic growth.

Foreign Trade

Due to its great importance for external and internal equilibrium, foreign trade was handled quite timidly. Changes were enacted in all spheres of foreign trade; however, they were not far reaching. A renewal of the linkage between domestic and world market prices with the help of a uniform foreign-exchange multiplier which was differentiated by the two large trade regions (CMEA and the West)[8] and valid for exports and imports alike was among the first goals. Importers (exporters) paid (received) the world price converted into forints by the foreign exchange multiplier, modified by import duties, taxes (subsidies/special taxes), which was calculated as a ratio of the average domestic cost of exported goods and the receipts in dollars (or roubles) in the 1964 trade structure. Some economists argued in favour of a marginal ratio, but adherents of the average ratio prevailed; apparently the reformers were afraid that some exporters would make large profits (Gadó, 1969, pp. 115–16; B. Balassa, 1970; Timár, 1973, p. 63–6).

The choice of an average conversion ratio meant that enterprises with higher than average costs could export only with the help of subsidies. The subsidies given to enterprises were of a size to allow them to achieve profitability of the same level as in the domestic market. The rationale of this provision was to prevent enterprises from switching from foreign markets – usually more demanding – to domestic markets. Originally, the subsidies were to end in three years. It soon turned out that, though the situation in foreign trade was at that time favourable, subsidies had to be continued. In the period 1971–75 uniform subsidies for sub-branches were applied, the rationale being to discourage uneconomical and encourage efficient exports. Subsidies were also applied to imports in order to shield the economy against high increases in prices (Czeitler, 1972, pp. 115–26).

Changes were instituted in the relationship between producing enterprises and foreign trade corporations (FTCs). However, only a few enterprises (primarily in engineering industry) obtained licences for direct access to foreign markets (10–15 per cent of exports). Other enterprises were allowed to enter into a contractual relationship with foreign trade corporations either in the form of agency contracts (commission) or partnership contracts. FTCs were supposed to carry on business on their own account only in the case of products of small domestic producers (Gadó, 1969, p. 15; Brown and Marer, 1973, p. 172; B. Balassa, 1970).

Planning in foreign trade was modified; enterprises were no longer assigned foreign trade targets. Foreign trade was to be managed by indirect and also by direct methods. The central authorities reserved, as already mentioned above, the right to impose targets on enterprises, if this was warranted by obligations following from trade agreements.

Exports and, especially, imports were subject to licensing. This had several purposes: to enable the ministry of foreign trade to influence the commodity and geographical structure of trade, the balance of payments and the role of imports in domestic markets. This activity was aided by, apart from subsidies, taxes and tariffs (Gadó, 1969, pp. 116–17; Brown and Marer, 1973, p. 172).

5.4 ORGANISATIONAL SYSTEM

With some simplification it is possible to argue that the economic reform left the hierarchical organisation of the economy intact. One of the elements of the strategy in implementing the 1968 reform was the principle not to antagonise any segment of the population, and an elimination or even a definite weakening of the hierarchical structure would have necessarily antagonised a great part of the bureaucracy. This position was taken despite the fact that in 1962–64 a great reorganisation of industry, which had already started in 1959 as a response to similar reorganisations in other countries, was carried out. This substantially reduced the number of enterprises – from 1039 in 1961 to 853 in 1964 and 811 in 1968 – and brought about the establishment of nation-wide enterprises in some cases and, in others, trusts, both directly subordinated to the branch ministry. The industrial reorganisation was supposed to increase concentration and specialisation and rationalise management of industry. Needless to say, the reorganisation contributed to centralisation of management and monopolisation of production (Wilcsek, 1969, pp. 194–5; Schweitzer, 1982, pp. 35–6).

The 1968 reform set the principle that all enterprises, regardless of their size or subordination, should enjoy the same autonomy. It did not, however, stop the process of mergers, though at the same time some new, independent enterprises came into being (Wilcsek, 1969, p. 195; Laki, 1983, pp. 88–9). When the reform came to a halt in 1972, a new wave of mergers started, initiated to a great extent by large enterprises. Many of them wanted to improve their financial situation by swallowing up thriving enterprises. There were also other reasons for more concentration; large enterprises were eager to put their hands on the surplus labour in the enterprises they integrated. And, finally, the desire to firm up their position in the market also played a role.

There were, of course, mergers initiated by small or medium-sized enterprises which were in a dire financial situation (Laki, 1983, pp. 126–7; Schweitzer, 1982, pp. 55–60).

Due to the elimination of the assignment of plan targets to enterprises a shift in the distribution of administrative authority over enterprises occurred. The role of branch ministries and the Planning Office was reduced in favour of functional authorities (ministry of finance, foreign trade, labour), banks and the National Materials and Price Office.

The 1968 reform did not bring, as already mentioned, important changes in workers' participation in decision making. Nevertheless it increased the role of trade unions. It is worthwhile mentioning that in the 1966 Party resolution, when the role of the trade unions is alluded to, their obligation to represent the interests of workers is mentioned in first place. Despite their increased role, the trade unions continued to be subordinated to the Party (*A gazdasági* . . . , 1966, p. 41).

5.5   CONCLUDING REMARKS

The reform brought about many important changes in the system of management: it expanded significantly the autonomy of enterprises, eliminated the assignment of binding output targets, which had paralysed the initiative of managers, and thus made room for direct ties between different enterprises governed to a great extent by market forces, introduced a market for producer goods, initiated flexibility in price formation, carried out some decentralisation in investment decisions and undertook the first steps in linking domestic production to foreign markets. All these provisions are more or less contrary to the traditional centralised system as it was known in the 1950s. In other words, the changes mentioned pushed the Hungarian system of management beyond the framework of the centralised system. If we apply Brus' classification of systems we can term the Hungarian system as having evolved, due to the 1968 reform, close to a decentralised system; however, if we use Antal's classification, then the Hungarian system can be called an indirect system.

Despite its shortcomings, which will be discussed below, the reform had a favourable effect on the economy. It reversed the declining trend in economic growth even with the reduction of the work week from 48 to 44 hours (in 1968–70), brought about improvements in productivity and in the balance of payments as well as an acceleration of real wage growth. What is perhaps of the greatest importance and lasting impact is that it improved the supply of consumer goods to the population and thus restored the market equilibrium in consumer goods. Credit for this is also due to the development of small-scale farming side by side with large-scale production in collective farms (B. Balassa, 1978; Friss, 1978; Tardos, 1982).

The reform was, of course, marked by shortcomings and contradictions, many of which resulted from compromises aimed at satisfying the conflicting interests of different groups. Besides, the economic policy was not always in tune with the direction of the reform. The reformers expanded the autonomy of enterprises by eliminating, among others, assignment of plan output targets, but hierarchical relations, which were the instrument for carrying out the disaggregation of output targets, were left intact despite the fact that at least a great part of the bureaucracy could not be expected to be enthusiastic about the reform to say the least. Apparently, in order not to antagonise the bureaucracy, part of which was afraid of losing its position and influence, the reform went only halfway (Antal, 1981; Szamuely, 1984).

The reform was intended to give much greater scope to market forces; this in turn required the creation of conditions for competition. However the excessive concentration in the economy which was the foundation of monopolisation, was left intact, or, more precisely, was allowed to continue (see Laki, 1983, p. 14). For various reasons imports were not allowed to play an important role in the generation of competition.

In order to smooth the transition to the reformed system, several brakes were applied. Some of them were later removed, but others remained in force as the formula for distribution of profit which was not eliminated until 1976.

In pricing, where changes were crucial for the working of the market mechanism, only small progress was achieved. Prices did not become a paramount factor in equating demand and supply, and even less in allocating resources. The renewal of the linkage between producer and consumer prices made some headway, but domestic prices adjusted little to foreign market prices. Quite strict limits were set to price flexibility, including producer prices. Fear of inflation and social tension encouraged the authorities to be cautious. Because the authorities failed to create a rational price system, profit could not fulfil the role of a guide for decision making (Nyers and Tardos, 1978; B. Balassa, 1978; Friss, 1978).

Enterprises were limited in their decision making about investment; in practice, financing of larger projects was possible only by bank credit, and this was available only with the consent of the branch ministry (Nyers and Tardos, 1978).

The 1968 reform did not put an end to the interference of the authorities. Ministries had ample opportunities to influence enterprise activities, and they used a broad range, from the most subtle to overt methods which were contrary to the law, the latter mostly after 1972–73. In addition, at consultations called to discuss the plans, the representatives of the branch ministry, the National Bank, and the ministry of finance had a good opportunity to spell out their expectations to managers. Enterprises were, and will be, in many respects dependent on the benevolence of the authorities. To mention the most important reasons: they may need government loans and bank credit to finance investment; if they are in financial difficulties they may try to get a subsidy or tax relief; if they want to import additional machines or raw materials, they need an additional allocation of foreign currency. All these cases offered themselves as an opportunity to remind enterprises of what the expectations of the authorities were. The authorities could also assert themselves because the founders continued to appoint the top managers and evaluate their performance. If the government apparatus could not assert itself, the party apparatus could be called on for help.

The influence from above and the quest of enterprises for subsidies and tax reliefs brought about a situation in which bargaining about output targets, which was characteristic of the centralised system, was replaced by bargaining about application of regulators, subsidies, tax reliefs and prices. Large enterprises, mainly if they were headed by directors who had important positions in the Party, had a good opportunity to influence the nature of regulators according to their interests. As a result, the original idea of the reform, to apply the regulators uniformly as much as possible, was eroded (Antal, 1981) and this made even more difficult the introduction of a hard budget constraint in enterprises.

Under the conditions described, the market could play a limited role. Bauer (1983) characterised coordination of economic activities in Hungary as being by neither plan nor market.

Finally, the traditional strategy of economic growth was not much changed. The authorities were still captives of the old thinking with regard to economic growth; only after the shocks of the 1970s did they change their minds (Szamuely, 1984).

In 1972–73 the reform came to a halt. There are disagreements about the reasons for this. Some believe that large enterprises undermined the reform for reasons mentioned above (Szalai, 1982). Others believe that the change in the international atmosphere and the abandonment of reforms in other countries of the CMEA finally caught up with Hungary and that political pressure from outside and inside reversed the trend in the reform. Still others believe that internal inconsistencies and deficiencies in the concept of the reform itself should be blamed (see Chapter 7). Antal (1985a, p. 254) takes the position that the hierarchical build-up which was left intact eroded the reform. It seems that all the factors mentioned had a certain share in the process of recentralisation in Hungary. But there were also other factors. No doubt the explosive increase in oil prices and greater increase in decentralised investment than had been assumed combined with the persistence of the old diseases, among others, huge fluctuations in the rate of investment growth, gave the authorities the 'moral' right to revert to some of the old methods of management (see Havasi, 1985, p. 10).

6 The Polish Economic Reform of 1973

6.1 INTRODUCTION

The riots in 1970 were a strong message to the Polish leaders that a rearrangement of priorities was needed and that workers wanted improvements without delay in the standard of living. They were no longer willing to sacrifice the present for a future which was, in their eyes, at best uncertain.

Gierek's leadership came up with a new strategy which was supposed to ensure high economic growth rates (an old dream of the planners) and at the same time improve the standard of living. The new strategy aimed at restructuring and simultaneously modernising industry with up-to-date technology imported from the West. In this way, Poland was finally supposed to embark on the path leading to an intensive type of economic growth. Naturally, Poland could not finance a strategy which assumed high rates of investment growth and real-wage growth from its own resources and therefore resorted to borrowing in the West. As to the repayment of the credits, the planners had a simple answer – exports of manufactured goods produced in the new and modernised plants had to accomplish the objective.

The new leadership committed itself to an economic reform which was supposed to back up the new strategy of economic development. To this end, in 1971 a committee for the modernisation of the system of functioning of the economy and the state was appointed in 1971. Its report was approved by the VIth Congress of the Communist Party in 1972, and in January 1973 the reform was put into effect. Certain elements of the reform which had been prepared earlier under Gomulka were integrated in the new reform.

The provisions of the economic reform were to be gradually expanded on a voluntary basis. This had to ensure that the provisions adopted would not be applied rigidly, but, in the process of their introduction, would be adapted to the needs of the economy. In addition, in the application of the new general rules consideration had to be given to the conditions in individual branches (Wojciechowska, 1978, p. 19; Pajestka, 1975, p. 9).

90

First, the reform was confined to 27 large economic organisations (called WOGs in a shortened form in Polish) as experimenting units, 24 of which were in industry. In the years following, further WOGs were subjected to the reform. In 1975 their number increased to 125; of these 110 were in industry, and their share in sales was 67.7 per cent (Mieszczankowski, 1984). The new reform was thus organisationally based on WOGs, which became the basic economic units in management (more pp. 102–3).

As will be shown later, this was not a far-reaching reform in the way the Czechoslovak or Hungarian ones were. In some respects it did not go beyond the centralised system, and in others it took solutions similar to the Czechoslovak and Hungarian reforms. The Polish leaders were reluctant to go too far. Some economists even believe that the decision to embark on a new strategy of economic development was also motivated by the consideration that such a step would make a genuine reform unnecessary.

The WOG system, as some Polish economists call the reform, went through three phases. In the first phase (1973–74), the principles of the reform were concretised and put into practice, whereas in the second phase (1975–77), when the economy deteriorated, many restraints were imposed and controls intensified to the extent that all that remained of the reform was its organisational framework. In 1977 the attempt was made to introduce a modified WOG system. In the last phase (1978–80), the reform faded away (Kierczyński, 1984; Brus, 1985a, p. 205; Holubicki, 1977b).

6.2 PLANNING SYSTEM

The reformers did not promise radical changes in the planning system. The document of the committee for reform even demanded a strengthening of central planning, though combined at the same time with an expansion of the autonomy of enterprises (Baka, 1978, pp. 53–4). Obviously, what the committee had in mind was to make planning more effective. To this end, the reform called for an extension of the time horizon in planning, for the five-year plan to become the basic instrument of planning, for the transfer of some planning rights to enterprises and for an improvement in the methods of drafting plans. The reform put great stress on drafting a long-term plan for 15–20 years (up to 1990), which was to become the basis of five-year plans. It is doubtful whether calling for the five-year plan to become the main instrument of planning had great practical meaning. At any rate, the annual plan remained the fundamental instrument for current management of the economy, but of course, in quite a modified form. It no longer included output targets binding on WOGs; however, there were many exceptions. As a result, the plans of WOGs and of the branch ministry which supervised them were no longer completely identical; they were identical only to the extent that the ministry's plans contained targets binding on WOGs. The objectives of the ministries' plans not covered by binding targets were to be achieved by economico-financial levers. The WOGs were obliged to work out their own long-term, medium-term and annual plans which reflected their own interests. The plans had to be submitted to the ministries as information, but not for approval (Marzec, 1974, p. 72).

The supervisory minister had the right to assign targets and limits regarding supply of certain preferential goods on domestic and foreign markets, to order the introduction of new products and investment projects important for the economy or the branch in question, and to set minimum value of exports to the East and West, limits on foreign exchange for imports and limits on materials allocated centrally (Marzec, 1974, p. 79). Obviously, the list of exceptions was broad enough to allow the ministry to interfere with WOGs to a great degree.[1]

The relationship between WOGs and enterprises integrated in them was not the same in all associations since this relationship was determined, not only by the authorities, but by the WOGs themselves. Generally, it is possible to say that problems of development and foreign relations were centralised in the hands of WOGs. Payment of taxes was made mostly by WOGs which had the right to redistribute them within the association. In most associations, enterprises were autonomous, financial units with their own funds. WOGs had to fulfil two functions; they had to see to it that enterprises followed branch policy and they had to represent enterprises *vis-à-vis* the ministries (for more see Jakubowicz, 1973; Wiesel, 1974).

6.3 REGULATION SYSTEM

First I will discuss the changes in the price and tax system which determine the environment in which enterprises have to work.

Price System

The reform brought about some decentralisation in decision making about prices, some flexibility in pricing and attempts to renew somewhat the linkage between individual price circuits. These were modest changes which could by no means bring about a rational price system. But even these changes turned out to be an impediment to rather than a catalyst of improvement in economic efficiency. New attempts to improve the wasteful structure of prices for consumer goods were not tried until 1976, when they failed.

Unlike other reforms under review, the Polish reform was preceded by a producer price revision in 1971, of which the aborted retail price revision was supposed to be an integral part. In connection with the 1973 reform, a new price revision was instituted, to be implemented in stages, first in WOGs and only later in other organisations. But even in WOGs, the revised producer prices were to be valid only for new products, since WOGs were not allowed to increase prices as a result of the revision (Kubiczek and Bazgier, 1975, p. 278; Tymiński, 1977).

In the producer price revision it is necessary to distinguish between the basic price (*cena wyjsciowa*), which was not often used as an operational price, and the price for individual products. The basic price was supposed to be a centre around which operational prices fluctuate. It was to serve planning purposes and especially the setting of the accumulation rate in individual prices of new products (Kubiczek and Bazgier, 1975, p. 273; Fedorowicz, 1978, p. 108). The basic price consisted of the average branch cost plus profit mark-up which was calculated according to the two-channel price-type formula, namely a percentage of fixed assets and inventories (8 per cent) and the wage bill (20 per cent). The prices of individual products were set on the basis of their average branch cost plus profit whose rate was set by the State Price Commission uniformly for all the products of a WOG. The rate was a ratio of the accumulation rate derived from the basic price to total costs minus material costs (*koszty przerobu*) (Kubiczek and Bazgier, 1975, pp. 272–5; Lipowski, 1975, pp. 161–3).

As to the pricing of new products a distinction was made between producer goods (machines and equipment) and consumer goods. Pricing of the former followed 1971 provisions in substance. If new machines or equipment were involved, the director of the producing organisation could set the price in agreement with the main buyer and after consultation with the ministry of foreign trade. The price could not be higher than the world price. In the case of modernised machines, prices had to correspond to prices of products with analogous functions, with the qualification that due consideration was to be given to their use value. Since it was expected that the use value of the new products would be higher than that of the old, the gains achieved were to be shared in a certain relationship by both the producer and the buyer. Such an arrangement had to spur interest in both in technological progress (Stolarek, 1978, pp. 233–5; Lipowski, 1975, pp. 158–60).

WOGs received greater decision-making powers with regard to new consumer goods which were in great demand because of their conformance to the latest fashion or because of their attractiveness. Prices for such goods were supposed to be determined by supply and demand. The profit so produced could all be pocketed by the producer. If the producer could not make enough profit, he could apply for a reduction in the turnover tax for three years. In order to encourage producers to renew products frequently, new products on sale for 2–3 years were to be burdened with a higher turnover tax, if their price did not decline (Stolarek, 1978, p. 237; Cholewicka-Gozdzik, 1974, p. 172).[2]

The new price system, which was crucial for the success of the reform, was far from rational; it was in substance a patchwork of elements, mainly from the old system, combined with some belonging to a market economy; in addition, the blending together was not very cohesive. Under such conditions output added, which was the main indicator, could not be a very reliable indicator of performance. The situation was compounded by the fact that the definition of the new performance indicator – output added – was differentiated by groups of WOGs, a recipe for inequities. The explosive rise in world market prices as a result of the oil crisis disrupted the price system and created conditions for even greater distortions in output added in individual WOGs. For example, some WOGs were importing materials at low domestic prices and exporting final products at high transaction prices (see p. 101); others imported materials at transaction prices and sold products for low prices in domestic markets (Holubicki, 1977b).

Tax System

The tax system underwent changes as a result of the reform. The previous tax on profit was abolished and replaced by taxes on factors of production: on net fixed assets (5 per cent) and on the wage bill (20 per cent), both payable from gross profit. Of the two only the latter was a new tax. Apart from the 20 per cent on the wage bill, WOGs also had to pay 15.5 per cent social insurance contribution and 3 per cent to other funds (the 18.5 per cent were included in production costs) (Fedorowicz, 1977, pp. 135–8). Taxation of factors of production was supposed to encourage enterprises to use capital and labour more economically and to be a criterion of minimal efficiency in the use of factors of production themselves (Topiński, 1975, p. 176). In addition, interest on investment credits (8 per cent) had to be paid from gross profit.

Net profit was used for two funds: the bonus fund for managers and the fund for development. The first fund was used, as its name indicates, for money incentives for the management of WOGs and units subordinated to them (more p. 98). What remained from net profit after making allocations to the bonus fund (provided that no other funds were financed from net profit; some WOGs used part of the net profit for stimulating exports, for improvements in quality, etc.) went to the development fund. This fund also included the remainder of the amortisation fund.[3] The development fund was subject to progressive taxation once it crossed the threshold normative, which mostly was 3 per cent of the average value of fixed assets, but in some organisations reached 8–10 per cent. In setting the normative the planners took into consideration the amount of fixed assets and inventories in the organisation in question. The progressive tax was quite high,[4] and the only way to avoid it was to channel the funds available above the normative into a reserve fund which organisations were supposed to have (Fedorowicz, 1977, pp. 149–53; Topiński, 1975, p. 189). From the foregoing it is clear that the development fund was designed in such a way that enterprises would be short of funds for investment.

Incentive System

Wage bill and bonus fund determination

The reformers put the new incentive system in the centre of the reform. In this respect they continued in the established tradition. What was remarkable in the 1973 reform was that greater stress was put on wage regulation as an incentive instrument rather than on the bonus funds themselves. Was this for public relations reasons? After all, the reform was a managerial reform; it was geared to the interests of managers from whom a turnaround in effeciency was expected. And this was also the reason why a special bonus fund for managers was instituted.

The new wage regulation system differed from the old in that the size of the wage bill was no longer dependent on the fulfilment of planned output targets; instead, it was linked to actual performance. Of course, this did not mean that the wage bill ceased to be centrally controlled. Control was retained through the assignment of the normatives '*R*' and '*U*' and later, as will be shown, through charges to the branch reserve fund as well. The Polish reform stopped short of the Czechoslovak (1966–69) where wage growth in most of the enterprises depended on produced gross income and was, for a certain period, regulated indirectly by taxation (instead of a normative).

In the new system, wage-bill growth was mostly linked to the increment in output added over the previous year. This was primarily in industry where an expansion of output usually brings about economies of scale (reduction in costs and employment per unit of production). In some organisations, mainly in construction where an expansion is not necessarily connected with a decline in costs, the wage bill was set as a proportion of output added. The following formulae were used for the computation of the disposable wage bill, that is the sum of funds to which organisations were entitled on the basis of their performance.

$$F_n = F_o \left(1 + R \frac{P_n - P_o}{P_o}\right)$$

$$F_n = P_n \frac{F_o}{P_o} U$$

where F_n = disposable wage-bill, F_o = wage-bill of the previous year, P_n and P_o = output added for the current year and for the previous year, respectively, R = incremental normative, U = proportional normative.

Output added was defined as the value of output expressed in realised prices (i.e. the prices enterprises got for their products), reduced by the value of used or purchased materials, used energy and services, annual amortisation of investment credit including appropriate interest and the turnover tax, and increased by subsidies. The given definition is a generalisation of the way output added was used in 1973. Associations which later converted to the system applied a definition of output added which was different in some respects. It is of importance to stress that output added was designed as a sales indicator, which is, no doubt, an advantage compared to an output indicator. A sales indicator discourages hoarding of inventories and 'doctoring' work in progress.

The branch ministries set the normatives 'R' and 'U' for WOGs in a differentiated way, depending on their possible expansion and increases in efficiency. WOGs had the right to differentiate the normatives for the units under their jurisdiction. Both normatives were supposed to be long-term, in the beginning for 1973–75. 'R' was usually set in the range of 0.5–0.9, whereas 'U' in the range of 0.95–0.99 (Fedorowicz, 1977, pp. 110–16; Topiński, 1975, pp. 130–4). Since both were smaller than unity, increases in output added brought about a relative decline in the wage bill as a share in output added (no change in prices is assumed) and, in the case of the proportional formula, where the normative was supposed to diminish annually, the wage bill as a share in output added declined even if the latter remained the same. This meant that profit could grow faster than the wage bill and, if employment did not change, average wage increases lagged behind labour productivity growth.

Taking the foregoing as point of departure the planners expected that the linkage of wage-bill growth to output added would be an incentive to an expansion of output and increases in productivity. The smaller the labour cost per unit of output added, the greater the benefit from such a linkage. Even production of the same output added with a smaller work force enables higher average wages to be paid. It was also hoped that the linkage of wage-bill growth to a sales indicator would induce managers to pay greater attention to consumer preferences. The long-term normatives were supposed to give managers a sense of greater certainty and predictability and thus make them more interested in long-term strategy than in the short term to which they were accustomed.

One of the main objectives of the 1973 reform, to achieve higher productivity through higher wages, was accomplished. Plan targets in productivity were overfulfilled in 1971–75. Yet average wage growth exceeded the plan targets by an even greater rate (Meller, 1977, p. 150). Since employment also grew faster than was planned, there was an acceleration not only in average wage growth but also in the growth of the global wage bill, phenomena which could not remain without an effect on prices (for the reasons, see pp. 98–9). The central planners tried to cope with the new situation by imposing in 1976 a linkage of wage growth to productivity growth (for experimenting organisations this linkage was binding, if it was not followed voluntarily) and by making charges for wage increases payable to a branch reserve fund. Beyond a certain point, these charges were progressive; when first introduced in 1974, they were proportional. Charges (*obciazenia*) were a Polish speciality; they were a quasi-tax which remained at the disposal of ministries which could use them for future increases in basic wages and/or for financing the creation of jobs. Their function was to restrain wage increases, mitigate inter-WOG wage differentials and also restrain employment increases. In a situation where many enterprises could easily have access to funds, as will be shown below, 'charges' turned out to be a not very effective tool (Gliński, Kierczyński and Topiński, 1975, p. 59; Bury, Karwanski and Migdal, 1976, pp. 54–8).

The new bonus fund for managers[5] (the term 'managers' was understood very broadly; it included top managers down to supervisors) was applied to the whole industry, unlike the new wage-bill regulation which was limited to experimenting units. The bonus fund was fed from profit, and its size depended on the amount of net profit produced and the proportional normative (percentage share in profit). Only in a few experimenting units was the bonus fund dependent on the increment in profit. The normative set by the ministry in a differentiated way was supposed to be valid for several years (Cichowski, 1973; Jędrychowski, 1973; Zawislak, 1973).

The bonus fund was subject to progressive taxation, but only the portion exceeding the amount paid out in the previous year. Sums from the bonus fund channelled into the reserve fund were also tax exempt and could be used in years of poor performance. The progressivity was quite steep.

Employment Regulation

The reform gave experimenting units the right to make decisions about employment; in other words, employment limits were abolished. The reformers believed that better labour economy would result from the new system of wage-bill regulation and managerial bonus fund; both had in theory a built-in stimulus for a better use of labour. Furthermore, the newly imposed tax on the wage bill combined with the social insurance contribution made labour costs more expensive, and this raised hopes for a higher substitution of capital for labour.

It soon turned out that the predictions were ill-founded. Employment in experimenting units grew much faster than in the rest of the economy. There were good reasons for this: many WOGs shared to a greater extent than other units in the huge investment activities which were also initiated to cope with the fast growth of the able-bodied population. But this was not the only reason. Many enterprises managed to acquire enough funds for wage increases without being under sufficient pressure to be concerned with the level of employment. This was possible due to manipulation of output added: some got away with price increases on new products which were not warranted by the additional costs, while others shifted to more profitable products. Some enterprises managed to turn to their advantage their involvement in foreign trade under inflationary conditions (Holubicki, 1977a; Gliński, 1977, pp. 40–1). Higher labour costs probably did not have an impact on labour economy either. Even if the favourable income conditions of enterprises are disregarded, the tax and social insurance contribution would have had to be much higher in order to have an effect (Kabaj, 1977, pp. 62–3).

In order to cope with the problems in employment the government resorted, on the one hand, to the imposition of employment limits and, on the other, to the introduction of a new disincentive in the form of an already mentioned, ineffective charge (a quasi-tax) on employment increases (*Polityka*, 1974, 10 August; Gliński, Kierczyński and Topiński, 1975, p. 59).

Investment Decisions and Financing

In investment regulation the reform introduced some new elements: one, the linkage of investment activity through output added to the wage bill, was not applied in any country of the CMEA (Gliński, Kierczyński and Topiński, 1975, p. 131). Otherwise, investment activities remained under the control of the central authorities, directly or indirectly through the banks. Decentralised investment was limited to replacement and modernisation investment (Jędrychowski, 1984).

The central planners retained decision making about developmental investments. A part of them were treated as 'priority' investments which meant preferential claim on supplies and inclusion in the state plan by name. In 1974 there were 109 such projects and they amounted to 22 per cent of all the investment costs. Less important investment projects included in the state plans were controlled by limits to the credit which the banks could extend. The central planners also set time limits for the completion of investment projects. It is not clear to what extent the central authorities interfered with modernisation investments; it seems that here organisations had quite a lot of leeway in decision making. Originally the planners pledged to eliminate altogether any limits on such investment in the near future. In 1975 these investments were redefined by being limited to replacement of machines and equipment. The rationale of this move was to restrain enterprises' tendency to use them for construction work (Gliński, Kierczyński and Topiński, 1975, pp. 122, 24). Needless to say, this move restricted decentralised decision making in investment.

The developmental investments were financed from bank credit. If the authorities deemed the development fund excessive to the investment needs of WOGs, they could make WOGs use the balance as a supplementary source of developmental investment financing. This 1975 measure reduced even more the rights of WOGs in investment activity (Brus, 1985a, p. 205). Budgetary funds were available if organisations could not muster enough funds from other sources. (Of course, unproductive investments were mostly financed by the state.)

Organisations had to repay the credit, extended on the developmental investment, including interest, within a set time limit after the project was put into operation. The repayment period varied from several years up to eighteen (Jędrychowski, 1984). The interest rate on investment credit was 8 per cent generally, but lower in some cases.

The annual amortisation of the bank credit including paid interest had to be deducted from the annual output added and, since the wage-bill growth was linked to output added, repayment of bank credit had a diminishing effect on the wage bill. The rationale behind this was the consideration that production in new capacities equipped with new technology would be less labour intensive. It was also expected that such an arrangement would exert pressure on organisations to use investment resources economically (Gliński, Kierczyński and Topiński, 1975, p. 131; Szydlak, 1972; Jędrychowski, 1973).

The effect of credit repayment on the wage bill could be reduced by organisations getting a higher normative 'R' (or 'U'), or lower interest rate, or by stretching out the repayment period, or by a combination of these three factors. No doubt, organisations used their bargaining power to achieve some relief. No wonder that Jędrychowski (1984), using the benefit of hindsight, maintains that credit was not really an effective form of investment financing and, because of the low level of interest rate, it did not help to select investments from the viewpoint of their effectiveness.[6]

Modernisation investment was financed primarily from the

organisation's own resources, from the development fund of the enterprise or association. Such self-financing was nothing new; it was already applied before the reform in a modified way (Fedorowicz, 1977, pp. 258–9).

From the foregoing, it is clear that WOGs enjoyed the rights in investment activity given to them by the reform for only a short period; they were soon eroded. In the beginning of the new development strategy, which was based on rapidly growing investment outlays, decentralised investment was not objected to. Once economic disequilibrium started to take on threatening proportions and the authorities began to tighten the control screws, decentralised investment was one of the first victims, all the more because economico-financial levers, which were supposed to lead WOGs to rational investment decisions, had failed.

Foreign Trade

In the planning of foreign trade no important changes occurred; the old system of assigning targets in exports and imports by the method of disaggregation was maintained. It was argued that, in view of the dramatic increase in foreign trade activities as a result of the new development strategy, indirect methods alone could not ensure that the objectives of the plan in foreign trade could be achieved (Walter, 1974, pp. 184–6).

In other important systemic matters pertaining to foreign trade, the Polish 1973 reform did not differ substantially from the Hungarian and Czechoslovak reforms. In common with the other two countries, though not to the same extent, the Polish authorities undertook measures to reduce the separation between domestic and foreign markets and to involve producing enterprises in foreign trade transactions, at least to a certain degree. To reduce the separation between the two markets, the so-called transaction prices (world market prices recalculated in zlotys on the basis of average cost conversion ratio)[7] were brought in for exports and imports after a partial introduction in 1971 in connection with the producer price revision. Needless to say, such determination of transaction prices could be maintained only with the help of subsidies and this turned transaction prices into a formality to a great degree.

In imports plain transaction prices were used to a limited degree. Some modified transaction prices were used for imports of certain raw materials. Official prices were used for imported consumer goods and for raw materials brought in for the purpose of producing goods for retail markets. In brief, the transaction prices had little impact on the industrial cost of production. In this way the central planners wanted to shield the economy from imported inflation (Walter, 1974, pp. 192–9; Sztyber, 1978, pp. 207–14).

Before the 1973 reform, very few production associations had direct access to foreign markets. With the establishment of WOGs, the involvement of producing organisations in foreign trade increased. WOGs which produced for foreign markets to a great extent were allowed to absorb foreign trade corporations which traded the products of WOGs. Foreign trade transactions were carried on the account of WOGs.

Other foreign trade corporations (FTCs) traded on their own account or on a commission basis or in the role of an agent (only a technical difference existed between the last two). If they traded on their own account, FTCs paid the producers (usually small producers or cooperatives) official domestic prices. Trade by commission was carried out on the producers' own account. According to one author, trade by commission was supposed to be the most important form of trade relations between the producer and the FTCs (Bialecki, 1986, pp. 148–50; H. Wojciechowski, 1986; Walter, 1974, pp. 199–201).

6.4   ORGANISATIONAL SYSTEM

Poland was the only one of the countries under review where the reform meant a considerable industrial concentration, more precisely, a culmination of this process. The WOG, as mentioned above, became the basic economic unit of the reform and, as such, a *khozraschet* unit.

WOGs were not internally uniform. In fact, they integrated various associated organisations which came into being after 1958 when Gomulka's leadership brought to an end the attempts to reform the system of management. With some simplification, it is possible to say that WOGs included three types of organisations: (1) industrial associations, in which enterprises had minimal autonomy; included were enterprises producing investment goods; they had a monopolistic position; (2) associations of enterprises (enterprises had quite a large autonomy; a separate administrative apparatus existed as in the former type; this type included consumer goods industries); (3) multi-plant enterprises – vertical and horizontal combines (mostly the administration was carried out by the leading enterprise; strict centralisation) and enterprises with several plants were included (Jakubowicz, 1975, pp. 255–61; Haus, 1983, pp. 38–50; Korsak, 1978, pp. 352–90).[8]

The question may be asked: why did the Polish authorities base the economic reform on WOGs at a time when it must have been clear that WOGs necessarily strengthen monopolisation and restrict the autonomy of enterprises? Interestingly enough, many economists in the beginning of the 1970s stressed only their positive advantages. According to Pajestka (1975, pp. 15–16), the emphasis on WOGs conformed to the requirements of modern production and the need for closer ties between science and research and production. He also favoured WOGs because they allowed an inner redistribution of funds.

Gliński (1977, pp. 108, 122) believed that with the branch ministries weakening coordination of inter- and intra-branch activities, new organisations were needed which would be responsible for the supply of goods. Giant organisations were also created in the hope that Polish enterprises would be able to achieve a stature like that of well-established foreign corporations such as Volvo and Siemens.

No doubt, all these considerations played a role, but one cannot get rid of the impression that a paramount factor was the reluctance of the authorities to carry out a genuine decentralisation. WOGs seemed to be a convenient organisational tool under these conditions; it ensured a more effective control and allowed the authorities to argue about the minimisation of bureaucratic control. Expectations of economies of scale from the new organisational system might also have been taken into account. Probably the trend to industrial concentration, which prevailed at that time in all the neighbouring countries including Hungary to some extent, also had a certain role.

6.5   CONCLUDING REMARKS

The reform was short lived, as soon as the economic situation deteriorated, it came to a halt, and a process of recentralisation began. It slowly faded away.

The main reason for the worsening of the economic situation can be traced back to a general disequilibrium which affected all important aspects of the economy (market for materials, labour, investment, foreign trade and, of course, consumer goods). Several factors can be blamed for this. The new development strategy, on which so many hopes were pinned, turned out to be a failure. The Polish central planners overestimated the capabilities of the economy; they stepped up investment activities to a level which became impossible to handle rationally (in 1973 the investment ratio was 32 per cent). The imported technology in the form of investment goods was excessive; it could not be properly absorbed. On top of this, investment decisions were made from above without sufficient knowledge of domestic needs and without due regard for export possibilities and needs (Fallenbuchl, 1986, p. 363). The assumptions that the imported technology would be paid off by exports of products, *inter alia*, from newly built plants financed by credits from the West, were refuted by the economy's inability to produce enough exportable products and by the developing slump in the West.

Though Poland as an important exporter of coal did not suffer a deterioration in terms of trade (in the period 1971–76 it. only experienced a worsening of terms of trade in 1973–74) as Hungary and Czechoslovakia did, nevertheless the trade deficit with non-socialist countries was increasing from year to year (in 1972 the deficit made up 13.2 per cent of the import, in 1976 39.8 per cent), one reason being that investment activities were more and more dependent on imports of material from the West with a resulting growth in indebtedness (for more see Fallenbuchl, 1986, p. 367).

After a long period of an austerity policy it was only natural (and political wisdom required it) that average wages were allowed to grow. The problem was, however, that they grew excessively, considering productivity increases and investment activities. Rapid increases in real wages, which, in 1971–75, reached an annual rate of 7.2 per cent, were not accompanied by corresponding increases in the production of consumer goods. The change in agricultural policy was partly to blame for this. In the beginning of the 1970s, the Polish leaders tried to appease the private peasantry with various provisions (abolition of compulsory deliveries, substantial increase in prices for agricultural products, extension of social security programmes to the peasantry, etc.). When the political situation was consolidated, the Polish leaders returned on the whole to the old policy. They again stressed socialised agriculture, and various provisions were made to back up this policy (insufficient supply of producer goods, reluctance to sell land from the State Land Fund). A combination of these policies with poor weather brought down agricultural growth rates in 1975–76 after impressive growth in 1972–72 (Brus, 1983, pp. 35–6).

The Polish central planners did not manage to tackle the problem of distorted consumer price relativities which produced a high consumption of food, especially meat, compared to the per capita of national income. True, the Polish leaders tried to change the price relativities in 1970 and again in 1976, but in both cases they failed.

From the foregoing it is clear that the economic policy was primarily to blame for the rise of the economic crisis. The question now is: what was the role of the reform in the economic development described? Some believe that it was not helpful and that it even contributed to the economic crisis (Mieszczankowski, 1984).

The reform gave economic units greater autonomy in matters of price setting, wage determination, employment and investment. This in itself is not a guarantee of higher economic efficiency. Reforms can act in such a direction only if they are combined with an environment in which economic units are pushed to behave rationally. The creation of WOGs did not contribute to the generation of such behaviour; on the contrary, by strengthening the monopolisation of the economy, a fertile soil was created for the maximisation of output added in money terms and profit by WOGs without really increasing production correspondingly. This maximisation was made possible by unwarranted price increases for new products, increases in transaction prices due to inflation in Western markets, worsening of the quality of products and collecting of unwarranted subsidies. The fact that output added was not uniformly and properly defined[9] and the normative was set differently for different WOGs also worked in this direction. As a result, average wages could also grow fast and thus contribute to market disequilibrium (Kierczyński, 1984; Mieszczankowski, 1984). For the same reasons, WOGs were not interested in labour economy at a time when labour shortages started to show up.

The reform was introduced by steps in the hope that this would enable the systemic changes to be adjusted to the needs of the economy. The piecemeal introduction of the reform did not prove an advantage since the planners did not manage to make the new rules consistent with the old (Brus, 1983, p. 34). Some authors believe that the failure of the reform was also due to its rigidity and the lack of what in the West are called stabilisers, which could mitigate shocks in the economy (Baka, 1978, p. 62).

The reform was a managerial reform; the incentive system introduced by the reform was geared to managers. The central planners believed that if managers were properly motivated, this would do the trick. This might be one of the reasons that the self-management bodies which had been dormant since the middle of the 1950s were not activated. Average wages outside WOGs grew at almost the same rate as in WOGs, and therefore there was no reason why workers in their minds should link wage increases to the reform and be interested in its fate. As a result of all this average workers did not even know that a reform was going on (Mieszczankowski, 1984).

In no country under review and least of all in Poland were managers excited about reforms, one reason being that adjustment to the new rules of the game introduces elements of instability to the running of enterprises. In Poland, where the reform in question was preceded by three short-lived attempts at reforms, which did little to improve the working of the management system, managers viewed the reform with a great dose of scepticism and indifference (see also Zieliński, 1978).

The hierarchical structure of the economy with numerous branch ministries was not weakened by the reform (on the contrary, WOGs meant a strengthening of the hierarchical structure) though it was clear that a great part of ministerial administration was not favourably disposed to genuine reforms (Baka, 1978, p. 63; Brus, 1983, p. 34).

Part III

Economic Reforms of the 1980s

7 Common and Contrasting Features of the Reforms of the 1980s

7.1 ECONOMIC CONDITIONS FOR REFORMS

In the 1970s the economies of the four countries grew quite rapidly in the first half, but in the second half, and even more in the beginning of the 1980s, they took a turn for the worse (see Table 7.1). Only in 1983 or 1984 did the countries experience some recovery. The decline was caused by both internal and external factors. In all countries the sources of extensive growth were largely exhausted. Labour shortages were compounded by declining growth rates in the working age population, a phenomenon which had started earlier and which had turned into negative growth rates in 1976–80 in general and in Czechoslovakia in the beginning of the 1980s. Increasing shortages of raw materials and energy were another important factor. The extraction of raw materials and fuels in the USSR, which supplies the other countries of CMEA, was more and more shifting to the Eastern regions with unpleasant climatic conditions and often difficult access to deposits; therefore productivity in the extracting industry was declining and cost per unit of production, also due to high transportation costs, was increasing. Expectations of more economical use of raw materials remained mostly behind planned targets. Though material intensity of products is much higher than in advanced industrial countries, CMEA countries have not managed to reduce it at the pace it is being reduced in the Western countries, one reason being that the former are lagging behind in the development of high technology industries which are less material intensive (Drucker, 1986).

The investment ratio continued to grow – in the 1970s in some countries it grew faster than the plan envisaged – but in the 1980s it substantially declined. The lower investment ratio had to bring down the rate of economic growth for the sake of coping with disequilibria, but at the same time it slowed down capital replacement which is a precondition for technological progress. The smaller countries were, in addition, affected by the explosive increases in oil prices which

Table 7.1 Selected performance indicators for 1976-85[a] (annual growth rates in per cent)

	USSR			Poland			CSSR			Hungary		
	1976–80	1981–85	1986–90 (planned)	1976–80	1981–85	1986–90 (planned)	1976–80	1981–85	1986–90 (planned)	1976–80	1981–85	1986–90 (planned)
1. National income produced	4.2	3.6	3.6–4.1	1.2	–0.8	3.1–3.6	3.6	1.8	3.4–3.6	2.8	1.3	2.9–3.2
2. Industrial production, gross	4.4	3.7	3.9–4.4	4.5	0.1	3.0–3.1	4.1	2.6	2.9–3.4	3.4	1.9	2.7–3.1
3. Agricultural production, gross	1.7	1.1		–1.7	2.1		1.9	1.8		2.4	0.7	
4. Employment in the economy	1.9	0.9		0.9	–0.2		0.8	0.7		–0.1	–0.6	
5. Investment in the economy	3.7	3.7		–3.0	–2.5		3.5	–1.1		5.5	2.3	
6. Social labour productivity[b]	3.3	3.1		1.6			2.6	1.1		3.9		
7. Capital productivity[c]	–3.0	–2.4		–6.3			–1.7	–3.5		–3.2	–3.1	
8. Balance of trade[d]	+1.5	+2.0		–2.9	+1.0		–1.2	+0.1		–2.6	+0.3	
9. Terms of trade[e]				–0.4	–0.9		–2.0	–4.0		–0.7	–1.7	
10. Personal consumption per capita[f]	3.4	2.1		3.3	–2.0		1.0	0.7		2.2	1.5	
11. Real wages	2.3	1.4		2.1	–4.1		0.7	0.0		0.8	–0.8	

Notes: See Table 2.1.
Sources: See Table 2.1.

resulted in worsening terms of trade in all the countries except Poland. The slump in the West, accompanied by protectionist tendencies, made the competition in Western markets more difficult for CMEA products. All this contributed to balance of payment deficits and indebtedness *vis-à-vis* the West.

The reaction to the external factors was slow; they were to some extent underestimated, perhaps because the effects of the explosive price increases were for some time cushioned by the price policies in CMEA and, when measures were taken, they were quite half-hearted; the countries were somehow reluctant to face reality (Urban and Lér, 1982, 1986; Höhmann 1985).

The situation was compounded by the fact that factor productivity worsened as a result of mentioned and unmentioned factors in all the countries.

Soviet Union

In the last three five-year plans economic growth rates have continued to decline and have always been lower than planned. However, they have never dipped below zero as they did in the other three countries. The Soviets are trying to offset the exhaustion of extensive growth sources by 'intensification' of the economy. To this end they have put greater stress for some time on using more efficiently investment funds by modernising existing enterprises instead of building new ones, on improving the quality of products, on importing new technology from the West and on economising on raw materials and energy (Rumer, 1985, p. 165).

Traditionally, investment outlays have grown faster than national income. The XIth five-year plan had to bring about a reversal in this relationship. (In 1981–85 investment outlays had to grow by 12–15 per cent, against 42 per cent in 1971–75.) The reversal effort, which failed, would also have been important in making sure that the 'social programme' would succeed and that improvements in the standard of living would be achieved even with declining economic rates. Part of this strategy for improving the standard of living was the food programme launched in 1982 and higher investments in agriculture (Abalkin, 1981; Pécsi, 1984, pp. 43–53; Höhmann, 1983, p. 115).

These efforts have not produced the expected results. As Gorbachev himself admitted at the June 1987 Central Committee meeting, the pace of technological progress has slowed down at a time when it is accelerating in the West. The quality and design of finished

Soviet products is not improving and, as a result, the USSR has few products which can compete in demanding foreign markets. On top of this, the Soviet Union suffers, as already mentioned, from shortages of different kinds, including consumer goods and labour. In 1971–85 money circulation in the USSR increased 3.1 times, whereas the value of consumer goods only doubled. The Soviet economy is, to use Gorbachev's words, in a precrisis situation (*EG*, 1986, no. 27).

In the XIIth five-year plan for 1986–90 the Soviets are continuing their intensification attempts with some new elements. They put greater stress on restructuring the economy, on promoting technological progress by shifting investment to the machine-building industry and accelerating the modernisation of capital stock (higher retirement rates for machines), and attempting to reduce the completion time for investment projects. The intended 'radical reform' is part of this strategy (Urban, 1987; Clement, 1986).

Hungary

In 1971–75 the Hungarian economy achieved higher annual growth rates than those planned (6.2 per cent against 5.4–5.7 per cent). Perhaps encouraged by this positive development, the planners envisaged the same growth rates for 1976–80 as they had planned for 1971–75 (Mosóczy, 1979, pp. 157, 170), despite the fact that great changes of a non-temporary nature had come about in international markets. The Hungarian leaders were reluctant to resort to any austerity which might interrupt the upward trend in the standard of living; they believed somehow that the new storm could be weathered by sticking to the old strategy of economic growth. As in the past, they started out with a huge investment drive, and the economy grew fast in the first two years despite a crop failure in 1976 (see Antal, 1985a, p. 302). The economic factors turned out to be stronger than the wishes of the Hungarian leaders. They had to recognise very soon that it was necessary to cope with the worsening economic situation. Starting in 1974, Hungary's domestic consumption exceeded the current national income. The difference had to be covered by imports financed by loans, primarily from the West (Havasi, 1985, p. 15).

In 1977 the Central Committee of the Party decided to concentrate on the renewal of external equilibrium by slowing down economic growth, intensifying the trend to structural changes in the economy and modernising industrial branches which could have a long-term comparative advantage. This was a decision of great significance since it meant setting a course for halting the old policy of import substitution and orienting the economy to export possibilities (Lázár, 1982; Berend, 1981).

As a result of the new measures, investment activity was curtailed, and the growth rate of national income started to decline; in 1980, Hungary experienced negative growth, and in the following years the economy stagnated. Real wages declined too, approximately by 10 per cent between 1978 and 1986.

Despite declining growth rates which curtailed imports no great change occurred in external equilibrium. The deficit in the balance of trade which started in 1974 and worsened in the following years and was caused primarily by the deficit in trade with developed countries continued to trouble the Hungarian economy; one reason being worsening terms of trade (compared to 1970 import prices in 1986 exceeded export prices by 41 per cent (*SE*, 1986, p. 24)). In 1984 the situation improved, but only for a while. Foreign debt again continues to grow, one reason being a decline in world prices for agricultural products, and the budget deficit rises despite the applied austerity policy.

Poland

Poland did not react quickly to the situation which emerged in foreign markets. Instead of investment, which was very dependent on imports, being scaled down, it continued to grow and with this growth foreign debts piled up. In 1973 foreign debts amounted to $3 billion and their servicing to 17 per cent of exports, still a bearable burden; in 1974 the debts amounted to $15.3 billion and their servicing required 55 per cent of exports, to increase in 1980 to 101 per cent. All this happened at a time when the terms of trade were not really deteriorating. In 1979, a year when the terms of trade did deteriorate slightly, they were the same as in 1970 (Mieszczankowski, 1984; Jędrychowski, 1982, pp. 99, 152–4).

The investment drive was the main cause of inflation. It was focused on huge new projects in metallurgy and engineering at the expense of modernisation of existing factories. Because of over-investment new productive capacities were put on stream with great delays while wages were paid. Market disequilibrium was compounded by the worsening situation in agriculture, for reasons discussed in Chapter 6 (Mieszczankowski, 1984; Kisiel, 1984).

Considering the situation in which Poland found itself, the approved five-year plan in 1975 for 1976–80 was still an ambitious one (Mosóczy, 1979, p. 136). Not until 1976 were the Polish leaders finally prepared to act; the so-called economic manoeuvre stipulated a substantial decrease in investment and a shift of resources to consumer goods industries in order to arrest the rapidly developing market disequilibrium, which was also worsened due to the failed attempt to increase prices of foodstuffs. Furthermore, it called for a reversal in the balance of trade deficit in order to arrest the increasing indebtedness. Even before this, some changes in the system of management, which in substance meant greater interference with enterprises, had been carried out. Again the leaders mismanaged their own decision; investment was reduced, but, at the same time, the construction of the second stage of the huge metallurgical combine in Katowice was started. In addition, imports were slashed in an arbitrary way which aggravated developing shortages (Kisiel, 1984; Fallen-buchl, 1986, p. 371).

As a result of all this, economic growth started to decline, and in 1979 Poland experienced negative growth accompanied by a decline in real wages. In 1980 the government again tried to reduce market disequilibrium by huge price increases. This was the last straw! Then came the social crisis which had been smouldering for some time. Solidarity appeared on the political scene, and the fight for free trade unions and economic and political reforms entered a new, unprecedented stage in post-war Poland. Solidarity's fight was accompanied by strikes and pressure for higher wages, activities which contributed to a decline in output and a deepening of economic disequilibrium. The decline in coal production in particular, combined with a reduction in material imports from the West, had a multiplying effect on total production. National income continued to decline, this time dramatically – in 1980, 6 per cent and in 1981, 13 per cent; only in 1984 was the decline arrested (*RS*, 1985. p. xxxv) (see Chapter 9).

Czechoslovakia

In the middle of the 1970s the economic situation in CSSR started to deteriorate; even the lower plan targets could not be achieved. In 1981 there was a slight absolute decline in national income. In the following years the economy stagnated; in 1984–85 there was, however, a recovery. As a result of this development, consumption stagnated and in some years actually declined.

The worsening economic situation was caused primarily by internal factors, among them labour shortage, and shortages of raw materials and fuels caused by the excessively high material and energy intensity of products played an important role. Furthermore, social labour productivity and capital productivity were declining. The situation was compounded by foreign trade developments. The terms of trade continued to deteriorate as a result of the oil price shock, whose consequences were not fully felt until 1980 (compared to 1970, import prices in 1975 exceeded export prices by 6 per cent; in 1985, the figure was 49 per cent), and the deficit in the balance of trade even with socialist countries was persistent enough for some time for debts to pile up (*SR*, 1986, p. 443).

The central planners tried to remedy the situation by an 'intensification' of the economic process (a more economical use of resources, and an increase in labour productivity) and, on the other hand, by a slowdown in economic growth which had to bring about a reduction in imports together with a spur of exports, even at the expense of domestic consumption, in order to improve the balance of payments. The expansion of domestic fuel production (coal) – though at the price of huge investment and pollution – also had to work in this direction. This strategy provided some breathing space, but only for a short time (Vintrová, 1984; Levcik, 1981; Urban and Lér, 1982; Kusín, 1982).

The only solution to the problems faced by Czechoslovakia is to restructure the economy: to stop the extensive growth of heavy industry in favour of modern, high-tech branches which promise to recover lost foreign markets. Heavy industry is the main reason for the Czechoslovak distinction of having much higher relative consumption of energy and steel than the most advanced industrial countries. Not only this; heavy industry requires a great deal of investment which could be used for better purposes. According to economic calculations, the present proposals for the further development of heavy industry and protection of the environment until the year 2000 would require approximately three-quarters of all industrial investment. If the proposals were to be accepted, few investment funds would be available for new, high-tech branches, and for modernisation of light industry (Soják, 1987; *Rudé právo*, 1987, 20 March).

These are not new problems. However, it took a long time for the political leadership to address them at least partially. Even if restructuring of the economy is included in the present five-year plan, progress is very slow. For example, the targets for 1986 were not fulfilled (Jezdík, 1987).

7.2 POLITICAL CONDITIONS FOR REFORMS

The 1968 developments in CSSR and its occupation changed the internal and external political atmosphere for economic reforms. Reforms started to be viewed, especially in conservative political circles, as a source of internal instability and an external threat to the already limited national sovereignty, and therefore as something to be shunned. In all the countries, which experimented with reforms, this activity came to an end. Hungary was also under pressure to follow its neighbours; though it resisted this pressure initially, the reform came to a halt in 1972 (see Chapter 4).

The favourable economic situation in the first half of the 1970s backed up the political thinking and attitudes to reforms. Poland was the only country which, in the beginning of the 1970s, embarked on a reform; but this had to do with its special political and economic problems.

At the end of the 1970s, under pressure of the deteriorating economic situation, the attitude to reforms slowly started to change. In 1979, still under the leadership of Brezhnev, who was known for his aversion to change, the Soviets came up with a package of provisions aimed at improving the 'planned management' of the economy. The unfolding political crisis in Poland may have had a certain impact on this decision. Czechoslovakia soon followed the Soviet provisions. The 1979 provisions had only a marginal effect on the economy. Andropov's leadership, marked by quite a penchant for letting the word spread around the world that it was interested in reforms, came up with an experiment which, at several points, went beyond the 1979 provisions. Again Czechoslovakia followed suit.

Though the Soviet changes remained within the framework of the traditional system, they improved the political climate for reforms which was also indirectly advanced by the Soviet inability or reluctance to dip deeper into its own resources for the sake of helping the smaller countries cope with the difficult economic situation, mainly external disequilibrium. Under such conditions, the Soviets could not object if the countries were looking for non-traditional ways of solving their problems.

Hungary was under heavy economic and intellectual pressure to change its economic policy (primarily the strategy of growth) and put the reform again on track. There was quite a lot of resistance in the Party, primarily to the latter demand. In the period 1979–83 the changes made in the system of management, though they included some new elements (as in pricing), were piece-meal and of no great consequence. Only when the economic situation worsened even more and pressure from the intellectual community increased, were more comprehensive changes decided on by the Central Committee of the Party in April 1984; these changes pushed the system of management beyond what brought the 1968 reform. This did not mean that the fight for reform was over; still more changes were needed to make the reform workable. In 1987, the authorities committed themselves to further changes.

Poland was under even greater pressure than Hungary to change economic policy and reform the system of management. Apart from economic pressure, the new, spontaneously arisen Solidarity movement pushed forcefully for economic changes. It hoped that, *inter alia*, the economic changes would help to back up the sought-after political changes. In the Communist Party itself, a strong current favouring reform came about. And soon the country was engulfed in preparations for a reform. This reform was soon eroded and a new fight began for a comprehensive reform. In 1987 the political leadership came up with a proposal for a second stage in the reform which goes beyond the original reform.

In Czechoslovakia, the pressure for reform was much weaker, an important factor being that Czechoslovakia was less indebted. In addition, in the leading circles of the Party, there was an aversion to further experimenting with meaningful changes. It is necessary to wait and see how Gorbachev's pressure for reform in the USSR will be reflected in the CSSR.

With Gorbachev's accession to power, the clamour to reform grew louder, to reach a peak with Gorbachev's pledge at the XXVIIth Congress of the Party for a '*radical reform*'. The documents adopted at the June 1987 Central Committee meeting are its most important product. The question is warranted: why did Gorbachev commit himself to a 'radical reform' if his predecessors rarely even used the word 'reform', let alone 'radical'?

The dislike for change, which was probably generated to some extent by the advanced age of Brezhnev and his team, and the fear of what a reform might do to their political standing, stopped them from taking action, even when they were faced with falling further behind the West in mastering high technology. Gorbachev and his colleagues are different from the old guard; they are not burdened by old guard worries (they bear little responsibility for the mismanagement and the mess in the economy) they are much younger, more dynamic and eager to show some results. And therefore they are more willing to face the gloomy reality about the technological gap, low economic efficiency, poor quality of products and shortages, and do something about it – all the more because, in the long run, it threatens the Soviet position as a superpower. Since they understand that without political changes the economic reform has little chance of succeeding, they are trying to change the political atmosphere, too, by more openness and some democratisation. Finally, the fact that the Soviets have reached strategic parity with the USA allows the new guard to devote greater attention to economic problems. This may change if parity is lost. And therefore Gorbachev is trying hard to achieve a disarmament deal with the USA which would sustain the parity. Regardless of how far the 'radical reform' goes, it has created a favourable climate for reforms for the time being.

The reforms of the 1980s differ in many respects from those of the 1960s. Here I would like to confine myself to the differences in the relationship between economic reform and the political system in Hungary and Poland. In the 1960s the political system underwent few changes in Hungary and Poland, and no great pressure was exerted on the ruling elite to change it. The intellectual community still believed that economic reforms were possible, even within the existing or a slightly changed political system.[1]

In recent years the situation has changed; in Poland and in Hungary there is growing support for the view that, without important changes in the political system and without bringing the ruling elite under social control, the market cannot take on a paramount role, the reforms cannot be made irreversible and the economy cannot be turned around.

There are several reasons for this change in thinking. The most important is, of course, the poor economic situation which is blamed by most economists on the failure of the ruling elite to guarantee the market a decisive role in coordinating the economy. The controversial document written for the Hungarian People's Patriotic Front, 'Turning point and reform',[2] states that large and medium-sized enterprises still depend primarily on the Party and on the state management authorities, and little on the market. A similar situation exists in Poland. There is no longer great faith in planning; it has been discredited, especially by the inability of the central planners to bring about structural changes in the economy in line with the changes in industrially advanced countries, and thus prevent a growing gap in technological progress between socialist countries and the West.[3] Such changes are imperative if external and internal disequilibria are to be removed. It is argued that in the present system the distribution of funds for investment is not governed by the needs of the economy, but rather by power relations in the Party.[4] Can a worse accusation than this be made against a system which pretends to base planning on scientific methods?

Considering the one-Party system as given, the reformers would like to bring it as much as possible under social control. There is great similarity between demands in both countries, among which the most important are: a call for greater power to elected representative institutions (Parliament) (in Hungary for a government responsible to the Parliament, thus eliminating the coalescence between the Party and government), for the abolition of the '*nomenklatura*', which ensures Party control over cadres, at least at the level of enterprises, and for the introduction of genuine pluralism in ownership by, among others, the elimination of many obstacles to the growth of the private sector. In Poland, unlike Hungary, there is, due to the strong influence of the outlawed Solidarity, a demand for a strengthening of the self-management system. In Hungary, many economists believe that economic efficiency considerations should be given priority in self-management over political considerations.

The USSR and the CSSR are not yet exposed to the problems mentioned above. In neither country does a political atmosphere exist which would allow far-reaching political changes to be formulated. In addition, the intellectual community in the USSR has not yet been exposed to the frustrations and intellectual fermentation which the fight for reforms produces and which may lead to demands for far-reaching political reforms.

7.3 COMMON AND CONTRASTING FEATURES OF THE REFORMS OF THE 1980s

Introduction

In the 1960s the Hungarian and Czechoslovak reforms were the most far-reaching and the Soviet the most modest, with the Polish somewhere in between. In the 1980s, the four countries under review are grouped differently from the viewpoint of reforms. The Hungarian reform remains the most far-reaching, followed by the Polish. The Soviet and Czechoslovak reforms make up the second group which still operates in the framework of the centralised system. The 1987 reform initiatives are here disregarded.

In the first group, the 1980s can be regarded as a second stage in the development of the environment needed for the working of the market mechanism. In the 1960s most economists believed that the abolition of binding targets and rationing of inputs, and some other changes (such as price reform) would be sufficient to create such an environment. Recently, more and more economists have realised that these expectations are unrealistic and that, without allowing a capital market and a genuine labour market – both regarded not long ago as strange elements in a socialist system – the market mechanism has no chance of working properly (see Tardos, 1987). Introduction of a capital market aims at expanding substantially the options which enterprises have in the use of profit and the raising of capital, whereas bringing in a genuine labour market should make hiring and firing dependent simply on economic efficiency. And, really, in both countries (to a much lesser extent in Poland) some progress has been achieved in developing capital and labour markets.

The second group is adopting some of the systemic methods applied in the first group. It is already clear that this trend will strengthen with the 1987 reform initiatives. At the same time, it is also taking over some of the methods of the German Democratic Republic, especially with regard to organisation of the economy.

Planning System

Compared to the second wave of reforms in Hungary and Poland, the reforms of the 1980s have given market forces greater room for manoeuvering by extending the autonomy of state enterprises and by allowing the expansion of private small-scale businesses. Yet, planning has remained the fundamental coordinating mechanism. It is necessary to wait and see whether recent promises in both countries to accelerate the economic reform and give more room to market forces will affect substantially the role of planning.

In both countries (to a larger extent in Poland) the governments have reserved the right to impose targets if certain plan objectives cannot be achieved by other means. National plans and enterprise plans (which are supposed to reflect their own interests) are coordinated by economic regulators and, in addition, by some other instruments such as consultations and agreements.

Neither in the USSR nor in Czechoslovakia has the role of planning as the main coordinating mechanism of economic activities been changed by the provisions of the 1980s.[5] Improvements in the management system are to be achieved without really reducing the role of planning. What the planners are after is to improve the process of planning and the implementation of the plan objectives. The former includes improving scientific methods used in the working out of plans, extending the time horizon in planning, strengthening the cohesiveness and interconnections between plans of different duration, and state and regional plans, and finally making the plans more balanced[6] and stable. The extension of the time horizon is to be achieved, on the one hand, by working out a long-term prognosis, and, on the other, by making the five-year plan based on the long-term prognosis the main instrument of planning. What the planners really have in mind, when talking about the management of the economy by five-year plans, is to draft annual plans on the basis of five-year plans and not on the basis of the achieved level of the previous year which, on the one hand, leads to deviation from the plan targets and, on the other, favours enterprises which conceal reserves. This is not a new demand, but its achievement has eluded the planners in the past.

Gorbachev's reform, as formulated in the approved documents of the 1987 June meeting of the Central Committee, and the Czechoslovak 'reform' as formulated in the 'Principles' (see p. 191) do not make any important changes in the fundamental question of the role of planning. Due to the intended expansion of enterprise rights and the permission for restricted private activities, it can be assumed that market forces will be given a limited role.

The most important change is in the way the state plan objectives are to be achieved. Targets will continue to be assigned; they will be, however, fewer and less detailed. Rationing of inputs will also be maintained for the time being. Normatives, which replace directive methods, will be used to a greater extent. All these measures will no doubt create a greater leeway for enterprise decision making and may have a slightly favourable effect on enterprise behaviour.

In Czechoslovakia and, to a lesser extent in the USSR, prices are supposed to play a more active role in formulating plans.

In Hungary and Poland, the personnel of most enterprises has been given the right to participate in decision making. The new management structures differ in the two countries, not only in name but also in organisation. Nevertheless, they have many common features with regard to authority as well as to objectives they pursue. One important objective is to make the authorities' interference in enterprises' affairs more difficult. More in Poland than in Hungary self-management bodies are viewed as an instrument of democratisation of the political system.

Gorbachev's reform counts on the institution of self-management bodies in enterprises too. As will be shown in the countries studies, the self-management bodies in Hungary and Poland play a very limited role for the time being. Since, in the USSR, it seems they are to be openly under the tutelage of the Party, it is doubtful whether they will be able to play any independent role. It can be assumed that the Czechoslovak self-management institution, which is presently discussed, will not differ much from the Soviet.

Regulation System

Compared to the 1960s, in the first group market forces have gained more ground and, as a result, profit motive has a greater role. Fiscal policy in the form of taxation has taken on importance and has replaced normatives in most instances. This is not to say that normatives have been removed for good; they still reappear if problems arise in certain building blocks of the system (e.g. in wage regulation). Monetary policy is more significant than before, but still has a small effect on economic activities, including investment. The reorganisation of the banking system, which is now in progress in Hungary and which is also promised in Poland, will surely promote the role of credit and the interest rate, and of market forces in investment activities. Not only this, it is assumed that regulation of the money supply will become a new tool for influencing economic activity. In the developing of the capital market, first steps have been taken.

If the autonomy of enterprises is to be meaningful, the old system of evaluating enterprise performance with indicators has no justification. And, indeed, in Hungary it has been almost fully, and in Poland partly, eliminated. Therefore the question of which evaluation indicator to use – a question which was passionately debated in the 1960s – is no longer an issue.

In the USSR and CSSR, the provisions of the 1980s put greater stress on indirect instruments of regulation than in the past and on the need for enterprises to rely on their own financial means resulting from performance. As a result, the role of money and profit has increased. The reforms initiated in 1987 make full *khozraschet*[7] and normatives the focus of regulation. The rationale of the idea of full *khozraschet* is that if enterprises have to rely solely on incomes which they obtain from the sales of their products, then they will be under economic coercion to work productively. To make this concept workable, it is first necessary for the principle of self-financing to be really respected and, in addition, for an environment to exist in which market forces can play an important part, an idea which both countries are reluctant to a great degree to follow. The idea of full *khozraschet* is to be strengthened by normatives which are supposed to give enterprises greater leeway and more choices, and expand their time horizon in decision making by giving them a feeling of certainty about the evolution of various funds and taxes. Normatives may also reduce bureaucratic arbitrariness. Needless to say, normatives can mean progress compared to targets set in absolute amounts, provided that they are set in advance, are stable for a certain period of time and are not applied to each enterprise separately.

In taxation, which is increasingly becoming the most important regulator, Hungary and Poland have taken different approaches. Hungary has opted for proportional taxation on profit and on some other variables, and Poland (at least for the initial period) for progressive taxation. Whether a tax on profit should be progressive or proportional depends on the objectives of the central planners. If they want to tax the ability of enterprises to pay or to avoid great differentiation in net profit or siphon off unjustified profits – achieved through price increases – progressive taxation is the correct answer. However, progressive taxation may discourage economic efficiency since it penalises success and rewards poor performance. As will be shown later, these considerations have been decisive in the two countries' options.

In 1988 a new tax reform, which replaces the existing turnover tax with a new value added tax and introduces a new income tax, will go into effect in Hungary. In Poland, the same is planned for a later time. The main purpose of the restructuring of the tax system is to help controlling subsidies, and curbing the fast developing inequalities in distribution of income and, of course, providing a new source of revenues for the government. In the USSR and Czechoslovakia, no important changes have occurred in this area, except that the Soviet Union has introduced for the first time a quasi tax on profit.

In pricing, though it is crucial for the development of the market, no great advancement has been achieved in the first group. Hungary experimented with some new elements which did not exist before in CMEA countries – so-called competitive producer prices in manufacturing and for energy and raw materials. The substance of this change has lain in an effort to link domestic producer prices more closely with world market prices. The Polish reform brought about changes in pricing which had already been applied in Hungary in the 1968 reform. For various reasons, the authorities have not managed to maintain the price flexibility they promised. Gorbachev's reform promises to apply greater flexibility in price formation, among others, by introducing the known price grouping. In Czechoslovakia, the only new element in pricing is that periodical revisions of wholesale prices have been replaced by continuous price adjustments.

The innovations are perhaps the greatest in wage regulation. They have not, however, been a success, either in Poland or in Hungary. They have not stimulated the expected economic efficiency; on the contrary, they have become a source of wage drift. In 1988 Hungary will even return to direct wage regulation, though only temporarily, until a new system is designed, which will not be an easy task. In the Hungarian system, for the first time in most enterprises, wage-bill growth is no longer linked to a performance indicator and a normative; instead it is controlled by progressive taxes. Enterprises have thus been given greater autonomy in wage determination, but the authorities have still reserved the right to impose additional taxes if the wage bill grows too fast.

Initially, enterprises in the Polish reform were given more leeway than Hungarian enterprises in wage-bill formation, but gradually their rights – due to wage drift – were restricted. The present Polish regulation system resembles the Hungarian of the 1970s. However, Polish enterprises may have more rights as to determination of wages for individual workers.

Already the 1980s provisions in the USSR made the wage-bill growth dependent on an indicator of actual performance over the previous year (which, in most cases, is net output instead of gross value of output) and on a normative. This means that the institution of overfulfillment has been discontinued. In Gorbachev's reform, the wage bill is dependent simply on actual performance and the normative. In Czechoslovakia, wage-bill regulation is moving in the Soviet direction.

Apart from pledges, in none of the smaller countries has any serious effort been undertaken to do something about the narrow wage differentials, let alone the low level of wages (see pp. 228–9).

In Hungary, the incentive system for personnel is determined by enterprises themselves, and they also decide how much of the incentive fund is used for bonuses. (Only the incentive system of top managers – directors and chairmen of cooperatives – is determined by the authorities.) The same is true in substance in Poland, the difference being, however, that in Hungary the size of the bonuses is controlled by taxes on earnings (wages plus bonuses), whereas the bonus fund in Poland is controlled separately by taxes.

Historically, innovations have been first introduced in bonus fund formation. Yet in the 1980s, the USSR, as well as Czechoslovakia, has stuck to the traditional methods of bonus fund formation. Gorbachev's reform expands the authority of enterprises in this area by making the bonus fund simply dependent on the balance of profit and the normative. The Czechoslovak 'reform' makes the bonus fund dependent on disposable profit.

In employment regulation, the differences in practice, as in the 1960s, are not as large as one would expect. The situation in the labour market has almost the same impact as systemic considerations. In Hungary, enterprises are free to hire workers; the Polish 1982 reform promised the same, but, when the situation in the labour market worsened, restrictions were imposed in some counties. In the USSR already the provisions of the 1980s have given enterprises some latitude in hiring and Gorbachev's reform promises to lift remaining controls. The CSSR has several times changed its policy and now promises to impose employment limits only exceptionally.

As to incentives to labour economy, not much has changed; the stress is still on the stimulating potential of the profit motive, especially in Hungary, and on wage regulation. Considering the latter in isolation from other factors, it has nowadays a greater potential to be an instrument for inducing labour economy, since the four countries are now more willing to allow the use of savings from work force reduction for wage increases (in Hungary and Poland it is an integral part of the reformed system). This is, however, offset by the planned small increases in wages.

In Hungary, labour economy is to be helped by allowing enterprises to treat employment from the viewpoint of microeconomic efficiency, whereas the concern for full employment is to be the business of the authorities.

In the 1960s reforms in the smaller countries, the promised autonomy to enterprises in investment activities was substantially undermined by the banks using the extension of credit to make enterprises follow the objectives of the state plan. This arrangement was much criticised and was recently almost abandoned in Poland and Hungary. In both countries, however, the expansion of enterprise autonomy in investment activity has been hindered by the high taxation burden (in Poland also by the obligation to first take care of the old centralised investment and by great shortages) which was, on the one hand, the result of the austerity policy and, on the other, a safeguard against wage drift and price abuses.

In the USSR and the CSSR in the 1980s, the rights of enterprises in investment activities and financing have been somewhat extended, but investment as a whole is still under the strict control of the centre. Enterprises have been given greater rights in decision making about investment in modernisation and reconstruction which is becoming the focus of investment activities in the effort to accelerate technological progress. There has also been an attempt to use bank credit more for the regulation of investment activity, but with no great success. The 1987 Soviet reform does not envisage important changes in the rights of enterprises in investment activities.

In foreign trade, the differences between the two groups are among the greatest. In Hungary, and in Poland to a much lesser extent, the state monopoly in foreign trade has been reduced to a great degree. With Gorbachev's accession to power the Soviets are starting to change their view on the role of foreign trade and the first cracks in the state monopoly have shown up, whereas in Czechoslovakia nothing has changed in substance. In Hungary, and in Poland to a lesser extent, the domestic markets are partially exposed to the effects of foreign markets. In the USSR, and in Czechoslovakia to a lesser extent, domestic markets are sheltered from the effects of foreign markets.

Organisational System

Here the differences between the two groups are the greatest; it can be said that they march in different directions. In the first group, there are strong pressures for deconcentration in industry. In addition, in Hungary, entrance into an association has become the prerogative of enterprises and they are supposed to exercise it on the basis of their interests, and the number of industrial ministries has been reduced to one. In Poland, voluntary associations coexist with compulsory associations.

In the USSR, associations (more or less compulsory) in industry and construction are expanding rapidly and Gorbachev's reform intends to accelerate this process with some modifications. In Czechoslovakia, perhaps because concentration is more advanced, there may be a slight reversal.

The purpose of deconcentration in Hungary and Poland is primarily to create a more competitive environment. At first glance, one would expect that the USSR and Czechoslovakia will imitate the first group, though very slowly, since in all other aspects, if there is some movement, it is in the direction of coming closer to the institutions in Hungary and Poland. In this case, however, the USSR and Czechoslovakia behave differently and thus strengthen monopolisation. It seems that both countries try to avoid far-reaching reforms through more concentration whose purpose is apparently to simplify the hierarchical build-up and to harness economies of scale.

7.4 CONCLUDING REMARKS

The reforms of the 1980s are evaluated in country studies and in the conclusion, and therefore, here, only a few words are needed. Compared to the reforms of the 1960s, the reforms of the 1980s have registered progress in all the countries under review, except in Czechoslovakia. What is also important is that the political atmosphere for reforms, with the Soviet Union coming on board, has considerably improved. This, combined with the pressure of the critical situation in the economy, guarantees that the reforms will continue for some time.

The fate of the reforms is, of course, in the political sphere. Without changes in the political system, the reforms cannot properly unfold. It is evident that most political leaders are nowadays more disposed to political changes than in the past. They have learned that some liberalisation does not endanger their positions. There is also a need for the political leaders to have the courage to tackle such problems as restructuring the economy, reducing labour shortages by reallocating labour and decreasing the huge number of inefficient and obsolete enterprises. Without a solution to these problems, disequilibria in the economy, a lagging in technological progress and weakness of incentives, due primarily to narrow wage differentials, cannot be coped with. The changes in the system of management cannot by themselves bring about a turn-around without an active economic policy. Yet, tackling the mentioned problems means engaging in a fight with powerful lobbies concerned with maintaining the old structure of the economy and also with workers who are the mainstay of the regime. The situation is complicated by the fact that the success of the reforms depends also on the extent to which the political leaders manage to gain the support of workers. And this is not an easy undertaking since the reform expects from workers various sacrifices, among others, hard work (which the majority is no longer used to) and, what is offered to make up for this is belt-tightening for some time.

8 The Hungarian Economic Reform in the 1980s

8.1 INTRODUCTION

At the end of the 1970s, under the pressure of worsening external disequilibrium, the Hungarian authorities decided on important changes in economic policy, the most remarkable being the abandonment of the old strategy of economic growth, and embarked on some systemic changes including a competitive price system, the weakening of the hierarchical system and the expansion of small firms. This trend also continued in the beginning of the 1980s; its most important product was the expansion of the private sector. It soon became clear that all these systemic changes were not sufficient to create an environment in which enterprises could enjoy autonomy and which would force them to behave rationally (Antal, 1983). Pressure for further changes led to the April 1984 resolution of the Central Committee of the Party (hereafter the changes resulting from this resolution are called '1985 provisions') which, in its conceptual outlines means a consistent return to the principles of the reform of 1968 and which, in many respects, goes beyond that reform.[1]

Since the new provisions were introduced slowly and not always consistently and did not produce the expected results, and the economy, despite expectations, not only did not improve but worsened, the political leadership was again pushed, to a great degree by the urging of the intellectual community, to new action. And so came about the Party's Programme on economico-social development (hereafter the '1987 Programme') which was later translated into a Government Action programme approved by the Parliament (*Nsz*, 1987, 4 July and 19 September). Both documents promise to stabilise the economy, accelerate its restructuring and continue the reform with greater speed by giving greater room to market forces and competition.

In this chapter I will discuss the changes in the management system which occurred in the 1980s, primarily those which resulted from the

129

April 1984 resolution of the Party and the legislative provisions base on it as well as the provisions to be implemented in 1988.

8.2 PLANNING SYSTEM

Compared to the 1968 reform, the 1980s have not brought substantial changes in planning which still determines the objectives and the direction of economic development. These are pursued in the Hungarian system as much as possible by indirect methods, though direct methods are also used. The latter are applied to investment in energy production and its distribution, the extractive industry and important infrastructure projects, and foreign trade. In the competitive sphere (manufacturing, agriculture, construction, services) the market mechanism plays an important role; it is, however, regulated on the basis of the plan, and this means in practice that the government also interferes in the competitive sphere; it supplements the market especially where it is not well developed; but it also makes direct decisions for the sake of accelerating foreign trade, technological progress and economic growth (A. Balassa, 1984, pp. 29–31).

The annual plan, though it no longer contains targets for enterprises, still continues to be drafted. It contains intended government objectives in economic growth, production, investment, standard of living as well as in economic policies including economic regulators the government intends to apply in order to achieve its goals. The state budget policy as well as the credit policy are closely intertwined with the annual plan. The central authorities reserve the right to interfere operatively with enterprise activities, not only indirectly by modifying the regulation methods, but also directly. They have the right, under certain conditions, to order enterprises to perform certain targets if the plan objective cannot be achieved by other means. The order must be given in writing, and losses arising from such orders should be paid by the ordering authority, which can be the founding body (the branch ministry or local government), the foreign trade minister or the body in charge of market supervision, usually the Material and Price Office. If the order is issued by the government council no compensation for losses can be claimed (*Magyar Közlöny*, 1984, no. 47).

In the effort to orchestrate the central plan with enterprise plans in order to encourage enterprises to follow the objectives of national plans, the old instruments (applied since 1968) are used: apart from economic regulators, a system of dissemination of information, consultations and agreements. The role of information is not supposed to be a one-way activity; the centre supplies information about its plans in the annual plan which can be of great importance to enterprises when drafting their own plans, but at the same time it wants information about enterprise plans. Consultations are a follow-up of the process of information. In the past consultations were often used as a forum for influencing enterprises' activities. It seems that the old practice has not yet come to an end (A. Balassa, 1984, pp. 38–31).

Needless to say, many economists do not agree with the combination of planning and the market mechanism as practised; they would like to see a greater role carved out for the market mechanism at the expense of planning. Of course, concrete views on the division of the roles are quite divergent, as the volume of contributions on the role of planning published by the Economic Institute of the Hungarian Academy of Sciences shows (*Vita* . . . , 1984). In the document mentioned, 'Turning point and reform', which presents a radicalisation of views on the role of the market compared to the document above, the authors call for a replacement of the existing planning (whose focus is on planning of economic growth, macroproportions, investment activities, etc.) with financial planning whose centre would be the planning of internal and external financial equilibrium. Though the '1987 Programme' as well as the Government programme promises to improve planning and give greater room to the market mechanism, this by no means indicates the adoption of the demands in the 'Turning point and reform'.

New Management Structures in Enterprises

In the long debate in 1981–84 which preceded the 1985 provisions, one of the main demands was to separate government administration from enterprise business. Such a provision is viewed as a guarantee against government interference in the affairs of enterprises. In response to these demands the rules for exercising property rights have been changed. The management of enterprises is allowed to exercise property rights with certain qualifications and is supposed to be no longer responsible to the authorities for its decisions and performance. Auditing rights of the authorities are limited to an examination of whether the enterprises obey the laws of the land. What is of great importance is the gradual introduction of the new management structures on the level of enterprises.

In large and medium-sized enterprises important policy decisions rest in the hands of an *enterprise council*. This council consists of representatives of management (the director can appoint up to one-third of the management representation) and employees. The latter must make up at least 50 per cent of the members of the council; they should be blue- and white-collar workers. Managers, other than top managers, can sit on the council as representatives of employees. Party and trade union representatives participate in the deliberations without having the right to vote.

The second new management structure is designed according to the working of cooperatives. The management can rest in the hands of a general meeting of all employees or in the hands of representatives of employees. In both cases an executive management must be elected.

In the two new management structures the director is elected; however, the founding body has the right to veto anyone on the list of candidates for a directorship as well as the dismissal of directors. The Party exercises its influence through the founding body.

The two new management structures have rights which are denied to state supervised enterprises (enterprises with the old structure of management); they can make decisions about issuance of bonds for investment purposes, transfer of assets, mergers with other enterprises, and about important employment problems. They are also entitled to elect and dismiss the director with the mentioned qualifications, determine his jurisdiction and evaluate his performance.

In the new managment structures the job of the director must be advertised, and he should be usually appointed for a period of five years (and the founder of the state supervised enterprises can do the same if he so wishes) (*Magyar Közlöny*, 1984, no. 46). Advertising, however, is only necessary if the present director is not re-elected in the transitional period to the new management structures. And the authorities have made it known that they prefer to have the present directors re-elected and really only a few new directors were elected.

According to 1986 figures, 62 per cent of industrial enterprises are managed by enterprise councils and 15 per cent by collective management. Only 23 per cent of enterprises (primarily those in poor shape) remain under the direct supervision of the ministry. Enterprise councils have become the prevailing management form in industry also because directors preferred them due to their looser structure (*F*, 1987, no. 2). It seems that the situation in other sectors is not substantially different.

The question may be posed: are the provisions mentioned sufficient to discourage authorities from interference in the affairs of enterprises and to ensure the personnel's participation in decision making and thus its interest in the promotion of economic efficiency (see Chapter 7)? Apart from the already mentioned instruments for influencing enterprises' decision making, the authorities can use the dependence of enterprises on the benevolence of the authorities for asserting themselves (since enterprises may need government loans, authorities' support in getting foreign exchange and construction capacity, and, last but not least, subsidies, tax exemption or reduction). Finally, the founder still has influence over the selection of the director and can prevent his dismissal.

On the other hand, the present austerity policy, which is reflected in, among others, restrictions on earnings increases, creates a favourable atmosphere for a voluntary solidarity between enterprise councils and directors, the latter being able to use this as a shield against the authorities' interference.

There is a danger that primarily the new management structure[2] headed by an enterprise council, which is the more important of the two, will be reduced to a formality. The experience with Yugoslav workers' councils shows that a shrewd director is, for known reasons, in a position to manipulate the workers' council. In the Hungarian system the possibility of manipulation is eased by the provision that the council need not be convened more than once a year, managers can sit on the councils as representatives of employees (Sárközy, 1985) and the old directors may remain in their positions. First experience shows that the composition of industrial enterprise councils is of a kind that makes manipulation easier. The percentage of genuine blue-collar workers sitting on the councils is small; the councils (as well as their chairmanships) are packed with subordinates of the director (managers, engineers, administrators, etc., whose promotion depends on the director). This is probably also the reason why a predominant number of councils are content to play a rubber-stamp role; to the extent that they are active, they concentrate primarily on the determination of earnings and distribution of bonuses (Bossányi, 1986; Pető, 1986). Under such conditions, it cannot be expected that the new management structures will bring about an increased employees' identification with enterprise interests.

8.3   REGULATION SYSTEM

Regulation of Incomes of Enterprises

Incomes accruing to enterprises from sales of goods and services have been regulated since 1968 by taxes levied on gross profit. Since the purpose of taxation – besides being a source of revenues for the state – has not been to mitigate differences in enterprise profit but to be a criterion of economic efficiency, all taxes are proportional, with the exception of taxes on earnings. Such proportional taxation has to reward enterprises which are able to produce more profits. In reality, this principle has been grossly violated, as will be shown later.

Disregarding the local tax, enterprises pay a tax on profit (after several increases, in 1987 it was 55 per cent) and on factors of production (on wages paid out – 10 per cent – and on property – 3 per cent – as well as an entirely new tax on accumulation (up to 25 per cent)) (*Magyar Közlöny*, 1984, no. 47; Bossányi, 1984; Balázsy, 1987). All these taxes are paid from profit, directly or indirectly, from the incentive fund.

The tax on profit, together with other taxes paid from profit, make up more than 80 per cent of the profit produced by enterprises.[3] It is generally accepted that the tax burden is too high and hampers the autonomy of enterprises. However, the authorities have been reluctant until recently to ease it because of the state budget deficit and the desire to have the level of enterprise purchasing power under control. For more, see later.

After the payment of taxes (local, profit and wage) enterprises are free to use the balance of profit according to their own considerations – with some limitations. The 1968 reform's division of profit into two funds has been abolished and instead a new incentive fund has been introduced. The new fund is made up of profit after taxation, the full amortisation fund (before 1985 enterprises had to surrender 40 per cent of the amortisation fund), and receipts from sale of fixed assets and some other sources. It can be used for investment and bonuses as well as for payment of some taxes as in the past. Taxation is still differentiated, not according to the funds the profit is channelled into, but according to the purpose for which profit is used. The incentive fund, like the sharing fund in the past which was used for all other allowable purposes except development, must be used in a certain order. First, it must be used for payment of taxes: property, accumulation and, what is the most important, taxes on earnings.

Bonuses for top managers can be paid from it if the enterprise has fulfilled all other obligations (Kolarik, 1984, p. 61).

Starting with 1988, the incentive fund as well as other funds which enterprises have (welfare and culture, and technical) are to be replaced by one single property fund from which all enterprise activities will be financed. The rationale behind this move is to give enterprises greater leeway in decision making (*F*, 1987, no. 28, p. 7).

Overhaul of the Tax System

In 1988 the tax system is to be overhauled by the introduction of a new general turnover tax which is nothing but a value added tax and of an income tax payable by wage and salary earners and the self-employed. The purpose of the general turnover tax, which replaces the present turnover tax, is to give a clear view of the tax burden and indirectly provide control over subsidies. It is expected that no exemptions from the set tax rules will be given. If the extension of subsidies is warranted, it will be made in the form of profit tax reduction. The benefit of this approach will be that poorly performing enterprises will not be able to take advantage of it to any great extent (interview with L. Antal, 1987). Several existing taxes will be terminated (property tax, tax on paid out wages and accumulation tax) and others reduced (tax on earnings, and on profit to 45 per cent). This has to make possible, on the one hand, a reduction in the huge tax burden of enterprises (the finance minister promises a reduction to 70 per cent, *Nsz*, 1987, 19 September) and, on the other, a reduction in producer prices in order to accommodate the new general turnover tax. The price reduction will be differentiated, since the overhaul of the turnover tax and the transformation of the present net earnings into gross earnings (see below) to be financed by enterprises do not affect all the branches to the same extent. In addition, the changes in prices are also to be used for changing price relativities and reducing subsidies. The producer price reduction is to be carried out in an administrative way, with the help of indexes which will be applied to the prices of 31 December 1987, in the range of 80 to 110 per cent. The rates of the new tax are to be almost as before: 25 per cent (normal), 15 per cent (reduced) and zero for many services (*F*, 1987, no. 28, pp. 7–11).

In 1988 Hungary will cease to be a country without income tax. In order to neutralise the impact of income tax on earnings, which are low anyhow, the net earnings achieved by individuals in their main jobs in the state sector in 1987 are to be increased sufficiently by enterprises to cover the new income tax in 1988. The income tax is to be progressive (from 20 per cent on earnings which make up 64 per cent of the average earnings in 1987 to 60 per cent on earnings exceeding ten times the average). The purpose of the new income tax is primarily twofold: on the one hand, to find a new source of state revenues in order to cope with the growing budget deficit, and, on the other hand, to mitigate the income differentials between the state and the private (legal and illegal) sectors.[4]

It is too early to predict the extent to which the tax overhaul will promote the economic reform. What is clear is that the new turnover tax will upset, at least for some time, the efforts to rationalise the price system. The tax overhaul will also add considerably to inflation (it assumed that in 1988 inflation will reach at least 15 per cent and 7 per cent will be due to the tax reform) and generate social tensions. Apart from padding costs, usual in price revisions, enterprises will look for compensation for higher costs in higher prices. As a result more controls will be needed to hold down inflation.

Regulation of Earnings in Enterprises

The new system of regulating earnings (wages plus bonuses), introduced in 1985, is a mixture of old methods and new approaches; if it had been implemented in 1987 in the form promised, it would have meant quite a dramatic break with the past. The new methods have not worked as expected – a very frequent phenomenon – and therefore controls which are a reminder of the past could not be eliminated.

According to the 1985 provisions in most enterprises (in 1985 this was 60 per cent) managers, in cooperation with trade union organisations, *are free* to set wage increases according to their own consideration; the only constraint is a progressive tax. The levying of taxes is done in two ways. In the two-thirds of enterprises where the new earnings regulation is applied, up to 1987 the progressive tax was levied on the earnings of each employee (regulation of earnings level, hereafter REL) and in one-third of enterprises the tax was levied on the average increments in earnings of the employees as a collective compared to the previous year (regulation of earnings increases (REI)). The progressive tax is quite high. In the remaining enterprises (coal industry, metallurgy, transportation, public utilities, etc., where no favourable conditions for competition exist) a version of the pre-1985 government earnings regulation system is applied (Borlói, 1984; Pongrácz, 1984, p. 71; Sebestyén, 1985).

In order to make sure that wage increases do not get out of hand, a back-up system has been built into the earnings regulation system for the competitive sphere. For the years 1985–86 a surtax was payable if average earnings increased more than 3 per cent and the value added grew at a slower rate than earnings compared to the previous year (Borlói, 1984). It was assumed that no surtax woud be paid in 1987; an assumption which has not materialised.

The new earnings regulation system, particularly REL, which is more closely tied to profit, was evaluated positively by many economists and enterprise directors; they saw it as an important step in the direction of loosening government control over earnings (before 1985 the growth of the wage bill depended on a performance indicator and normative and both were set from above) and a new opportunity for widening wage differentials, primarily for skill. They believed that REL especially would have a favourable effect on economic efficiency; it would bring about a movement of workers to enterprises which are short of labour but can afford to pay higher wages and thus exert pressure on lagging enterprises.

The excitement for REL was dampened by the earnings development in 1985 to 1987. Earnings grew much faster, particularly in enterprises applying REL, despite high taxation, than was envisioned in the annual plans. This in itself would not be so bad were it combined with corresponding increases in productivity, which was not the case, or at least with a realistic expectation that increases in the wage bill would soon be followed by increases in productivity. After all, average wages in the Hungarian state sector are low considering the national income per capita and in addition quite compressed (Révész, 1986).

There are several reasons for the generous wage policy practised by managers: competition for more labour (or for keeping workers on the payroll) which is still in short supply, pressure for parity in wage increases once wages start to grow fast in some enterprises, also because prices increase fast too, and reciprocation for the 'generosity' of the enterprise councils towards the top managers.[5]

The drift in earnings, and even more the deteriorated economic situation in 1986, prompted the authorities to increase restrictions on earnings growth through a short-term quasi-wage freeze in 1987 (in the official version a postponement of wage increases) and a tightening of the rules for earnings increases.[6]

As usual, when shortcomings in earnings regulation appear, a discussion about its overhaul arises. This time the trade unions have taken the initiative. Their proposal, in a nutshell, suggests that the trade unions, with representatives of enterprises (perhaps the Chamber of Commerce), will agree once a year on the minimum tax free increase in wages which will be related to consumer price increases. On top of this, branch agreements will be concluded on wage increases linked to a certain level of performance (Nagy, 1987).

In my opinion the idea that wage increases should be subject to an agreement among interested parties (as in Austria and Sweden) has no great chance of working under the existing conditions in Hungary. Managers in Hungary, and even more in other socialist countries, are not a sufficient restraining force in the absence of objective restraining forces (preferably the market) especially when self-management bodies are in existence. In addition, the government at present intends to slow down increases in earnings and reduce real wages (in order to mitigate inflationary pressures and reduce the budget deficit) and this is usually not an opportune time for easing control.

Indeed, starting with 1988 Hungary will embark on a direct regulation of wages which resembles in some respects the pre-1968 wage regulation. Most enterprises will be assigned rate limits for wage-bill growth, which means that the wage bill will no longer be linked to the performance of enterprises. The wage-bill regulation has been chosen in the hope that this will stimulate enterprises to reduce the work force since the saved money will be available for wage increases (this is at least what the government promises). In enterprises which suffer from labour shortages, average wages will be regulated. Exceeding the targets will be heavily penalised, probably by taxes. Bonuses will probably be linked to the produced profit of enterprises (*F*, 1987, no. 32, p. 7). This provision, which is supposed to be only temporary, is dictated by the fear that, under the austerity policy which the government pursues and whose integral part is a reduction in real wages, managers will be in no position to resist the pressure for wage increases, and may even be reluctant to do so.

Employment Regulation

As is known, Hungary, perhaps less than other socialist countries, still suffers from a paradoxical situation in which some industrial branches are plagued by labour shortages whereas in others or even in the same branches labour is underutilised. For some time the authorities have not done much for the sake of stimulating labour economy, if promises and statements are disregarded. They have apparently assumed that some of the systemic changes would do the job, that enterprises, in their efforts to maximise profits, would try to reduce labour costs, all the more because these costs due to higher taxes are increasing and also that earnings regulation would have a favourable effect on labour economy since this time enterprises are free to use savings from work force reduction as they see fit. However, under conditions of labour shortages and low labour costs (despite increases they are still not high enough to make enterprises interested in substituting capital for labour, see Balázs, 1984) enterprises value labour reserves more than savings.

Under the pressure of the precarious economic situation, the authorities have recently accelerated the restructuring of the economy and have started to act on their promise to make the government responsible for full employment and to let enterprises in their decisions about employment consider primarily economic efficiency (rational employment) (Havasi, 1984; Rácz, 1984a). Plans have been worked out for a reallocation of 200 000 workers and a cut in employment in industry of 90 000 (Kozma, 1987). (For example, the metallurgical enterprise in Ózd is going to dismiss 3000 workers.)

The Party has been persuaded that the restructuring of the economy cannot be accomplished without transitional unemployment and that legislation on unemployment benefits is needed. However, for ideological reasons, the decree on 'support for finding a job' is only a half solution. It can only be applied if at least ten workers are dismissed from an enterprise and, since enterprises are eager to avoid the paper work connected with such dismissals,[7] they have a tendency to dismiss fewer than ten workers at one time with the consequence that such workers are not entitled to benefits.

The Hungarian leaders deny that the new employment policy means an abandonment of the principle of full employment. However, at the same time, they do not omit stressing that the interpretation of full employment in the sense of job security for an indefinite term and of claim to a job corresponding to qualifications is unattainable under the new conditions (Faluvégi, 1984; Rácz, 1984b).

The authorities are not properly prepared for the new employment policy and changes in the labour market which are marked by creeping unemployment.[8] They have not yet enacted a proper law on unemployment benefits and they do not yet have a well-thought-out retraining programme for displaced workers and those newly entering the labour force. (The present programme is not satisfactory.) Yet they have made some provisions. If dismissed workers require retraining in order to be placed elsewhere, the government foots the bill. In some regions quasi-public works are organised, primarily for youngsters, and investment for job creation is planned where, otherwise, unemployment could not be avoided. The authorities also count on the increased role of the private sector in job creation (Pulai, 1987).

Price System

In 1980 further changes in the price system were enacted; their focus was on further restoration of the linkage between domestic and world market prices and thus the linkage between the domestic economy and the world economy. This was a response to the balance-of-payments troubles the economy experienced. In 1980 so-called competitive pricing was introduced which is no longer in force; it set the rules for forming producer prices in competitive branches of manufacturing where free prices are applied.

Competitive pricing consisted of three rules, the first of which refers to products and is still in force, whereas the other two were applied to enterprises. The first rule, which was introduced before 1980, meant that prices of products in the domestic market could not be set higher than the actual or assumed import price. The second rule established that enterprises were allowed to increase prices in the domestic market at the most to a level which they could achieve in the convertible currency market. According to the third rule, enterprises were allowed to earn a rate of profit on domestic sales to the maximum rate they could achieve in the hard currency market (see Csikós-Nagy, 1980, pp. 169–85; Horváth, 1980, pp. 25–31; Marer, 1986, pp. 258–61).[9]

The rationale behind the last two rules was to prevent a situation in which exporting enterprises would compensate losses in foreign markets by price increases in domestic markets. At the same time they had to serve as a stimulus to some enterprises to keep abreast with the productivity increases and to others to catch up with the level of productivity of their foreign competitors.

In non-competitive branches, and also for agricultural products and construction, producer prices are calculated as before on the basis of average cost plus profit. An adjustment of retail prices to producer prices would require huge price increases and therefore the decision was taken to adjust primarily retail prices connected with foreign tourism (Csikós-Nagy, 1980, pp. 122–4). The 1980 reform also brought to an end the huge differentiation in turnover tax rates as an important step to improve price relativities.[10]

Because the new competitive prices were not market clearing prices, but only simulated foreign market prices, the Material and Price Office had to interfere in the pricing process with many administrative regulations and restraints which were often changed. Problems also arose from the fact that enterprises started to drop less profitable exports (in order not to suffer losses in domestic markets) at a time when the government was interested in maximising exports. Therefore the third rule was dropped in 1984. In 1987 the second rule was abandoned due to two devaluations of the forint (in 1986 and 1987) for the sake of promoting exports. This was a logical provision if the government wanted to prevent enterprises from increasing prices in the domestic market as a result of devaluations – which enterprises, according to the second rule, were entitled to do – and thus to avoid destroying the whole purpose of devaluations.

With the abandonment of the second rule, the Price Club, which grouped competitive enterprises freed from administrative constraints in pricing, became superfluous and ceased to exist (see Adam, 1987).

The authorities maintain that competitive pricing was intended as a transitional measure to genuine market prices and that it has fulfilled its purpose which is exemplified by the fact that many enterprises, under the pressure of competitive prices, have managed to narrow the gap in the level of productivity between them and their foreign competitors.

Most prices belong to the category of free prices (in consumer purchases it was 58 per cent in 1987). To make sure that price movements do not get out of hand two methods are used. For certain groups of products where the Material and Price Office feels that there is a danger of a disequilibrium advance notice about intended price increases can be required. The Office can impose on the enterprise a one-year postponement of the price increase. The second method is a control imposed on domestic trade. Wholesalers and retailers together are not allowed to charge a higher profit margin than 15–21 per cent. If they exceed the rate without good reason they can be charged with violating the law on unfair prices.

In the area of consumer prices the Hungarian authorities are also trying to eliminate subsidies where they feel that this is politically possible.[11] Though this action contributes to the fuelling of inflation (Szikszay, 1985), the authorities are determined to go ahead with it, though slowly, in order to reduce government spending and eliminate an anomaly in pricing – in many cases wholesale prices exceed retail prices. There is also a tendency to continue to improve retail price relativities which in recent years have apparently become worse, because retail prices of foodstuffs have grown slowly, whereas prices of industrial goods (belonging mostly to the category of free prices) have grown much faster.

The existing price system, though more flexible and more market influenced, is far from rational. Many prices are still based on domestic costs, and price movements are regulated 'not by demand but by administrative controls' (Tardos, 1987) including agreements with enterprises.[12] Without a rational price system neither enterprises nor central planners can make rational decisions. There are, however, many obstacles to a rational price system including the absence of proper domestic competition, persisting shortages (in spare parts and some raw materials), and obstacles to free imports. To leave prices to market forces under such conditions would necessarily produce severe inflation which the government cannot afford. The situation mentioned will not soon alter, therefore no radical changes can be expected in the price system.

In its 1987 Action Programme (*Nsz*, 1987, 19 September) the government promises to free the prices of all products whose producers do not have a monopolistic position in the domestic market. For the time being, however, the introduction of the general turnover tax with its price indexing, set by administrative methods, means a return to the old method of price setting. Since the indexing is differentiated and the products of one group of enterprises serve as inputs for other enterprises, there will be many disparities in indexing, which will surely impede the process of price rationalisation. Therefore one may question the wisdom of introducing the general turnover tax at this juncture or at least its method of implementation.

Banking System

After long debates and manoeuvring, the mono-bank system is coming to an end and with it a further important feature of the centralised system. Starting with January 1987 the National Bank is in substance exercising functions of a Central Bank in a condition of central planning. Credit functions *vis-à-vis* state enterprises and cooperatives are now fulfilled by five fully-fledged commercial banks. After a short transitional period, in which enterprises will have to deal with a commercial bank assigned to them, they will be free to deal with the bank (or banks) of their choice. The new banks are joint stock companies; the main shareholders are the state treasury, enterprises and organisations. Private persons will probably not be able to be shareholders; it is, however, assumed that the banks will issue bonds accessible to private persons.

The new commercial banks are not supposed to be administrative institutions, as the National Bank has been, but rather partners of enterprises. They are supposed to extend credit strictly on a commercial basis and have some leeway in the determination of the interest rate. If this assumption is borne out in practice, one source of soft budget constraint will be plugged. However, due to the difficult economic situation and very limited possibilities of credit expansion, the changes in the banking system will not be instantly very noticeable (Radnótzi, 1986; interview with M. Timár, president of the National Bank (1986)).

Investment Decisions and Financing

The 1985 provisions limit centralised investment activities to large investment projects in the non-competitive sphere of material production and to projects in the non-material sphere where territorial governments are also active. The new investment legislation promises to reduce central interference in investment, separate central and enterprise investment and give enterprises in the competitive sphere greater autonomy in decision making about investment. Enterprises themselves are supposed to determine the methods of preparation of investment projects, their approval and supervision (Kardos, 1984).

Compared to the 1968 reform, the 1985 provisions brought some innovations to the financing of enterprise investment. They gave enterprises access to the whole amortisation fund and promised an extension of credit on a commercial basis. Due to enterprises' increased dependency on bank credit, as a result of the heavy tax burden, and the austerity policy in force for sometime, the National Bank has not been in a hurry to adjust its credit policy to the new requirements. As a result of the reorganisation of the National Bank credit should be available on a commercial basis.

The 1980s have also opened new sources of investment financing to enterprises; some of them however, are at an embryonic stage so far. Enterprises are allowed to issue two kinds of bonds, one exclusively for the population and one for enterprises – a novelty in the CMEA economies – for acquiring capital for investment purposes. The issuance of bonds for the population is subject to a permit from the ministry of finance, and so far very few have been granted, almost all to utility enterprises and the retail trade. Since the yields from bonds are much higher than from bank deposits, and for the time being they are guaranteed by the state, there would be no shortage of would-be investors. Behind the ministry's cautious approach is primarily the fear that a generous permission policy might substantially reduce savings deposits by the population, which are used for loans for housing construction where the interest rate paid is very low. In addition enterprises are for some time allowed to pool resources for joint projects, or invest in other enterprises. And finally enterprises can apply for World Bank credit (Bódy, 1984, pp. 128–9).[13]

The 1985 provisions promised to increasingly use fiscal and monetary policies for influencing the investment activities of enterprises in the direction of plan objectives. As to fiscal policy, the main instrument was supposed to be the tax on accumulation (it was first set at 18 per cent and later at 15 per cent) which is, however, going to be short lived, since it will cease in 1988. Not much is known about its impact. Interest rates on credit were increased several times (in 1985 they were 13 per cent); it is, however, not clear whether they had a great impact on decision making of enterprises, rather the recent reduction in investment activities was achieved by administrative methods (Kornai, 1986).

It is necessary to wait and see to what extent the expanded enterprise autonomy in investment activities will promote rational investment decisions. There are still factors which hamper the rational investment activities of enterprises, for instance market forces are still weak, and pressure for wage increases is strong. Investment decisions are not motivated primarily by the desire to maximise profit (Matits, Temese 1986). They often result from the fear that the idle funds may be withdrawn by the authorities – a quite frequent practice in the past. The developing capital market could counter such tendencies.

Foreign Trade

The 1980s have not brought important changes to the principles adopted in 1968, with two exceptions, which will be discussed below. Exports, and especially imports, are still subject to licensing, and foreign exchange control is exercised. Licensing of imports before 1987 went through several stages depending on the balance of payments. In 1982, when the balance of payments was most critical and efforts to increase exports to the West did not succeed, the licensing of imports became more comprehensive and the granting of licenses more selective. In 1985–86, when the balance of trade has deteriorated again, imports are subject to stricter screening.

In 1981 the Hungarians introduced a uniform exchange rate for convertible currencies, thus abandoning the practice of having one exchange rate for foreign trade and one for the other transactions.[14] The value of the new exchange rate is based on the average cost incurred in producing a unit of a basket of convertible currencies in exports and fluctuates with the fluctuations in the exchange rate of the basket. Because it is based on an average cost conversion ratio, subsidies for many exports are needed.

Further cracks in state monopoly in foreign trade have occurred; the number of enterprises which have direct access to foreign markets has increased substantially. Starting with 1986 all enterprises which fulfil certain conditions should be given a licence for direct trading (*F*, 1986, no. 5). (In the fear, however, that some enterprises may abuse the licenses by allowing superfluous travel abroad, the authorities are circumspect in the granting of such licenses.) Most foreign trade operations are still carried on by state trade corporations.

It can be expected that, as a result of the recent adoption by the Central Committee of a Programme for economico-social development (*Nsz*, 1987, 4 July), some further liberalisation in the regulation of foreign trade will occur.

8.4 ORGANISATIONAL SYSTEM

The organisational system went through some changes in the beginning of the 1980s, and the provisions of 1985 have strengthened the trends in the changes and added some new ones. Generally, it can be said that the process of concentration in industry which continued in the 1970s was reversed. In addition, the tendency to give more power to functional ministries at the expense of branch ministries has continued. All this has been done for the sake of making the economy more competitive and flexible.

In 1980 the government began to dismantle trusts (associations which had quite a great administrative power over enterprises in their jurisdiction). According to Wass von Czege (1985) in the period 1980–85 fifteen trusts out of the existing twenty-four were dismantled (most of them in the food industry) and, as a result, one hundred and fifty new autonomous enterprises came into existence. In addition several large enterprises were dissolved, and, in their place, new autonomous enterprises emerged (cf. Gyurak, 1984). Enterprises have been given the right to enter into loose associations according to their own economic interests. The deconcentration in industry which has taken place is still not enough for the creation of a competitive environment. There are calls for further deconcentration (see, e.g. 'Turning point and reform', 1987).

The abandonment of the assignment of output targets to enterprises and the coordination of economic activities by economic regulators has reduced on the one hand the role of the branch ministries, and on the other increased the role of the ministry of finance, the National Bank and the Material and Price Office. Management of industry nowadays rests in the hands of one ministry, instead of the three which still existed in 1981. The number of industry ministries was reduced not only because their jurisdiction and as a result their duties had shrunk, but also in order to avoid temptation on the part of the bureaucracy to seek out new regulations and rules.

8.5 CONCLUDING REMARKS

I have explained how the provisions of the 1980s change or intend to change important aspects of the system of management in order to expand the autonomy of enterprises and create more room for market forces. The provisions viewed from these aims raise many questions, especially how they can be evaluated in systemic terms, what their influence on the economy is and what the future of the reform will be. The questions will be analysed in the order they have been raised.

The reform in the form in which it now appears is a result of many compromises in order to accommodate the conflicting interests of various parts of the government administration, social organisations and groups involved through their representatives in the design of the provisions. Compromises usually generate inconsistencies; indeed, the Hungarian reform is marked by several, among the most important being that the planners would like to achieve higher economic efficiency but are reluctant to liquidate obsolete enterprises;[15] would like to achieve more competition but no decisive actions have been taken to limit monopolisation. There are, of course, also inconsistencies which result from the unfavourable economic situation. The tendency to compromise has been one of the main reasons for the slow pace of the reform; many needed changes have been unnecessarily delayed.

Compared with the 1968 reform, the changes in the 1980s have increased primarily the role of fiscal policy. Normatives are to a great degree replaced by taxes. Monetary policy, in the explained meaning in the introduction, is not yet very developed. It can be expected that the changes mentioned in the banking system will eventually give a boost to monetary policy. Some progress has been achieved in the creation of a capital market, and it can be assumed that some of the obstacles to its further development will be gradually removed.

In the organisational system some progress has also been achieved. Hierarchical relations which some critics blame for the erosion of the 1968 reform (Antal, 1985a, pp. 45–9) have been weakened. Most of the trusts have been dismantled, many large enterprises dissolved and the number of branch ministries reduced. Separation of government administration and enterprise business has been carried through to a great extent.

Taking all this into consideration one can argue that the reform goes beyond the original principles of the 1968 reform in several aspects. It gives in brief greater autonomy to enterprises and creates more room for the market. Despite this progress, market forces are still weak. Though the 1980s introduced some new elements in the system of management which aim at expanding the autonomy of enterprises, the authorities continue to interfere excessively in the business of enterprises. This interference is not strictly one-sided; enterprises also protect their interests, as in the traditional system by bargaining, but this time, about regulators, subsidies, tax breaks and prices. They try to influence the design of the regulators in their favour or at least to obtain some privileged position. Consequently, as during the 1968 reform, the regulators, despite promises, are not applied uniformly.

As a result of bargaining which is made easier by the relatively huge industrial concentration, many enterprises still have easy access to subsidies and tax reliefs and can increase their receipts by price increases.

Weakness of the market undermines the role of profit as a guide to decision making. The profit motive has also been weakened by the behaviour of the government; whenever it has been faced with a budget deficit, it tried to enhance its revenues where it could, regardless of the accepted rules of the game. Thriving enterprises which managed to make more profit than other enterprises have been the first targets. The profit motive has also suffered because it has been possible to achieve profit unjustifiably (by juggling prices, bargaining for subsidies and/or tax reliefs – phenomena quite widespread). Under

such conditions optimal spending of profit is a secondary consideration, the first being quick spending. Needless to say, such behaviour
does not favour the expansion of the time horizon in decision making,
and thus interest in long-run profitability must suffer. It is no wonder
that Hungarian economists have for some time been absorbed with the
idea of what they call 'interest in property', or, more precisely, how to
make enterprises interested in expanding capital (Antal, 1985b).

The upcoming tax reform, according to its architects is supposed to
strengthen the market in the long run. In the short run, however, it
introduces disturbing elements in the working of the market.

The Hungarian reform has been long enough in operation to justify
the question about its influence on the economy. Has the indirect
system of management, brought about by the reform, helped the
economy in the long run? Needless to say, statistical figures alone
cannot give the correct answer, primarily for two reasons. Hungary,
like many other countries, went through turbulent years as a result of
explosive price increases in oil, a development not of its making. It is almost impossible to say in what different a position the economy would
have been if it had operated under the traditional system. This is all the
more difficult in that the development of the economy may be even
more influenced by economic policy than the system of management
and to distinguish the separate effect of each factor is very hard.

Secondly, the objective of a reform is to create an environment for
new behaviour by economic units, but some of such changes are
difficult to quantify. Judging the reform simply on the basis of
statistical figures, its record does not seem to be good. However, if we
compare Hungary with its neighbours, the favourable effects are quite
noticeable. The reform has brought about a change in the behaviour of
many managers in the direction of entrepreneurship; in many
enterprises profit increasingly acts as a guide to decision making. The
reform is instrumental in maintaining quite an acceptable micro-
balance in consumer and producer goods. Technological innovations
have improved also because foreign technology has become more
accessible (Bauer, 1987). Last but not least, the reform also shares in
the credit for the relatively liberal atmosphere in Hungary, which has,
no doubt, a favourable effect on some aspects of the economy.

From the foregoing it is clear that the reform has not yet been
completed. The question 'what now?' is complicated by the present
critical situation in the economy (see pp. 112–13). Political leaders and
a majority of the intellectual community are at loggerheads about the
strategy for coping with the twin problems (economic reform and

economic situation). After quite considerable hesitation, the political leaders, under pressure of the worsening economic situation, are slowly adopting measures which will give greater room to market forces (reorganisation of the banking system, greater stress on rational employment, greater willingness to liquidate obsolete enterprises, restructuring of the tax system). At the same time, by austerity policies (*inter alia* a reduction in real wages), boosting of exports, changes in the structure of the economy, etc., they are trying to cope with the slowly growing foreign indebtedness and the danger that Hungary may not be able to honour its commitments to foreign creditors.

The intellectual community calls for a second reform which would in substance create a market economy, change the role of planning (see p. 131), expand pluralism in ownership and the capital market, institute central bank independence and a more realistic exchange rate, liberalise imports, dissolve most large enterprises, etc. and democratise the regime ('Turning point and reform', 1987; see also Bauer, 1987, Kornai, 1986).

As to the problems in the economy, the intellectual community calls for stronger medicine in order to cope rapidly with the problems mentioned. It believes that higher rates of inflation than at present will be needed in order to restrain consumption and higher than frictional unemployment are unavoidable if structural changes are to be carried out rapidly. It insists that structural changes should be in line with export potentials to Western markets ('Turning point and reform', 1987).

Probably a compromise will be struck; the political leadership will accept some of the demands for expansion of the market environment and democratisation. The recent decision of Central Committee on the programme of economico-social development attests to it.

9 The Polish Economic Reform of 1982

9.1 INTRODUCTION

The political and economic crisis in Poland intensified the debate about the need for an economic reform. There was almost a consensus that only a reformed management system of the economy could cope with the problems facing the economy, namely low economic efficiency, market disequilibria and inadequate structure of the economy. In contrast to the past, several institutions and organisations came up with their own concepts of economic reform. In this way, they intended to influence the official concept of the economic reform which was worked out under the leadership of the Party. Among the several projects presented, one by the Polish Association of Economists and another by some authors from the Chief School of Planning and Statistics deserve special attention. The latter project was supported by Solidarity (Pysz, 1983).

The present economic reform was preceded by the Politbureau's appointment in September 1980 of a Commission for the preparation of an economic reform. In January 1981 the Commission published its first proposal which was followed by a debate. Soon a new document called 'The directions of economic reform' (hereafter 'Directions') was worked out; this document was approved by the IXth Congress of the Party in July 1981 and thus became the official document serving as a platform for working out legislation.

All this happened before the declaration of martial law, which took place in December 1981, and therefore was still much influenced by the aspirations of Solidarity. The reform had its beginnings in a new political atmosphere which developed during and after the abolition of martial law which had outlawed Solidarity. This was reflected in the implementation of the reform; its original principles, as formulated in the 'Directions', were modified in both minor and major aspects in 1982–84 (which was supposed to be the transition period) and in 1985–86 at the expense of the autonomy of enterprises. Though the authorities have characterised many modifications as temporary measures, dictated by the disequilibrated economy, the public,

150

enlightened by past experiences, has been highly skeptical about government intentions.

To calm the criticism of and dissatisfaction with the development of the reform, the central authorities in 1987 came up with 'Theses about the second stage of economic reform' (hereafter 'Theses') for public debate (supplement to *Rzeczpospolita*, 17 April 1987), in which they promised to continue the reform. Most of the intellectual community, which in the meantime has become quite radical, has seen in the 'Theses' a new manoeuvre of the ruling elite without great consequence for the economy. Due to the worsening economic and political situation, the authorities in October 1987 brought in a programme (hereafter the '1987 Programme') to carry out the second stage of the reform which promises to accelerate it and should include, *inter alia*, an expansion of the autonomy of enterprises and a greater role for market forces. The latter should be backed up by an easing of entrance into the private sector and dropping of any discriminatory provisions against it. In the sphere of economic policy, the '1987 Programme' promises to renew market equilibrium (in three years), accelerate the restructuring of the economy and stop the growing indebtedness by 1991 (*TL*, 1987, 27 October; see also the report of the Politbureau, Supplement to *TL*, 1987, 18 November).

An examination of the 'Directions' makes it clear that the architects of the reform did not want a kind of market socialism. At most they wanted an integration of planning with a self-regulating market, an integration in which planning would play a leading role. The 'Theses', mainly the '1987 Programme', go beyond the legislation of 1981–82 in many respects. However, they are only promises, and, at the time of completion of this book many details are not yet known.

9.2 PLANNING SYSTEM

The 'Directions' and the new act on socio-economic planning based on the 'Directions' make it clear that the central plan continues to determine the goals and most important proportions of the economy as well as the conditions under which enterprises work. Compared to the pre-reform state the objectives of the central plan are not to be accomplished by direct methods with the exception of some targets in investment (and other targets to be discussed later), enterprises are to become autonomous and different forms of ownership have to have the same conditions for development, a promise which has not yet been honoured. All this should create room for the working of the market mechanism. Enterprises are to be influenced by the central plan as well as by the market mechanism, which is, however, regulated by the plan (Baka, 1983a, pp. 62–7, 118, 131–3; *Reforma Gospodarcza*, 1983, pp. 61–73).

The 'Theses' do not bring any important change to this concept except that they are more specific. They promise that the market mechanism will gradually expand from areas where it now dominates (vegetables and fruits) to food and light industry. Production of producer goods and, of course, the infrastructure remain in the domain of the authorities. The '1987 Programme' promises to focus the state annual plan gradually on financial plans (budget, credit plan, balance of payment plan, etc.) at the expense of physical planning.

The planners are no longer allowed (with some exceptions) to assign targets to enterprises. The annual plan, which is a concretisation of the five-year plan and is supposed to be the main instrument of planning, is binding only for the government and can be regarded as an internal government document. The abolition of target assignments is of great importance for the autonomy of enterprises if it can be combined with a market for inputs. Since inputs in Poland are rationed to a great degree due to shortages, there is a good opportunity for interference in enterprise affairs, and the authorities use it fully.

The national plan and plans of enterprises (which may reflect their own interests) are coordinated through economic regulators applied by the authorities, including banks. Three additional methods of control are used: voluntary agreements (arising when the government places orders for certain products), non-voluntary agreements (resulting from the branch ministry's right to impose certain activities because of natural disaster, for the sake of national security and the fulfilment of international obligations) and exchange of information (which aims at helping the state as well as enterprises in drafting their plans). All three methods give the authorities enough opportunities – and they use them – to continue interfering with enterprises' autonomy. Government contracts (orders) for production, which were introduced in 1983, deserve special mention. Originally they were to be limited to structural changes, to improvement in market supply and to exports, but in the meantime they have been extended to other areas (Report . . ., 1984). Some enterprises are eager to get government contracts (this guarantees preferential supply of inputs) and some are under pressure to accept them. The 'Theses' promise to limit government contracts. It should not be forgotten in this context that the founder has the right to control enterprise activities, evaluate the work of the director, and participate in decisions about granting subsidies and other advantages to enterprises (Golinowski, 1982; Baka, 1984b; *Reforma Gospodarcza*, 1983, pp. 13–14).

The Role of the Enterprises

Polish enterprises are supposed to be autonomous (self-regulated), self-managed, and self-financed. The Polish planners like to stress that enterprises' activities under new conditions are marked by 'The three Ss'.

Autonomy (independence)

Autonomy generally means that enterprises have the right to set policies with regard to what to produce, how to produce (what kind of technology to use), where to buy inputs, how much to pay in wages, how many people to employ, what price to charge, etc. The autonomy which enterprises have been given in Poland is much, much narrower. Some of the constraints have already been mentioned. But they are much more numerous: enterprises are not free to change their production profile and they may be forced to join a certain association for five years. Furthermore, they must arrange their plans, establish and use funds, charge prices and perform some other activities according to existing government regulations. Autonomy has not been granted to all enterprises. Some industrial branches (mining, energy, sugar-refining, meat) are still subject to the old administrative system (Józefiak, 1986).

Self-management

The self-management system resembles to a great degree the Yugoslav system of the initial period before 1964. The Act on self-management gives the self-management bodies (general meeting, the assembly of delegates in enterprises with more than 300 employees, and the workers' council – the executive body of the first two) quite far-reaching rights. In certain cases the self-management bodies have the right to make decisions, in others to express views, initiate actions and exercise control. The general meeting approves the distribution of profit earmarked for the employees, carries out annual evaluations of the workers' council as well as of the director, and approves the long-term plan and status of the enterprise as well as the status of the self-management system.

The rights of the workers' council refer to the basic policy problems of the enterprise; the council approves the annual plan and changes to it, changes in the direction of activities, distribution of receipts into funds and investment projects, and decides about the enterprise joining associations, etc. In many other important issues it has the right to be consulted (*Reforma Gospodarcza*, 1983, pp. 18–20).

Viewing the self-management system simply from the stand-point of existing legislation, one can see that it is far from perfect. In important enterprises including those providing essential public services, the director is appointed and dismissed by the founder (branch minister or territorial council). Only in the remaining enterprises is the director elected by the workers' council, but even there the authorities can veto his election (Baka, 1984a). The founding body has, as already mentioned, the right to evaluate the activities of the enterprises and their directors. The self-management bodies are not responsible to the authorities for their decisions. However, the director has the right to hold up the implementation of a decision made by a self-management body if he feels that it is contrary to the law. If a disagreement arises as a result of the director's decision, the courts make the final decision (*Reforma Gospodarcza*, 1983, p. 25).

Experts in the field maintain that almost all enterprises now have self-management bodies. However, in only a small percentage of enterprises – approximately 15 per cent – are they really active and where they are active, the former functionaries of Solidarity can take credit for it. (According to Z. Sadowski, the new deputy prime minister responsible for the reform, the number of active self-management bodies is 30 per cent (*TL*, 1987, 29 October). In the other enterprises they confine themselves to the role of rubber stamps.

There are indications that the authorities would like to trim the rights of the workers' councils. The 'Theses' call for an increased role for managers, and the '1987 Programme' pledges to come up with provisions after the reasons for the conflicts between managers and workers' councils have been examined. Z. Sadowski calls for a partnership between managers and workers' councils in which managers would have the authorisation to act as a real decision maker and make risk-taking decisions. Only in this way, he argues, can efficiency be improved (*TL*, 1987, 29 October). The opposition, which sees in the workers' councils primarily a political instrument, demands free elections, the result of which cannot be overturned by a veto, of managers in all enterprises by employees and thus an abolition of the '*nomenklatura*'. There are also some fears that the authorities, which increasingly push the brigade system (contracting out of work for certain groups during normal working time), intend to put it in place of the self-management system.

Self-financing

Self-financing means that enterprises must cover all the costs from their own receipts and that they are responsible for their activities. Subsidies and tax breaks are not excluded. The authorities would like, however, to apply them *ex ante*, that is in cases where it is warranted, and not *ex post*, which would mean an approval of the enterprise's poor showing. Self-financing also implies letting enterprises go bankrupt if they are not able to meet their financial obligations. Formally bankruptcy is possible, but there are good political reasons for the authorities' reluctance to act (cf. Pajestka, 1985). Up to 1987 very few enterprises went bankrupt.[1]

The idea of self-financing also means creating an environment in which enterprises will be under pressure to work efficiently, i.e. to look for ways to use resources, including human ones, economically. It also involves eliminating conditions which allow enterprises to achieve good results by manipulating prices and getting subsidies, tax breaks, etc, in brief, eliminating what J. Kornai calls 'soft budget constraint'.

All this is to be achieved by exposing enterprises to elements of market forces (making the financial performance of enterprises dependent on success in the market) combined with economic regulators whose task is, *inter alia*, to regulate those forces. Central to these incentives (and disincentives) is profit which is supposed to be an indicator of performance and thus a guide to decision making.

9.3 REGULATION SYSTEM

I will start with prices and taxes which create the environment in which enterprises work.

Price System

The Polish reform introduced three groups of prices: fixed (so-called official), regulated, and contractual. The first are set by the authorities and applied to foodstuffs and services which are a major factor in the cost of living, producer goods which have a great impact on the cost of output, and to the principal agricultural products. Fixed prices for foodstuffs are set on the basis of cost plus profit. In warranted cases they may be set below cost, which in practice is often done. Fixed prices for raw materials and semi-finished products produced at home or imported must be calculated on the basis of prices in foreign markets (transaction prices, world prices converted into zloty on the basis of the official exchange rate). Regulated prices were set by sellers according to rules laid down by the authorities for the calculation of costs and profit. They were applied to subsidised goods and services, rationed goods, and also to less important consumer goods, primarily industrial consumer goods and producer goods. Contractual prices were to be negotiated between sellers and buyers and thus were to be determined by supply and demand; the negotiation referred in substance to profit[2] (*Reforma Gospodarcza*, 1983, pp. 74–9; Koziński, 1984; Zdyb, 1985).

The planners assumed that, as market equilibrium improved, contractual prices would expand; in turn, they expected that contractual prices would help achieve this market equilibrium. The expectations of the planners were dashed. Contractual prices developed according to a pessimistic scenario, which the planners could have predicted on the basis of previous experience. They contributed to price increases. Great shortages and a lack of competition allowed suppliers to impose prices, and therefore they were not forced to economise on costs. These price increases followed the enormous official price increases in 1982 aimed at achieving market equilibrium and improvement in price relativities.[3]

Nor did regulated prices develop as the planners expected. In this case too, a tendency to inflate costs and prices asserted itself. Some argue that the progressive tax on profit, whose purpose was to siphon off huge profits, at the same time encouraged price increases. No doubt faster wage increases than those envisaged in the annual plans also contributed to price increases (Wojciechowska, 1984; Report . . ., 1984).

The provision to apply transaction prices to imported raw materials and semi-finished products brought official prices closer to transaction prices over the years. Since the transaction prices are based on an overvalued zloty, the difference between world market prices and domestic prices is still huge (Józefiak, 1986; Ledworowski, 1986).

In order to cope with the problems mentioned the authorities made several provisions. Already in 1982 costs had been more precisely defined and the concept of unjustified costs introduced. In the period 1983–86 a further series of measures, which are difficult to monitor, was decreed. In some cases contractual prices were replaced by regulated prices; in others contractual prices were calculated on the basis of cost plus profit. Thus the difference between the two groups of prices was blurred. In addition, annual price freezes were imposed. The turnover tax, which was originally supposed to be uniform, with some exceptions, is now used as an instrument of price determination (Cias, 1983; Kalinowski and Karpiński, 1984; Lipiński and Wojciechowska, 1985).

Obviously the measures which were undertaken are contrary to the spirit of the reform and some have not turned out to be very practical. For example, the introduction of 'unjustified cost' does not prevent enterprises from including all the cost in prices (Report . . ., 1984). The measures undertaken have further postponed the achievement of the goal of the reform: to make the price system more rational. In conditions of distorted prices it is difficult to evaluate correctly the financial results of enterprises and to determine to what extent the amount of produced profit correctly reflects performance. As a result, prices and profits cannot fulfil their role as guides, either for enterprises or for central planners, to rational decision making. The central planners are also deprived of reliable guides for granting subsidies or liquidating inefficient enterprises.

The 'Theses' promise to introduce equilibrium prices (the time and the methods to be determined in the debate) in order to help bring about economic equilibrium. At the same time they vow to expand contractual prices which are nowadays partially frozen for most producer goods and to drop regulated prices which have been already replaced by maximum prices for consumer goods at the level of producers. Some prominent economists suggest limiting the price reform to producer prices since they doubt whether an attempt to restructure retail prices as well will really bring about market equilibrium. To achieve such a restructuring of retail prices under the existing conditions would require limiting the purchasing power of the working population and they doubt that the public and the trade unions would agree.[4] Nevertheless, the '1987 Programme' promised to carry out a radical price reform including huge retail price increases in food, coal and energy in 1988. Compensation was to be given for wage and salary earners and pensioners, and also for a depreciation in savings (within three years) (*TL*, 1987, 1 November). Considering the historical experience which Poland has had with price increases, one wonders why the Polish leaders wanted to re-embark on such a potentially explosive course. Probably the desperate economic situation was one of the reasons; another was the hope that a better psychological preparation of the public for the upcoming shock and the expected endorsement of the provision by a referendum would substantially reduce the probability of an explosion. It seems that pressure by the IMF and the World Bank to put the economy in order also played a role. Now, when the referendum in November 1987 ended in failure, the Polish leaders will have to spread out the price increases over a longer period. Anyhow the rate of inflation will be high, probably more than 40 per cent against the estimated 26–27 in 1987.

Taxes Paid by Enterprises

In the 'Directions' the stress was on taxing factors of production, that is fixed assets, land and labour costs; the possibility of taxing profit was only mentioned in a footnote. It was assumed that such taxation would make enterprises more economical in their use of factors of production. The taxation legislation took a different turn. Profit defined as the audited balance sheet profit became the main source of taxation. The reform also introduced a 20 per cent tax on paid out wages and a tax on land and buildings (both includable in production costs), and also a charge (a quasi-tax) on wage increases payable from profit. The 50 per cent share of the state in the amortisation fund can also be regarded as a tax (Directions . . ., 1983, p. 147).

The most controversial tax was the tax on profit. Many argued against its progressivity and the way it was calculated. The architects of the reform argued that progressive taxation was needed in light of the uneven growth of prices and the danger of great differences in profit not justified by performance. They suggested mitigating the possible discouragement produced by progressive taxes by granting tax breaks (Baka, 1983b). The progressivity of the tax depended on the rate of profit; on the whole it was steep. Profitability was defined as the ratio of gross profit to what the Poles call *koszty przerobu* – production costs minus material costs. This calculation of profitability was objected to because it was seen as working against labour economy and encouraging higher wages.[5]

In 1984 the government dropped the progressive tax and replaced it by a proportional tax of 60 per cent with many differentiated reductions, which was increased to 65 per cent in 1985 in order to cope with an increasing state budget deficit as well as with the 'soft budget' of enterprises (Szczepanski, 1984; Cichowski, 1985).

From the after-tax profit, enterprises must feed the reserve fund[6] (used primarily for covering losses) and the development fund (which is earmarked principally for investment and composed of allocations from profit and amortisation funds). Enterprises can, if they wish, form an employee fund for bonuses, and a social and housing fund (*Reforma Gospodarcza*, 1983, pp. 119–31).

The 'Theses' promise an overhaul of the tax system in the beginning of the 1990s. The present turnover tax is to be replaced by a value added tax, probably along the lines of the Hungarian reform, and income tax is to be reintroduced and, simultaneouly, the tax structure mentioned will be changed.

Regulation of Earnings

This is another important area where the central planners have not managed to find a satisfactory solution. With the start of the economic reform enterprises were given the right to determine the funds for wages (the Act on finances of enterprises uses the term 'means for remuneration') according to their possibilities and needs. The average growth of wages as well as the growth of the employee fund were controlled by heavily progressive charges payable up to 1986 to the State vocational activisation fund which is used, *inter alia*, for financing changes in the structure of employment.

The applied wage regulation was motivated by the desire to curb any great wage differentiation and the fear that the reformed system of management combined with the economic crisis might generate unemployment (Kabaj, 1984), a fear which was soon proven to be ill-founded. A temporary reduction in the retirement age, the introduction (in 1981) of an allowance for women on prolonged maternity leave and the expansion of the private sector were the most important factors which averted unemployment (for more see Adam, 1984, pp. 173–4).

Since taxation of average wage growth encouraged the hiring of workers who could be paid wages below average and thus compounded labour shortages, it was abandoned in 1983 and replaced by taxation of the wage bill. The progressive taxation[7] was retained, but for both wage bill and employee fund growth it was eased. At the same time, a new element was introduced in wage regulation, which meant a return to the former WOG system of wage regulation. Payment of taxes was linked to an indicator, mostly to net production, through a normative. For each percentage increase in net production over the previous year, the wage bill could increase by 0.5 per cent (the authorities could increase it in justifiable cases to 0.8 per cent) without enterprises paying taxes. Increases in the wage bill beyond this limit were taxed heavily (Penc, 1983).

The system introduced in 1983 is also applied in 1986–90 with some modifications. In addition four new methods of determining the wage bill have been introduced. In one method, applicable to a limited number of enterprises, the Polish central planners are apparently experimenting with a Hungarian instrument according to which enterprises are free to determine average wages. The only constraint is a progressive tax on the earnings of every employee separately, payable from profit. In the other three methods, which differ in some details, the growth of the wage bill is linked as before to an indicator (usually net output sold) and a normative. The size of the normative also depends on the percentage share of the wage bill in production costs beyond 15 per cent in 1984–85; for each percentage beyond this figure the normative increases to a maximum of 0.15. (The rationale of this measure is to take account of different enterprises' labour intensity, a measure which may become an obstacle to substitution of capital for labour.) Increases in the wage bill matching the increases in net output are free of taxes; further increases in the wage bill are taxed as before ('Directions in changes . . .,' 1986; Juchnowicz, 1985).

The 1982 wage regulation system was abandoned because the government failed to generate proper market pressure to force enterprises to keep wage increases in line with increases in productivity. The system introduced in 1983 and the modifications for 1986–90 have not brought about an improvement in the relationship of wage growth and productivity growth. What it has done is offer the bureaucracy new avenues for interference.

Because of the strong wage drift, the central authorities instituted drastic measures for controlling wage increases; enterprises which increase basic wages in 1987 by more than 12 per cent compared to 1986, are, with some exceptions, obliged to pay a 500 per cent tax on the increased wage costs (supplement to *Rzeczpospolita*, 1987, 14 May). (According to some computations, the limit was already exceeded in the first quarter of 1987.)

A decree of June 1982 gave enterprises the right to determine payment forms and also wage rates within set limits for minimum and maximum wage rates. A new system of determination of individual wages which came into force in 1984 extends the rights of enterprises provided they first fulfil certain conditions, such as the revision of work norms, the establishment of norms for employment, etc., and have the approval of the trade union organisation. The government has reserved the right to determine minimum wage rates (in the case of white-collar workers also the maximum) and the minimum span in wage rates (for blue-collar workers, 1:1.6). In addition, the law obliges enterprises to make supplementary payments for certain activities (overtime, night-shift) and to grant workers certain benefits (on retirement). Otherwise enterprises are free to arrange the determination of individual wages according to their own consideration and, of course, in agreement with the trade union organisations (Pancer, 1984).

The 'Theses' pledge to cease linking wage increases to performance and regulate them simply by taxes. In other words, the central authorities would like to return to the methods used in 1982, but probably only if they manage to put enterprises on a 'hard budget constraint'.

Employment Regulation

The 1982 reform gave enterprises the right to determine the number and the structure of the work force. It was assumed that the profit motive, combined with a 20 per cent tax on wages and the built-in incentive in wage regulation to labour economy, would induce enterprises to follow a rational employment policy. Despite all the mentioned provisions and incentives, labour economy has not improved markedly.

The profit motive has not proven to be a powerful incentive since, when market forces are weak, profit can be achieved by price increases, as well as by production increases. The high social insurance contribution, paid by enterprises (43 per cent of the wage bill) and the 20 per cent tax on wages have not turned out to be strong incentives either. Both can be included in production costs, and increases in production costs are of no great concern to enterprises under conditions of lack of competitive pressure. In addition, labour costs do not make up a large proportion of the total cost of production, and, in the beginning of the 1980s, the proportion even declined Szczepanski, 1985; Kabaj, 1984).

Theoretically, the strongest incentive to economise on labour is the wage regulation system, especially, the one before 1983, when enterprises still had a free hand in determining wages. It is, however, apparent that, when labour shortages exist, enterprises prefer labour reserves to some labour cost savings for wage increases, all the more since funds for wages can be acquired more easily than labour.

Because the incentives did not have the expected effects, and labour shortages[8] continued to persist, hampering a more vigorous recovery, the government in 1983 limited the freedom of enterprises in many regions to hire workers by introducing compulsory labour exchange (Report . . ., 1986). The 'Theses' promise that the government will take care of full employment so that enterprises can concern themselves with labour economy. It is necessary to wait and see how this promise will be translated into practice.

Investment Decisions and Financing

In the 'Directions' it is stated that enterprise investment will not be subject to 'any limits or directive targets. The enterprises will make decisions in this sphere autonomously'. Investment activities would be regulated by economic instruments, which would influence the size of the development fund, and by credit policy.

The Act concerning enterprise finances promises to confine central productive investments to megaprojects or projects of strategic importance. Some of them have to be approved by the Sejm and the rest by the government only. They are to be financed from bank credit repayable from the development funds of enterprises, to whom the investment projects will accrue. Only unproductive (for infrastructure purposes) investment is to be financed by the State or local governments or both. Other investment projects are to be decided upon and financed by enterprises from their own resources, from the development fund and also from repayable bank credit (*Reforma Gospodarcza*, 1983, pp. 124–5).

In reality, the situation was quite different from what the provisions called for. Enterprises were obliged to finance former central investments, some of them of doubtful value, started in the 1970s as their own. In 1983 50 per cent of all enterprise investments were old central investments (Karpinski, 1985). In addition, the vast majority (90 per cent) of bank credit was also used for this purpose (Staniek, 1984). Finally, investment in the fuel and energy industries increased substantially (in 1976–80 it made up 25 per cent of the total industrial investment calculated in 1982 prices, whereas in 1982–85 it was 37.4 per cent) as a result of increasing costs due to the exhaustion of easily accessible deposits of coal. All these phenomena created shortages of funds for other investments, including investments by enterprises in new capacities and in modernisation of the existing ones. Some enterprises did not have enough resources for a simple reproduction of productivity capacity. Many economists feared that this development would have dire consequences for the expansion of the economy in the future (Report . . ., 1986; Bobrowski, 1985).

Since 1986, the situation has changed; banks have more credit available for investment and under more favourable conditions. Interestingly enough, the demand for credit is lower than one would expect after a period of scarcity. There are several reasons for this. Many enterprises are afraid they will not be able to repay the credit on time (Bartoszewski, 1986). Others prefer to use their own funds (as long as they have enough) because they are reluctant to expose themselves to the strict perusal of their project with which extending of credit is connected. Economists who should know maintain that extension of credit simply depends on the effectiveness of the projects.[9] The objectives in national plans are, namely, formulated so broadly that they cannot really be a guide for the banks. Another reason for low demand for credit is a shortage of construction capacity and foreign exchange for import of machines.

Perhaps the rudimentary beginnings of a capital market have also had some effect on the demand for credit. Enterprises which have idle amounts in their development fund are allowed to lend to other enterprises. In addition, enterprises are allowed, with the permission of the ministry of finance, to issue bonds for investment purposes (see Zdyb, 1986); however, up to now there have only been a very few cases. Enterprise investment grew a bit faster in 1986 than central investment (investment in the state sector as a whole in 1986 for the first time grew more slowly in real terms than national income) and also exhibited more rationality in financing (Report . . ., 1987).

The planned reorganisation of the banking system, promised by the 'Theses', will increase the role of interest as a regulator of investment activities. The new commercial banks are to extend credit simply on a commercial basis. Interestingly enough, the Central Bank is to continue lending money to sectors of the economy.

Foreign Trade

The reform promised to bring about a reduction in the state monopoly of foreign trade, introduce a full range of economic instruments for the stimulation of exports and rationalisation of imports, and a proper exchange rate which would become the basis for transaction prices, thus allowing foreign trade to exert pressure on the domestic market.

The reformers also considered using imports as an instrument for enhancing competition in the domestic market and for achieving market equilibrium (Directions . . ., 1983; Baka, 1983a, pp. 71, 149; Report . . ., 1984).

The reform has allowed the existing foreign trade corporations to be replaced by joint ventures (*spolky*) with limited liability, in which the government's share is 51 per cent (the '1987 Programme' promises to reduce government's share) and the rest is in the hands of enterprises. This reorganisation has been steered from above and offered primarily to enterprises which have been trying for direct access to foreign markets (usually profitable enterprises) since it allows the authorities more or less the previous control. It is, however, possible for some enterprises to receive a licence for trading in certain products in certain countries. By the end of 1985, only 102 enterprises were in possession of a trading licence. Other enterprises can select the corporation with which they would like to carry on foreign trade transactions (*Warunki* . . ., 1984, pp. 118–26; Sobota, 1985; *RS*, 1986, p. 379; Ledworowski, 1986).

One of the incentives to export to nonsocialist countries is the permission to retain a portion of earned foreign exchange which can be used for imports and investment. The retention rate was quite differentiated depending on the import content of the exported products, their profitability and, of course, non-economic factors, etc. In 1984 it made up 12.3 per cent of exports. Recently, the incentive was changed in the sense that the retention rate is now equal to 20 per cent of export earnings for all exporters, with some exceptions.[10] What is also of interest is that export earnings can be sold at market prices (this means on the black market) to state enterprises. The rationale of this change is to boost exports; enterprises are, namely, not very eager to export, especially to the West. There is a strong demand in the domestic market for whatever is produced and no need to be much concerned with quality. The change also means a response to the criticism that making the retention rate depend on import content may encourage exports with higher imports contents (S. Gomulka and Rostowski, 1983).

The idea of bringing domestic enterprises under the pressure of foreign markets has hardly materialised. Despite several devaluations, the zloty is still overvalued; in 1985 only 62 per cent of exports to convertible currency markets was profitable if calculated in transaction prices (against the original goal of 75–85 per cent) (B. Wojciechowski, 1986). In the effort to reduce the rate of inflation, the government is reluctant to adjust the exchange rate to a level corresponding to the goal it set itself. No wonder that under such conditions enterprises insist on selling their products earmarked for exports to foreign trade corporations at domestic prices (Sobota, 1985). Needless to say, imports too cannot play the role the central planners wanted them to; due to large foreign indebtedness imports have been slashed and subjected to strict control.

9.4   ORGANISATIONAL SYSTEM

In view of the huge concentration in industry, economists called for the liquidation of existing associations, the division of huge enterprises wherever it is economical into small and middle-sized ones in order to create competitive conditions, and for the reduction of the existing number of branch ministries (Józefiak, 1986). The reform responded to these calls only partially and insufficiently. The old associations were liquidated, but, at the same time the Act on enterprises brought into being new associations (called '*zrzeszenia*' instead of '*zjednocze-nia*' as the old ones were). They are of two kinds: voluntary and compulsory. Enterprises can join more than one voluntary association whose purpose may be the pursuit of some joint interests, such as coordination of activities in foreign markets, investment, training, etc. The act stresses that compulsory associations should be created only in exceptional cases, for the purpose of certain activities. The 'Directions' indicate that in the first stage of the reform, when shortages in producer goods exist, the associations can be used for distribution of producer goods from the centre (Baka, 1983a, pp. 138–9; *Reforma Gospodarcza*, 1983, p. 15).

With the start of the economic reform a huge number of new voluntary associations came into being. In most cases they include enterprises from the old associations, and the managerial personnel of the new associations is mostly from the old ones. The new associations are not, however, a link in the management chain. The associated enterprises themselves make decisions (Sadownik, 1984, p. 141). Some enterprises join new associations in the realistic hope that large units have easier access than small units to needed inputs (Report . . ., 1984).

In the framework of the '1987 Programme', some important changes in the organisation of industry have been carried out. A newly established ministry of industry replaces branch ministries in industry. The majority of industrial enterprises have been transferred to the jurisdiction of regional governments, and the rights of the founders have been restricted. These changes are intended to, among others, reduce the great influence of branch interests at the expense of the national interest, a phenomenon which has often been criticised. Understandably, the new changes increase the decision-making power of functional institutions, mainly the ministry of finance.

9.5   CONCLUDING REMARKS

The Polish reform, as it was formulated in the 1981 document 'Directions' and in the ten laws based on it, resembles on the whole the 1968 Hungarian reform and thus is much superior to the WOG system (see Chapter 6). In some respects, for instance management of enterprises (self-management) and wage regulation in the first stage (no normatives, uniform application across the economy), the Polish reform went even further than the Hungarian, and in others such as pricing (in Hungary a better linkage to foreign market prices), defining the role of government, it lagged behind the Hungarian. Using Antal's classification, the Polish system could be characterised with some qualification as an indirect system. Of course, reforms must be judged not according to the intentions of their architects but on how well they do in practice. The present Polish management system is in many respects different from the one projected by the reform. A smiliar fate befell the 1968 Hungarian reform in the 1970s; however, the Polish reform has been eroded much more than even the Hungarian.

At present, plan targets are no longer assigned to enterprises. But government contracts and rationing of inputs, both vehicles for government interference in enterprise affairs, are still in use. Bargaining about plan targets, which is characteristic of the centralised system, has been replaced by bargaining about regulators, normatives, tax rates, subsidies, raw materials, foreign exchange, etc. As a result of bargaining, normatives, subsidies, tax breaks and other related instruments are applied in quite a differentiated way, and very often granted on unwarranted economic grounds at the expense of thriving enterprises. Such conditions, combined with the failure to produce a more rational price system, which in turn reduces the chances of making profit a guide for decision making, do not create an economic environment necessary to make enterprises seek increases in economic efficiency, especially since they are in a position to manipulate costs, profits and prices. The unfavourable environment is also caused by the failure of the government to put enterprises on a 'tight budget', a result, of course, of the irrational price system, but also of its inability to design a balanced system of distribution of profit which, on the one hand, would ensure enterprises the funds needed for investment without really allowing them to enjoy a 'soft budget', and, on the other hand, would allow the government to receive adequate revenues. The authorities try to counter the problems mentioned by limits and restraints, resulting in an excessive over-regulation of the economy (Mieszczankowski, 1985; Nasilowski, 1985; debate about the reform in *ZG*, 1985, no. 13). This is reflected in the tremendous number of legislative documents, not always consistent internally.

In brief, the original intention of the planners to integrate planning with the market mechanism has not been achieved. The market is weak and replaced to a great extent by bureaucratic interference, which is also bolstered by the insufficient elimination of hierarchical relations. But even planning is not of the kind the theoreticians have in mind. It is more *ex-post* (rather than *ex-ante*) planning for the purpose of coping with imbalances which arise, *inter alia*, as a result of the planning process. This is not to say that the reform has been entirely unsuccessful. Even the harshest critics of the whole concept of the reform admit that enterprises now enjoy more autonomy than before, in many respects, one should add (see debate on the reform *ZG*, 1985, no. 13).

To what extent can the reform be credited with the improvement in the economy? The three-year plan for 1983–85 was fulfilled in many of its important aspects.[11] In 1986 the economy continued more or less in the same trend. However, many problems which plagued the economy before 1986, have not been removed or solved. Economic equilibrium has not been achieved. Inflation is still double digit – and there are no chances of bringing it down very soon. On the contrary, it started to grow again (26–27 per cent in 1987 against 18 per cent in 1986 and 13 per cent in 1985). Wage growth has not been brought under control. What is also worrying is that wage growth is marked with growing inequities in the distribution of income. Exports to nonsocialist countries are not increasing and foreign indebtedness continues growing. Imports from nonsocialist countries have been slashed to an extent that they may have an unfavourable effect on the further development of the economy. In restructuring the economy little progress has been achieved (Report . . ., 1987). It seems that the economists who argue that the reform has not been very helpful in improving the economy are close to the truth.

What are the chances of the Polish economic reform? Will the '1987 Programme', which is still in the stage of promises, introduce a new momentum in the process of the economic reform? There is some chance that this may happen provided that the political leadership manages to convince the public, including the intellectual community, that it means business. Considering the existing disillusionment with the regime and the distrust of the ruling elite this will not be an easy job, even if the regime can claim credit for the present, relatively liberal atmosphere in the country. The political leadership will have to prove its commitment to a genuine reform by deeds, by agreeing with certain political changes which will bring the regime under some social control. In the economic sphere this will require measures which will give more room for the market mechanism (*inter alia*, expansion of the capital and labour markets) and the renewal of market equilibrium. Of great importance is the removal of obstacles for the further development of the private sector. The latter provision may not only contribute to the renewal of the market mechanism, but also help to increase productivity in the state sector and, with it, to create a basis for higher real wages.

10   Gorbachev's Economic Reform

10.1 INTRODUCTION

In the beginning of the 1970s, the 1965 economic reform, which had raised some hopes for the future, was more or less dead; it had been gradually emasculated so that, several years after its introduction, little of it remained. With the deterioration of the economy in the second half of the 1970s, the Soviet leaders were again willing to make some changes in the system of management. In 1979 they came up with a package of provisions which aimed at improving the system of planning, the incentive system and investment activities in order to make the economy more efficient, or, to put it in Soviet parlance, to 'intensify' the performance of the economy (*SEG*, 1979, no. 32, 1979 – hereafter the '1979 decree'). Needless to say, the 1979 changes were not intended to transgress the framework of the centralised system. It soon became clear, as could be expected, that these changes had no great effect on the economy (Aganbegian, 1983).

In the beginning of the 1980s, several experiments, usually confined to a certain sector or branch, were conducted in the economy. In January 1984, a much more comprehensive experiment was initiated by Andropov's leadership in a resolution of the Party and Government 'On the extension of the rights of associations (enterprises)' (hereafter the '1983 resolution') (*EG*, no. 31, 1983). At first it covered five all-union and republican ministries, and in 1985 it was expanded to twenty-six. In January 1986 the experiment, with some modifications, was extended to many new all-union and republican ministries, and, in January 1987, it was to be applied to all ministries on the basis of a resolution of the Party and Government 'On a further expansion of new methods of management and an acceleration of scientific-technical development' (hereafter the '1985 resolution') (see *SEG*, 1985, no. 32).

In his report to the XXVIIth Congress of the Party (February 1986) Gorbachev (1986a) committed himself and the Party Leadership to a 'radical economic reform' with the aim of creating favourable conditions for increasing economic efficiency, plugging the gap in technological progress and improving satisfaction of consumer demand. For some time, Gorbachev's real intentions could only be guessed at. At the 1987 June meeting of the Central committee, the speeches presented, especially Gorbachev's (1987), and the two documents approved – Principal provisions for a fundamental restructuring of the management of the economy (hereafter '1987 Provisions') (*EG*, 1987, no. 27) and the Law on the state enterprise (Association) (*P*, 1987, 1 July) – give an insight into Gorbachev's concept of reform, though still only a rough one, since many details are missing. At the end of 1987 new documents, based on the Law on state enterprise (hereafter '1987 Law'), were published; more are to follow in 1988. These documents are to be the rules for the transfer of enterprises to full *khozraschet* in 1988–89. This is a follow-up to the 1987 transfer of several ministries and their enterprises to full *khozraschet* on the basis of rules slightly different from the ones decreed in the '1985 resolution' and very similar to the ones issued at the end of 1986. In 1988 60 per cent of industrial enterprises in terms of output will work according to the rules of full *khozraschet* (interview with S. Sitarian, 1986). On the basis of available information it is possible to assert that the intended changes are remarkable and, if implemented, they will take the management system beyond what was intended in 1965. The 'reform' attests to the Soviet determination to abandon many economic misconceptions, products of the centralised system; however, in its present intended structure it is by no means a radical reform; it does not go beyond the framework of a centralised system of management in many crucial aspects. It is a good beginning, which, if its architects continue to pursue the goals to which they have committed themselves, may lead, after further changes, to a more far-reaching reform.

In this chapter I will discuss the changes carried out in the 1980s and Gorbachev's intended reform, which is supposed to be fully in effect by 1991.

10.2 PLANNING SYSTEM

I have already explained on a general level in Chapter 7 how the provisions of the 1980s and Gorbachev's reform affect planning. Now I will elaborate primarily on the mechanism used for achieving the objectives of the state plan.

In the 1980s the old system of target assignment – though with a much smaller number – and rationing of inputs have been maintained with some minor modifications, the most important being changes in the structure of indicators. For the first time, net output has become a success indicator, and the role of supply-contract fulfilment has been signficantly enhanced, in the hope that this will contribute to a better satisfaction of consumer demand. After long debates and experimentations, the 1979 decree called for the use of net output as an indicator of plan fulfilment. It was, however, not the exclusive indicator; in some branches of industry, the old indicator was used in a modified form. Considering the known shortcomings of gross value of output, which net output replaces, this was no doubt a step in the right direction. It could help to reduce material costs and unwarranted cooperation between enterprises. The 1984 experiment pushed net output into the background by making supply contract fulfilment with regard to structure, quality and timeliness of deliveries the main output indicator, and thus gross value of output in a modified form returned by the back door; the supply contracts were considered in terms of volume of realised production (Bunich, 1980; Hanson, 1983). Net output still plays an important role; it is used by most enterprises for the calculation of labour productivity and serves as a regulator of wage-bill growth.

In Gorbachev's reform enterprises will be allowed to work out and approve their own five-year and annual plans. However, for five-year plans they will have to do so on the basis of non-binding control figures, serving informative purposes, mandatory state orders (contracts), limits and normatives. The control figures include indicators of production in value terms, profit, indicators of technological and social progress, etc. State orders are defined quite broadly; they are to ensure the preferential needs of society. They include, on the one hand, orders paid from the state budget (defence, social sphere) and, on the other hand, orders paid by enterprises (as investment, significant technical programmes). They are supposed to take up only part of enterprises' output capacity; the rest is to be used by enterprises on the basis of contracts with buyers. The planned state orders for 1988 have, however, absorbed almost all the capacity in many enterprises and thus have become a cover up for the former assigned targets. Limits refer to inputs and to some investments. Thus rationing of inputs will continue; only in 1992 will two thirds of them be available in wholesale trade (interview with Sitarian, 1987). The 1987 Provisions also call for the creation of an environment for competition – a new phenomenon – but they do not make clear how this objective should be achieved. Under the existing shortages and intended acceleration of concentration in industry, even the freedom to select the supplier will not improve the position of the buyers very much.

Gorbachev's reform put great stress on economic normatives which are not a new instrument.[1] The 1983 resolution and the subsequent documents already promised that in experimenting ministries, and from 1987 in all ministries, the normatives, supposed to be valid for five years, would be handed down to economic units in the form of directive figures before the start of the five-year plan (*EG*, 1983, no. 31; Bazarovová, 1985).

Enterprises are to work out annual plans on the basis of their own five-year plan and contracts with other enterprises. The targets of the annual plans should be coordinated with supervisory authorities. (See also Chapter 7.)

The assignment of binding targets necessarily results in an evaluation of the economic units' performance; it is supposed to be on the basis of fulfilment of state orders and contracts between suppliers and buyers. Control figures are not supposed to serve as evaluation indicators. It is not yet clear how the planners intend to enforce the fulfilment of the assigned targets. There is no direct link between fulfilment of targets on the one hand and the wage bill and/or bonus fund growth on the other. During a transitional period for internalising the new management system, economic units can be evaluated on the basis of productivity growth and the level of material intensity (*EG*, 1987, nos. 27 and 28; *P*, 1987, 30 June and 1 July).

The 1987 Law promises to democratise the management of enterprises simultaneously with the extension of their rights. To this end, the 'working collective' of the enterprise is going to participate directly or indirectly in decision making about enterprise affairs. The participation should not, however, infringe on the principle of one-man management. The organisation of 'self-management' is quite different from that in Poland and Hungary. In contrast to those countries, the Party organisation in enterprises in the USSR is to steer the work of the self-management bodies.

The rights of the self-management bodies are surprisingly not very much restricted. The general meeting of the working collective (or conference of delegates) elects the director for five years (his election as well as his dismissal must be confirmed by higher authority), considers and confirms the enterprise plans, approves collective agreements and considers all important problems of enterprise activities. But its function is also to determine the methods of increasing productivity, efficiency and quality, activities which one would assume are in the purview of the director. It elects a council from the representatives of workers, management (maximum 25 per cent), the Party and trade unions. The council is the executive body of the general meeting and has to see to it that its decisions are implemented. In addition, it is to be involved in activities to improve the performance of the enterprise.

It is too early to draw conclusions about the future role of self-management. Judging simply from legislation one can see contradictory elements in the law. On the one hand, the law on enterprises gives quite great power to the working collective in cases of conflict between the enterprise administration and the council; namely, the general meeting is the arbiter. (But why not the founder?) On the other hand, the self-management bodies are given the function of mobilising the personnel for a higher performance, a function which recalls the position of trade unions and thus forewarns that self-management may be relegated to the role of trade unions. The fact that the party organisation is to steer the self-management bodies does not promise that they will be really independent bodies, free of manipulation.

10.3 REGULATION SYSTEM

The 1979 decree and the 1983 and 1985 resolutions put increasingly more stress than previously on indirect methods, as tools of regulation. They also attached importance to the principle of self-financing. Gorbachev's reform makes full *khozraschet* (see Chapter 7, note 7) the centre of regulation and thus profit receives a greater role.

In the next pages I will discuss how the principle of full *khozraschet* is intended to be implemented, and what are the tools to be used in the regulation of economic activities. Let me stress here right away that in Gorbachev's reform enterprises are given many more rights than they had before, and indirect tools (normatives, prices, money incentives, profit, taxation, credit, interest rate) have a much bigger role.

Distribution of Enterprise Profit

The Soviet authorities would like to make enterprises interested in maximising profit. However, the system of distribution of profit between the state budget and enterprises, existing up to 1981, did not promote the profit motive; enterprises were obliged to surrender to the budget the free 'remainder' of profit after making payments on loans including interest, channelling money into enterprise funds and financing some investment activities according to the rules set by the central planners. The 1979 decree was intended to rectify this situation, but it did so only partly. The distribution of profit by five-year normatives, applied to the planned and not actual profit,[2] was limited to ministries (Bornstein, 1985a).

The 1984 experiment brought further changes; the distribution of profit by differentiated normatives was applied directly to experimenting associations and the normative was set, however, for only one year; the authorities apparently realised that it would be more expedient to stick to real possibilities. In a situation where the amount of planned profit very often changes several times during one year (Ignatushkin and Filatov, 1984), it is an exercise in futility to set five-year normatives in an administrative system. In some branches the normative continued to be applied to the planned size of profit, unless the underfulfilment fell below a certain limit, in others, however, to the actual size (*EG*, 1983, no. 31; *EG*, 1984, no. 5; Bazarovová, 1985). The provisions for profit distribution for 1986 for experimenting enterprises did not make any importnt changes (*EG*, 1986, no. 2).

The distribution of profit by normatives has had no great effect on the behaviour of enterprises since it has been up to now more or less a formality, a smoke screen behind which an old, administrative redistribution of profit within ministries and associations has persisted (see Bunič, 1987).

Gorbachev's reform will bring changes to the distribution of profit between the state budget and enterprises. This is to happen on the basis of long-term normatives applied to actual profit. What is not clear is whether the normative will be uniform. There is strong pressure for differentiation as it was before and as it is in the current five-year plan (Bunič, 1987), all the more because it is difficult to design a long-term uniform normative. If the normatives continue to favour poorly performing enterprises, the 'radical reform' will lose its 'teeth'.

What remains of profit after payment of 'taxes' and interest on credit is to be divided on the basis of normatives into enterprise funds: for the development of production, science and technology, material stimulation, social purposes and for other purposes. The balance of profit plus wage bill constitutes *khozraschet* income. Enterprises may be allowed to pay a tax on *khozraschet* income instead of on profit. Enterprises are also obliged to pay a tax on fixed assets, on human resources (for the purpose of reproduction of the labour force) and on natural resources (whose purpose is to withdraw the differential rent) (P, 1987, 1 July).

Price System

Neither the decree of 1979 nor the 1983 and 1985 resolutions caused any deviation worth mentioning from the traditional systemic approach to prices. In 1980–81 the Soviets carried out the normal industrial wholesale price revision; the new prices went into effect in 1982. The new wholesale prices affected neither consumer prices nor agricultural procurement prices. In the calculation of the new wholesale prices, some costs were included which in the past were fully or partially paid from the budget; geological prospecting cost, stumpage fee and a charge on water. Also the social insurance contribution was increased to 14 per cent on the average to make the production costs a better reflection of the real social costs (Bornstein, 1985b, pp. 160–4; Schroeder, 1982, pp. 76–7; Kapustin, 1984, p. 559).

Gorbachev views a radical price reform as an important, integral part of the economic reform. Indeed, the reform promises quite far-reaching changes compared to the traditional price system. The mutual linkage of domestic price circuits (between wholesale and retail prices, and between agricultural procurement and wholesale prices) is to be restored. Though this is a very complicated and lengthy operation charged with political dangers, due to the great irrationalities especially in consumer prices, no clue is given about how it will be achieved (see pp. 34–5).

As to price formation, it seems that the Soviets intend to take much the same path as the other three countries are taking, or took at one time, i.e. they intend to decentralise it. Only prices for goods of national economic and social importance are to continue to be set from the centre (fixed prices). Otherwise sellers can agree with buyers about prices under the watchful eyes of the ministry (contractual prices) or can independently set prices (I will call them free prices). Contractual prices can be set on technical products produced to the specification of the buyer, new products, etc. Free prices can be applied to consumer goods and services as well as to producer goods, to which fixed prices do not apply.

A revision of wholesale, agricultural and also consumer prices is to be carried out. The new prices are to reflect not only costs (which should also include payments for use of the environment) but also use value, quality and effective demand. The purpose of the revision of wholesale prices is to improve their relativities (an increase in prices of energy and raw materials is expected). Revision of consumer prices is apparently to bring down the huge subsidies amounting to 73 billion rubles (*EG*, 1987, no. 27 and 28; *P*, 1987, 1 July).

At present, wholesale price mark-ups (rebates) are used as an incentive to promote technological progress, primarily through producing high quality goods. Up to a 30 per cent mark-up can be allowed for such production. Part of the profit so produced can be channelled into the bonus fund. In Gorbachev's reform prices are supposed to continue being a stimulus to technological progress. However, this will be limited to fixed prices (*EG*, 1987, no. 28).

To pass judgement on the price reform, one would have to have at least an idea how extensive fixed prices will be and how free 'free prices' will really be. Considering that the price revision will be carried out in the old way, the separation of domestic from world prices will be preserved and the huge concentration in industry will even accelerate, it is clear that the new price system cannot become an important factor of technological progress and economic efficiency as it is expected to.

The intended direction of consumer price revision is not yet clear. Apparently Gorbachev would like to renegotiate the 'social contract' which includes some very low prices for certain foods, mainly meat. The question is: will he have the courage to increase food prices, at a time when this is possible only at the expense of real incomes, due to great market disequilibria? According to Soviet computations existing supplies of consumer goods including unsalable goods use up only 85 per cent of the purchasing power of the public (Varga, 1987). Probably he would like to see the burden of the increased prices borne by higher income groups. If this is the case, what about the promised wage differentiation?

Wage Regulation

The 1979 decree dropped gross value of output as a regulator of wage-bill growth and replaced it with net output. The wage bill was, however, still dependent on the fulfilment of plan targets, in this case planned net output. In the 1984 experiment and in provisions for 1986–90 (valid only for enterprises not transferred to full *khozraschet*) including those for enterprises which have been transferred to full *khozraschet* in 1987, the growth of the wage bill depended and *depends* on the actual (and not the planned) increase in net output over the previous year. This means that the institution of overfulfilment, which was a source of various inefficiencies (encouraged labour hoarding, production of unsalable goods, etc.) in the traditional system is finished.

In the 1984 experiment, the wage-bill of industrial workers, engaged in production, for the annual plan is divided into two parts:[3] the sum of the wage bill of the previous year and the increment for the current year. The former is guaranteed, provided enterprises manage to maintain the rate of labour productivity growth at least at the average level of the last five years. The size of the increment in the wage bill is linked as before to an indicator which serves as a numerator in the productivity calculation formula, and this seems mostly to be net output. For each percentage increase *in net output* (not planned net output) the wage bill of the previous year increases by a normative, a certain fraction of a per cent.

The linkage of only the wage-bill increment to a normative was probably done in the belief that, under such an arrangement, it would not be so difficult to guarantee its stability and also that the need to design a separate normative for each economic unit would no longer be so important. And so, in the 1984 experiment, the normative was supposed to be stable for five years and the same for a certain group of similar economic units (Rzheshevskii, 1984; Volkov, 1985), which seemed to be a good compromise. A single normative for all the economic units in one ministry may generate dissatisfaction, since it necessarily leads to great differentiation in wage increases for reasons which may be beyond the control of enterprises. A separate normative for each economic unit may make the normative a useless instrument, since it opens the door to bureaucratic arbitrariness.

Two documents, one on wage regulation for 1986–90 and the other on the same problem for economic units transferred to full *khozraschet* in 1987, again give the ministries and the associations the right to differentiate normatives by economic units (*EG*, 1985, no. 49; *EG*, 1986, no. 52). Apparently the central planners have come to the conclusion that the introduction of group normatives has after all turned out to be unrealisable. The normatives are to be stable for the period of the five-year plan.

In setting the normatives, the planners take into consideration the planned macroeconomic relationship between average wage growth and labour productivity growth (in 1986–90 it is supposed to be 65 per cent) and the planned relationship for the economic units in question (Deripasov, 1986).

According to the 1987 Law, economic units in the reformed system will have a choice between the applied wage regulation system with important modifications (the whole wage bill, not only its increment, is determined by a long-term normative related to actual net output) and the new one in which the wage bill will be a residual of the gross income of enterprises after taxes and interest are paid and enterprise funds replenished (*P*, 1987, 1 July). The latter system was used in the Czechoslovak reform of the 1960s with the difference that the wage-bill growth was regulated by taxation. It is not yet clear how the Soviets intend to control wage-bill growth. At any rate, the idea of self-financing is pushed quite far here. The new wage-bill regulation will surely give managers more leeway in determining wages, provided, however, that the normatives are at least group normatives and stable.

Already, in the first half of the 1980s, one could detect a more favourable inclination to the idea of widening wage differentials, which was reflected in differentiated supplements to wage rates for highly skilled workers, and for highly qualified engineers and technicians. This trend has also been confirmed in the present revision of the wage system, confined to enterprises which are able to produce funds for the higher rates. By the end of 1987, 19 million workers had been transfered to the new wage rates (*EG*, no. 52, 1987). In previous revisions of the wage rates, the percentage differences between the rate of the lowest grade and the rates of succeeding grades were declining. In the new wage rate system they are increasing. What is of no less importance is that the average increase in rates of white-collar workers is higher than that of blue-collar workers (30–35 per cent against 20–25 per cent) (see interview with I. I. Gladkii, 1986).

The measures mentioned may serve as an indication of Soviet intentions, but they in themselves can at most be regarded as a first step in restructuring wages and bringing them closer to performance.

Substantial widening of wage differentials will not be so easy. The conditions which gave birth to levelling tendencies in wages have not changed. There is popular resentment against widening of wage differentials. The intended introduction of self-management may also work against wage decompression. Finally, the slowdown in wage growth works in the same direction.

Bonus Fund Formation

In this area, no important systemic changes have occurred in the 1980s.

In 1981–85 the bonus fund was, in substance, assigned as before to enterprise units as an absolute sum which was the planned bonus fund. The actual bonus fund depended on the fulfilment of a set of indicators and normatives, and was fed from profit.[4] However, changes have been made several times in the nature of the indicators; the most important have been kept, though with a changed role. The rationale for these frequent changes has lain in the planners' illusions that a restructuring of the indicators in themselves can improve the economy markedly. It seems that, on the whole, the movement to more synthetic indicators predominates. The new incentive system for 1986–90 resembles in some respects the new wage regulation system.

The 1979 decree mentioned growth of productivity and growth of the share of quality output as the most important indicators. Profit could be regarded as a third indicator, since in most industries the normative was expressed in terms of a fraction of a percentage of profit. Apart from these main so-called fund-forming indicators, there were also corrective indicators. Compared to the 1965 reform the number of indicators was quite high; the planners apparently suffered from the illusion that the greater the area of the economy covered by indicators, the greater the chance for coping with the problems of the economy.

In the 1984 experiment, the fulfilment of plan targets, as agreed upon in supply contracts with regard to structure, quality and time of delivery, became the most important indicator. The role of quality of output as an independent indicator declined once the planner realised that it could be integrated into contracts. Apart from the main indicators, the ministries could set other indicators which were suited to the specificity of the branch in question (Bazarovová, 1985).

The 1984 experiment has also brought about changes in the distribution of bonuses, primarily for top managers. This bonuses depend on the fulfilment of a maximum of three indicators instead of five or six as before. The main indicator is, of course, fulfilment of supply contracts. If these are not fulfilled, bonuses for the fulfilment of other indicators cannot be drawn (Rakoti, 1984a,b).

For the XIIth Five-year Plan (1986–90) there is a new incentive system valid now only for enterprises which have not been transferred to full *khozraschet*. The new system, which is to be applied by ministries and associations and enterprises, is similar to the wage regulation system in that the bonus fund now consists of two parts: the basic part (which is the bonus fund of the previous year) and an increment. The basic is guaranteed provided productivity growth does not decline below the average rate of productivity growth in 1981–85.

The main indicator for the determination of the size of the increment in the bonus fund of industrial branches is the cost level of one ruble of commodity output or accounting profit. (Other indicators can also be applied.) Both indicators are measured according to the traditional principle, in comparison with the plan targets in the previous year and not with the actual performance, as it is in the case of wage-bill regulation.[5] The normatives are set in advance for five years (they can, however, be refined when the five-year plan is approved) and can be differentiated by associations (*SEG*, 1986, no. 8).

Gorbachev's reform brings a considerable simplification to the formation of the incentive (stimulation) fund. The fund is simply formed from the balance of profit on the basis of a long-term normative. It is not yet clear to what extent the normatives will be differentiated. This even represents progress over the system set up for enterprises switching to full *khozraschet* by January 1987. In such enterprises, the normative is related to the planned balance of profit (*EG*, 1986,. no. 47).

In the new management system it will be left to enterprises to divide the bonus fund according to their own consideration. They are allowed to create, instead of a separate wage bill and incentive funds, a single fund for rewarding labour (*P*, 1987, 1 July).

The new approach to bonus fund formation perhaps characterises the best the nature of Gorbachev's reform in several important aspects of the management system. Before, the authorities, through linkage of the bonus fund formation to indicators, tried to cure the main ills of the economy though with little success, and that was the reason for the great number of indicators. The intended simplification of the bonus fund formation attests to the belief of Gorbachev's leadership that the creation of an environment for self-financing, combined with greater leeway in decision making for managers, has a better chance of curing the ills of the economy than the old system with many indicators.

Employment Regulation

The 1979 decree did not make important changes in the regulation of employment. Assigned limits on employment of blue- and white-collar workers, which were abolished in the 1965 reform, but which were gradually reintroduced, were reconfirmed. In addition, the five-year plan was supposed to contain a target for a reduction in manual labour.

Apart from these administrative measures, the 1979 decree

contained some incentives to improve labour economy. Workers' wages could be increased substantially if they fulfilled the assigned output volume with a smaller number of workers, a provision similar to the known Shchekino experiment. Finally, the increase mentioned in the social insurance contribution had, apart from a fiscal objective, the task of encouraging enterprises to substitute capital for labour.

The 1984 experiment brings about changes in employment regulation. According to Rzheshevskii (1984), employment limits and targets for the reduction of manual labour are no longer assigned to associations and enterprises. This does not mean, however, that economic units are free to hire labour just as they like. They themselves must set limits on the basis of targets in the annual plans and discuss the limits with the regional government during the drafting of five-year and annual plans (Bazarovová, 1985). Therefore it is difficult to say to what extent the change is important; maybe it is only of a psychological nature.

Compared to the 1965 reform, the changes in incentives for labour economy in the 1980s are of no great importance. Even the increase in social insurance contributions does not make a great difference, since it does not change labour cost significantly; in addition, the increased labour costs can be included in production costs. Furthermore, labour reserves are of great importance in planning from achieved level. It is necessary to wait and see whether the workplace certification, which has been going on for some time, will have a favourable effect on labour economy (cf. Hewett, 1987).

Gorbachev's reform gives enterprises the right to determine the size of the work force and its structure. It apparently relies on the full *khozraschet* principle to induce enterprises to save labour. The new tax on wages, apart from being a source for the reproduction of the labour force, probably has the same function.

It is doubtful whether Gorbachev's reform will noticebly succeed where the present system has failed, as long as, *ceteris paribus*, labour shortages exist side by side with overemployment. Managers value labour reserves more than some wage savings. The situation may change if the planned huge relocation of labour in connection with restructuring of the economy becomes a reality.

Investment Decisions and Financing

As is known, the Soviet economy is plagued by a high volume of unfinished investment projects which lead to an extension of the lead time beyond the set deadlines with all the consequences for efficiency. No wonder that in such a situation many projects become obsolete before they are put into operation, as Gorbachev himself admitted in one of his speeches (*EG*, 1986b). This is also confirmed by Investment Bank figures which show that, among projects transferred to the XIIth Five-year Plan, 25 per cent were designed 10–20 years ago (Serov and Borodin, 1986). One of the reasons for this situation is shortages, resulting primarily from overinvestment. The planners are trying to remedy this situation by a better coordination of investment projects with material and financial resources as well as with construction and assembly capacity. They are also trying to reduce the volume of unfinished projects by limiting the number of projects to be started, but with no great success.

The 1983 resolution and, even slightly more, that of 1985 extended the role of enterprises in decision-making and in the financing of investment. The central planners are now apparently willing to give enterprises more say in technical modernisation and reconstruction by allowing them to work out and approve plans for technical modernisation, as long as smaller projects are involved (in 1984 it was 4 million roubles). Larger projects have to be approved by the branch ministry after being scrutinized for the extent to which they are in line with the planned development direction of the branch or sub-branch in question. Such enterprise investments are included in state plans as decentralised investment.

Associations' (enterprises') projects are financed from their own resources, i.e. from the development fund and a single fund for research and development (a fund formed by the ministries from the profit of enterprises), and from bank credit. The latter is to be repaid from the development fund and the profit which remains with the economic units (*EG*, 1983, no. 31; *EG*, 1985, no. 32; Bazarovová, 1985). A part of centralised investment is also financed from the development fund.

The precise formation of the development fund, which consists of a portion of profit, a portion of the amortisation fund and proceeds from the sale of redundant assets, has changed several times. The authorities have not been able to make up their minds about the role the two, often conflicting, criteria should play: namely, should the development fund be fully linked to performance, or should investment needs be decisive (see *SEG*, 1985, no. 32; Matuliavichus, 1984; Rotstein, 1985). In the end, a compromise has been reached. New provisions for the formation of the development fund, published in 1986, stipulate that the five-year normative for allocation from profit should be the same for all enterprises in one ministry, whereas the normative for the allocation from the amortisation fund (which makes up the largest part of the development fund) can be differentiated according to enterprise plans for technical retooling, and the extent of machinery and equipment utilisation (*SEG*, 1985, no. 32; *EG*, 1986, no. 8).[6]

Gorbachev's reform, though less specific in this area than in others, brings few innovations. It reconfirms and expands the right of enterprises to make decisions about modernisation and reconstruction of their plants. Such investments are to be financed from the single fund for development, science and technology, which consists of a portion of the balance of profit allocated by a long-term normative as well as depreciation deductions (amortisation fund) determined by a normative, and from bank credit. Budgetary assistance is only available for large projects and they must be included in the state plan.

What is not yet clear is whether the normatives are uniform; in enterprises switching to full *khozraschet* in January 1987 the normatives are to be differentiated depending on the extent of wear and tear of fixed assets (*EG*, 1986, no. 49). Probably the same rule will apply here. It can be expected that the distribution of the development fund within associations will continue, but will be discontinued within branches.

The stress on self-financing in investment is understandable in light of the desire to make investment more efficient. The question is, will it really help to make investment more efficient? It is not yet clear to what extent the central planners will manage to impose on enterprises a hard budget constraint. Differentiation of normatives is not very helpful since it opens the door to bureaucratic arbitrariness and bargaining; on the other hand, the new provision to allow enterprises to handle the amortisation fund is a positive step. It is also progress that money accumulated in the develoıment fund can be carried over to the next year, a provision adopted some time ago (*SEG*, 1983, no. 32). However, this advantage is offset by the fact that enterprises have no free access to machinery and equipment and therefore buy what is available instead of what is needed (Rotstein, 1985).

In the provisions of the 1980s the Soviets always stressed the need for bank credit to play a role in the decisions of enterprises about the size of working capital, including inventories, and investment. For the time being, efforts in this direction have not been successful, the most important reason being that the interest rate on long-term credit is still low (1 to 2 per cent) and financial assets are redistributed within associations and branch ministries (Rydko-Silivanov, 1984; Zacharov, 1986). The 1987 Provisions and the law on enterprises put great emphasis on credit. Since the mono-banking system is going to be undermined by the creation of six branch banks which are to be put on full *khozraschet*, it can be assumed that interest rates will substantially increase, and therefore credit may play a somewhat greater role as a regulator.

Foreign Trade

It has taken a new leadership to realise that 'intensification' of the economy is not possible without changes in the regulation and organisation in foreign trade. The changes carried out hitherto are very moderate but remarkable because they have taken place in a previously entirely static sector. Starting with January 1987, twenty ministries and seventy associations have the right to engage directly in foreign trade operations. The existing foreign trade corporations for products which are traded by institutions allowed direct access to foreign markets have probably been integrated in these ministries. Associations and enterprises will have the right to enter into direct cooperative and trade relations with enterprises of the CMEA countries.

There are also some new incentives for promoting exports. Associations and enterprises involved in exports to the non-CMEA countries will be allowed to keep a certain percentage of foreign exchange for purchase of machines and equipment for the technical retooling of their own enterprises. There is, however, apart from the carrot, a stick in the provisions. If enterprises do not meet their obligations in foreign trade, the resulting losses must be paid by them. Finally, the Soviets intend to enter into joint ventures with capitalist countries (*EG*, 1986, no. 40).

The 1987 Law contains nothing new except to lay down the principle that economic units with a considerable stake in exports and imports can claim a licence for direct trade with foreign firms (*P*, 1987, 1 July).

The provisions mentioned, if really implemented, will introduce some flexibility in foreign trade operations. However, they do not eliminate the separation of domestic production from world markets, and thus enterprises are still not exposed to the pressures of foreign markets (*EG*, 1986, no. 40; *P*, 1987, 1 July).

10.4 ORGANISATIONAL SYSTEM

In the 1980s the process of industrial concentration has continued; the number of production associations (PAs) grew fast, of course, at the expense of enterprises. In 1964 their number in industry was 410 and in 1983 4202; approximately half of the industrial-production personnel worked in associations. Associations employing more than 20 000 people produce more than 65 per cent of the total production of all associations (Cheblakov, 1984, pp. 55–64; Kovalev, 1986; *Istoriia* . . . , 1980, vol. 7, p. 103). There are also, however, small production associations as well as scientific-production associations. The All-Union Industrial Associations which were introduced in the 1970s with great fanfare were quietly liquidated.

Needless to say, the rise of PAs is a result of administrative decisions; PAs include enterprises from the same ministry and region without due regard to economic and technological needs. The position of enterprises depends on the legislation as well as on the decision of the individual PA. In recent years, particularly, after the 1983 resolution, the authority of PAs has been extended. On the whole, it is possible to say that the present PAs centralise in their hands decisions about capital investment, supply, marketing and redistribution of various funds. In other words, the authority of enterprises, as a result of PAs, is quite restricted (Cheblakov, 1984, pp. 82–5).

The fast increase in industrial concentration has given the impression that the Soviets are attracted by the East German experience with 'Kombinae' and intend to go this route (see Gvishiani, 1986; Hanson, 1986). The question is, what is the direction of Gorbachev's reform? In their speeches at the June CC meeting, both Gorbachev (1987) and Ryzhkov stressed the importance of industrial concentration. Apart from production associations[7] and scientific-production associations, which are already in existence but which will be reorganised with obstacles to their becoming interbranch and interregional removed, new state production associations are to be established. Associations, enterprises and other organisations which will belong to the new state associations will be allowed to keep their independence. The new associations are apparently to take over the jobs of the chief departments of ministries which are to be gradually dismantled. They are not supposed to be administrative bodies, but an important part of the production mechanism itself. They should be capable 'of implementing the entire cycle of research – investment – production – marketing – maintenance' (Gorbachev, 1987). These new associations are to be served by tens of thousands of medium sized and small enterprises. Is this an attempt to imitate the USA or the GDR? In my opinion, the latter is more probable. The ministries are to become branch scientific-technical and planning centres and should also be engaged in managing foreign trade.

The concentration of industry is to be accompanied by a centralisation of ministerial administration. Many branches of heavy industry which have been subordinated to union-republic ministries during the 1965 reform will return to the jurisdiction of all union ministries (*EG*, 1987, nos. 27 and 28; *P*, 1987, 1 July). It is not yet clear what the division of decision making between recently established superministries[8] and the state planning committee and ministries will be.

The rapid expansion of PAs has had to bring about greater specialisation and accelerate technological progress with all the consequences. Few authors believe that PAs have achieved this goal (Subockii and Siginevich, 1985, pp. 301–11). What is certain, however, is that they have strengthened monopolisation in production which will undoubtedly increase with the intended acceleration of concentration.

10.5 CONCLUDING REMARKS

I will first discuss very briefly the systemic changes of the 1980s and then turn to Gorbachev's reform. The changes in the 1980s have been piecemeal and have not really affected the whole system of management. In addition, they are marked by contradictions.

This is not to say that they have not introduced some new elements in the system of management. They have extended the authority of economic units in matters of wage-bill formation, employment and investment decisions. The dropping of gross value of output as a numerator in the calculation of productivity and as a regulator of wage-bill growth, and its replacement by net output is, no doubt, a step in the right direction. The same is true, with certain qualifications, about the great stress on normatives. On the other hand, by continuing with industrial concentration, the central planners have strengthened monopolisation and thus undermined their own endeavour to make enterprises more interested in satisfying market demand. The systemic changes have had, on the whole, only a marginal effect on the economy. The Soviets themselves more or less share this view.

It is too early to pass judgement on Gorbachev's reform. First, many details are still missing and, once they are known, they may change the picture. Second, what is even more important, Gorbachev's reform is still at the stage of promises; it is not yet sure whether all of them will be put into effect. There are many examples of decisions of the highest bodies of the Party and government which have not been implemented or, if implemented then only formally. With these reservations in mind, I can now start the evaluation.

From the foregoing it is clear that Gorbachev's reform is a hybrid, consisting of incompatible elements. Some of its elements are really radical, compared to what exists now, and even more what used to be, in the USSR. The regulation system on the whole, as it seems from the legislation, is a pleasant surprise for all the adherents to a genuine economic reform, though it is not free of contradictions. On the other hand, the organisational system is from the old arsenal and exhibits strong features of the traditional system. Compared, however, to the 1965 reform, Gorbachev's reform presents progress; it is supposed to be more comprehensive, more far-reaching and is combined with political changes which make it less vulnerable.

Let me be more specific and commence with the assumed position of enterprises in the reformed system of management. On the one hand, enterprises are to be assigned targets, though in much smaller numbers[9] (see also p. 171) and without some of the features character- istic of the centralised system. The institution of overfulfilment is done away with, and the targets are mostly no longer to be related to the performance of the previous year. Still, enterprises will be restrained in determining the scope of their activities, though they will have more leeway and choices than before. What makes the situation worse is that rationing of inputs will continue because of shortages. (There is a promise to switch to a market for inputs within four or five years.) All this means that the authorities will continue to interfere with the day-to-day operations of enterprises with all the consequences of bureaucratic arbitrariness and bargaining, and strains on self- financing.

On the other hand, the rights of enterprises will expand substantially in the matter of prices, wages, incentives, employment, and use of profit, and somewhat in investment activities. The authorities are going to regulate all these important elements, except prices and employment, by normatives which will be related to the actual, not the planned performance. No doubt, this is progress and strengthens the idea of full *khozraschet*. However, if the normatives are going to be much differentiated, and there are signs that this is going to be the case, the significance of this innovation will be much devalued. One must also express doubts about the practicality of the concept of stable normatives, especially with regard to wages and incentives. A five-year period is too long for realistic normatives to be set.

The idea of self-financing, which is not new and which requires that enterprises be interested in economic efficiency, can be effective only under certain conditions. Among the necessary conditions is, of course, enterprises' freedom to determine what they will produce and where they will buy their inputs. It is also important that the tax burden is distributed equitably, not at the expense of efficient enterprises, and is not too heavy. And, finally, a rational price system is needed in order for enterprises to be able to make rational decisions. From the foregoing it is clear that, since the reform is not going to produce these preconditions to the extent needed, the idea of self-financing is unlikely to bring about substantial change.

The intended continuation of concentration in industry and centralisation do not bode well for the working of the reform. They will create conditions for tougher monopolisation and for greater vulnerability of buyers, all the more because shortages persist and the Soviet economy is not going to be opened up to foreign competition. It is doubtful whether the hugeness of the Soviet market makes a great difference. In addition, the gigantic associations are more difficult to manage and may have greater influence in bargaining at the expense of smaller units. What is no less important is that in most cases the expansion of the autonomy of economic units will benefit only associations.

The question is, are the intended systemic changes sufficient to bring pressure on enterprises in the direction of higher economic efficiency, innovations and a much better satisfaction of consumer demand with regard to product mix, quality and design? If the changes are carried out as promised, they will probably make some change for the better in the behaviour of enterprises.[10] The extent of the change will also depend on the degree of the determination of the authorities to hold the line even on the watered-down principle of self-financing, and whether they will honour their promise to liquidate inefficient enterprises (according to Ryzhkov (1987), they make up to 13 per cent of all enterprises) if various remedies turn out to be ineffective. The tremendous propaganda regarding the need for reform may also help for a while. To bring about lasting improvements, more systemic changes, including elimination of indicated inconsistencies, will be needed.

In my opinion, the Soviet reform can be regarded as a cross between the Hungarian and East German concepts of economic reform. (See Appendix for the East German concept of 'reform'.) Yet it is not entirely clear which influence is stronger. It would be wrong to liken it fully to the East German since in the GDR the Kombinate do not enjoy the rights promised to the Soviet associations. One can only speculate as to why the Soviets have resorted to such a hybrid system. One likely reason is that the reform is a result of compromise. Probably fears that the adoption of the Hungarian concept would have to be combined – if not immediately, then in the future – with some territorial decentralisation, not an attractive idea for a multinational country like the USSR, has also played a part. Furthermore, ideological inhibitions may also be involved; for many reformers and even for Gorbachev himself a strong orientation to the market may be too great a leap. Last but not least, more favourable economic results in the GDR than in Hungary in recent years make 'Kombinate' more attractive, all the more since the GDR system of management is probably closer to the thinking of Gorbachev and his associates.

From what is known at the completion of this book, it is clear that Gorbachev will not have an easy time implementing his economic reform. The success of the reform will depend on public support for the reform. This in turn will depend on how quickly he manages to eliminate shortages in consumer goods and improve their quality. And this is possible only with a reform in agriculture which again can be successful if the supply of industrial goods to farms substantially improves. With some simplification it can be said that success in reforming the management system in industry depends on a successful reform in agriculture.

11 The Czechoslovak Attempts to Improve the System of Management in the 1980s

11.1 INTRODUCTION

In 1969 the new leadership under Husak started to dismantle the system of management introduced in 1966–68 and replace it with the old, centralised system. In the beginning of the 1970s the economic situation improved: the rate of increase in national income grew, primarily due to faster growth in agriculture, the rate of inflation was substantially reduced, and the domestic market was better supplied with consumer goods. As a result, the political leaders were not very concerned with changes in the management system. In the middle of the 1970s, when the economic situation started to deteriorate, systemic problems again came to the forefront. In connection with the VIth Five-year Plan for 1976–80 the government came up with some provisions for the 'improvement of the system of planned management', which were nothing other than some minor changes in the system of success indicators, improvement in planning the targets in science and technology, incentives for exports, and so on (see Hûla, 1976; Lér, 1980). Apparently the changes did not have the expected effects, and since, at the same time, the economy experienced further deterioration, the government decided in 1978 to start experiments with some new provisions whose main objective was to promote economic efficiency and quality. On the basis of this experiment the Czechoslovak authorities prepared a Complex of provisions for the improvement of the planned management of the national economy after 1980 (hereafter 'the 1980 document') (see *SHN*, 1980, nos. 11, 12).

In 1984 the Government came up with a new document called 'The main directions of the further development of the complex of provisions for the improvement of the system of planned management' (hereafter 'the 1984 document') (*SHN*, 1984, nos. 42, 43). These new provisions were to take effect during the present VIIIth Five-year Plan for 1986–90.

The 1980 and 1984 documents resemble very much the Soviet 1979 decree and 1983 resolution (see Chapter 10) and they were more than probably inspired by them. The Czechoslovak planners took over not only the Soviet concepts of, and approach to, improving the system of management in many respects, but also many of the details. Of course, some differences between the systems remained, differences which have to do with the distinctive development of the systems in certain periods.

However, by the end of 1985 and the beginning of 1986 – as in the USSR – many provisions were somewhat modified. The modifications are summarised in a joint document of the functional authorities: 'Principles of Khozraschet' (hereafter 'the 1986 document') (see *SHN*, 1986, no. 14).

Gorbachev's commitment to a radical reform and the Soviet preparations for changes in the management system also prompted the Czechoslovak leaders to act. Judging on the basis of their statements, one gets the impression that Czechoslovakia is on the brink of a far-reaching reform. Husak promises that the reform in the offing presents the greatest interference with the economy since nationalisation (*Rudé právo* 1987, March 19). The official documents approved by the presidium of the Central Committee and the government – 'Principles for the Restructuring the economic mechanism in the CSSR' (hereafter 'Principles') (*SHN*, 1987, no. 5), and 'Concretisation of the principles for the restructuring of economic mechanism in the CSSR' (hereafter 'Concretisation') (*SHN*, 1987, no. 13) – do not bear out the promise. New documents are still to appear. In July 1987 a draft law on the status of enterprises was published for discussion (*HN*, 1987, no. 30); it is to be passed into law in 1988. The full extent of the change will not be felt until 1991, when the 'Principles' will be fully operative, so final evaluation must be reserved for a later date.[1]

The objective of all provisions and documents is the same: to put the Czechoslovak economy on the path to an intensive type of economic growth, help to accelerate the restructuring of the economy, intensify the process of innovations and modernise the industrial apparatus. In this chapter I will explain the changes implemented by the provisions in 1980–86 and discuss the changes promised in 'Principles' including 'Concretisation'.

11.2 PLANNING SYSTEM

Neither the documents of the 1980s nor the 'Principles' mean substantive changes in the role of planning. Since enterprises are promised greater rights, *inter alia*, by reducing the number of assigned output targets, one would expect that the 'Principles' would at least stress the role of the market. Interestingly enough, there is no mention of the market in the 'Principles'; only in the introduction is there a traditional call for the 'planned used of socialist commodity – money relations'. In many places, where one would expect the use of the word 'market', 'value relations' is used instead. Is this a camouflage in order not to give the opposition ammunition for arguing that the government after all must take the same route as the reformers of the 1960s, or are the central planners determined to allow market forces as little scope as possible? The latter seems to play a greater role.

The 'Principles' call for only a few changes in planning which were not included in previous documents, especially the '1984 document'. This is not to say that the 'Principles' simply repeat what was in the previous documents; in some cases, ideas for changes are developed or put in a slightly different context, and in others they contain more specifics. The changes in the 'Principles', as with the previous documents, cover improvements in the drafting of state plans, in their handing down to enterprises and in the position of enterprise (see pp. 120–1). What is a relatively new idea is the call in the 'Principles' for a diminishing role for physical planning. Financial flows and value instruments should no longer play a passive role in the sense that they simply adjust to set physical targets and proportions. On the contrary, in the drafting of plans they are to play an active role; equilibrium of the economy must result from equilibration of financial flows and material balancing.

No less important is the principle, already included in the '1984 document', that the decisive criterion for the inclusion of tasks in state plans and plans of organisations should be economic efficiency, and that it should be applied uniformly throughout the economy. On the national level, the criterion will be the increment in national income, and, on the level of organisation, profit. (In the '1984 document' the criterion was adjusted net output.)

The 'Principles' do not change markedly the role of economic units. Though the document promises an increased jurisdiction for enterprises, their autonomy is apparently not going to expand very much. Enterprises will continue to be assigned targets; one group will be assigned in the traditional way – though in a smaller number – through the chains of management, and the other group directly from above. The first group includes binding targets and limits which are to be broken down by the branch ministries, and the second, normatives and perhaps also criteria of efficiency which are not to be disaggregated, since they are supposed to be uniformly applied.

It is assumed that binding targets are to be applied in the fulfilment of important state programmes involving primarily structural changes, technical progress, foreign trade and defence. In the light and food industries binding targets need not be used if the organisations are able to supply the market smoothly. Limits should be used in the case of deficit inputs and foreign exchange.

Normatives, which determine the tax on profit and the funding of the wage bill and investment fund, to mention the most important, will be announced in the beginning of the five-year plan, and are to be stable for a long period. In principle, they will be applied uniformly. If enterprises are unduly affected by them because of lower receipts, other factors should be adjusted, such as prices and subsidies, but not normatives. It will be interesting to see if this new idea will work, if really applied.

Enterprises are to be given some leeway in the drafting of their plans, both five-year and annual. They are to have the right to draft their plans, taking into consideration contracts with their customers and orders, and can adjust them to changes in domestic and foreign markets provided they include all the assigned targets in their plans. It is not clear to what extent the contracts are the result of enterprise preferences.

After the Soviets decided to introduce self-management in enterprises, the Czechoslovak leaders felt that they could not remain behind; they tried, however, to postpone its introduction as much as possible. And it was for the first time incorporated in the bill on enterprises.

As in the USSR, the general meeting of the working collective (or conference of the delegates) is supposed to be the highest self-management body. It elects the director who must be approved by the founder, and the council which is the executive body, approves the five-year plan and year-end balance sheet, and discusses the long-term development plan and other important issues concerning the personnel. The director is responsible to the self-management body, but probably even more to the founder. If he gets into conflict with the self-management bodies, the founder is the final arbiter (in the USSR, the general meeting). The council controls the fulfilment of the general meeting's decision, approves the proposal of the director for the implementation of economic and social plans and is involved in the determination of the status of the enterprise (*HN*, 1987, no. 30).

Considering the historical experience with workers' councils in the 1960s, when they were the main centres of opposition to the so-called 'normalisation' process, it would be a great surprise if the ruling élite were excited about the idea of self-management. It is, therefore, no wonder that the bill considerably restricts the rights of self-management bodies; they are in no way to infringe on the principle of one-man management. They are much more restrictive than in the USSR. It can be expected that the execution instructions will put even narrower limits on their functioning. Probably they will try to use them as the USSR does, as an additional 'transmission belt' to the workers for the sake of improving performance. Of course, there is no hint in the bill about this; the Czechoslovak ruling élite is shrewder than to make such a public relations mistake. For the same reason, in distinction from the Soviet law on enterprises, the Czechoslovak draft law does not mention that the self-management bodies will be guided by the Party organisations.

11.3 REGULATION SYSTEM

The 1980s provisions bring some changes to the regulation system, but these by no means take the management system beyond the framework of the centralised system. The central planners now rely more on indirect methods and as a result profit has increased in importance. The 'Principles' promise to strengthen this line of management by introducing full *khozraschet* on the level of enterprises backed up by normatives.

Taxation of Enterprise Incomes

Though the reform of 1966 was dismantled, its system of taxes on economic units' profits, set in advance, has been maintained. The tax rate on profit has been quite high; most branches of industry have paid 75 per cent since 1980, most of the extractive industry 50 per cent and the food industry 60 per cent (Šourek, 1983 and 1985).

The setting of a tax on profit in advance can be a stimulus to profit maximisation. In Czechoslovak conditions, this stimulus is weakened considerably among others by allowing redistribution of profits within production economic units (PEUs) (see *SHN*, 1980, no. 12; *SHN*, 1985, no. 50). On the other hand, the fact that unused profit can be carried over to the next year by chanelling it into the reserve fund surely acts positively on enterprises' profit motives.

The profit[2] after taxation is used for several funds. All PEUs and their enterprises are obliged to form two groups of funds: one to provide financing of the construction fund (for investment), the fund for working capital, the fund for technical development (for non-investment outlays on science and technology, financed from the costs of production) and the reserve fund, and one for stimulation (the bonus fund), the fund for cultural and social needs, the fund for development (a new fund, for minor investment and since 1986 this fund has been merged with the construction fund into a single fund) and the fund for stimulation of exports. The last fund is new and is formed only on the level of PEUs (Šourek, 1981).

The 'Principles' intend to replace the tax on profit as the main source of state revenues with taxes (deductions) on factors of production: a tax on wages, a tax on the balance value of fixed assets, unfinished investment and inventories, and a tax for the use of the environment. The tax on wages is to cover state outlays on social insurance, health care, education and similar outlays connected with the reproduction of the labour force. From the tax on fixed assets centralised investments are to be covered.

The tax on profit will only be applied to that part of profit which remains after paying the mentioned taxes and making minimal allocations to the new investment fund (according to a normative), the fund for cultural and social needs and possibly other funds, such as the reserve fund. Naturally, the new tax on profit will be considerably lower than the present one and should be uniform. Whether it will be proportional or progressive is not yet clear. Enterprises should have some leeway in the use of the balance of profit.

That every tax is geared to a certain purpose is partly new, and the rationale behind it is to introduce discipline in outlays. There is also another innovation (already applied in Hungary) which is in line with the above-mentioned principle: in enterprises which are not destined for a contraction, the whole amortisation fund is to be channeled into the investment fund and used for enterprise investment.

Price System

The abandonment of the economic reform in 1969 also meant a stop to the changes in the price system and, in some respects, a return to the old system. In the meantime some changes in wholesale prices have been enacted. Explosive increases in the price of oil and some raw materials in world markets in 1973–74 forced the Czechoslovak government to embark on a wholesale price revision in 1977.[3] This traditional approach to price adjustments was replaced in 1981–85 by a so-called 'continuous updating' of wholesale prices which is to be carried on in the present five-year plan (Dvořák, 1985, p. 126). The price increases for inputs in 1977 were to be absorbed in the cost of production of processing branches by simply economising on costs or at the expense of profit. Price increases in 1981–85 were too large to be fully absorbed (only price increases of fuels and energy[3] had to be absorbed in order to motivate economic units to economise on them); as a result, wholesale prices were increased. Part of the price increases was passed on to consumers.[4]

It is known that the traditional rules of price determination hamper innovation, production of products with higher technical parameters and goods of higher quality. The so-called price stimulation introduced in 1978 is geared to coming to grips witht this problem. To put it briefly, stimulation of technological progress is to be achieved by the application of two-level prices and so-called stepped prices, solutions similar to those of the Soviets.

The two-level prices are applied to new producer goods, whereas the stepped prices are also applied to industrial consumer goods (the latest in fashion and luxury goods). The difference between the two is in who pays for the high initial costs due to the lengthy process of mastering production. In the first case the buyer pays a lower price or one which is expected to be valid once the product 'matures' (four years) and the difference between that cost price and the existing wholesale price is paid from the budget. Such an arrangement should make the producer interested in the production of and the buyer in using such products. Stepped prices are the same for the producer and buyer. With declining costs the price should decrease (Boura 1984; Sabolčík, 1984). Naturally, the system of stepped prices lends itself to many abuses. Therefore it is not allowed to be used for clothing and footwear for babies and children under fifteen years (*SHN*, 1984, nos. 42, 43; *SHN*, 1986, no. 16). In the current five-year plan, PEUs have the right to set the wholesale prices of certain new products, mainly if the prices are derived from world prices. In addition, they can set prices for the latest fashions (*SHN*, 1986, no. 16).

Not once do the 'Principles' stress the need for objectivisation of value instruments (prices, taxes, interest, exchange rate, etc.). Revision of wholesale and agricultural procurement prices is supposed to be the key to this objectivisation. Its purpose is also to facilitate a new arrangement of taxation which aims at a more objective evaluation of factors of production and thus at promoting their more economical use. The new prices are to be formed in the traditional way, costs plus profit. The profit mark-up is to be calculated in relation to the value of factors of production in which labour cost should be given a greater role in order to encourage substitution of capital for labour. These are not the only goals of the price revision; it is also supposed to create conditions for a reduction in costs, for bringing domestic prices closer to world prices and for the establishment of a more rational exchange rate. No explanation is given as to how and when this process of convergency of domestic and world prices is to come about. An official of the Federal Price Board suggests making the contractual prices applied in the trade between the CMEA countries the basis for pricing basic domestic products. According to him, the contractual prices are going to be improved; there is a good chance that world prices of the previous year will become the basis for contractual prices (Haluška, 1987). In other words, contractual prices are to link domestic with world market prices.

The price revision is not intended to affect retail prices; the separation of wholesale and retail prices is to continue.

From the foregoing, it is clear that the 'Principles' intend to change the role of wholesale prices, to make them more active, to change them from an instrument of planning to a criterion of planning and technological progress. This is not entirely a new idea (see Grünwald, 1984); it is, however, better articulated in 'Principles'. Considering that the price revision, the main instrument for reaching the goal, is to be achieved by old methods, the chances for success are slim. Even the promise to link domestic prices to world prices is not going to change much. It is reasonable to expect that such a linkage will be also effected by bureaucratic methods.

Regulation of Wages and the Incentive System

In 1970 the central planners returned to the traditional wage regulation system with some minor modifications (see Adam, 1979, pp. 171–2). The system applied in 1981–85 differed from the old in that wage-bill growth was linked to a net indicator, adjusted net output[5] – according to the Soviet pattern – instead of a gross indicator (marketed output). The rationale for this move was to strengthen the pressure on enterprises to reduce material costs and thus also nonwarranted cooperation with other enterprises. The wage regulation system for 1986–90 has again adopted some elements from the Soviet system as applied in the 1984 experiment. It is worth stressing that the progressive elements in the Soviet system, namely, the determination of the incremental part of the wage bill by *actual and not planned net output* so that the institution of overfulfilment no longer exists, have not been adopted. In addition the normative in Czechoslovakia is set for one year for the time being. The wage regulation system for 1986–90 is just as complicated as the previous one, the actual size of the wage bill depends on many factors, as if the planners wanted to solve all the ills of the economy by wage regulation.

The planned wage bill depends on the planned adjusted net output (or other indicator determined by the ministry) and the normative, which can be relative or incremental; in the first case, the normative determines the percentage share of the wage bill in planned adjusted net output and, in the second, the normative determines the increment of the wage bill over the previous year for a 1 per cent increment in planned adjusted net output. The incremental normative, apparently taken over from the USSR, is to be applied in organisations where the objective is to stimulate an increase in productivity by a reduction in the work force. The normatives are apparently not uniform; this is also clear from the rule that the incremental must be at a rate which would ensure that 'wage intensity' in adjusted net output does not increase.

The actual size of the wage bill depends on the extent of fulfilment of the indicator (and of course on the normative) and also on the so-called additive factors, for saving materials and energy (in 1981–85 from gains in stepped prices), and deductive factors, low technical level of products (in 1981–85 for exceeding employment limits) (Moravec and Hoffman, 1985).

The bonus fund is nowadays assigned to enterprises as a minimal share in the wage bill and is no longer a separate economic instrument. Before 1981 the incentive fund was assigned as a percentage share of profit. In 1981–85 the incentive was assigned as an absolute sum; the actual size depended mostly on the fulfilment of the profitability target and on additive and deductive factors (according to the same principles as the wage bill).

The 'Principles' bring some changes to wage regulation, the most important being that the wage-bill growth is going to be dependent, as in the USSR, only on *achieved* net output (defined rather differently from before) and thus no longer on plan targets, and that preference will be given to the incremental normative. (In the distant future the normatives are to be dropped and the level of basic wages regulated on the basis of the tariff system plus other regulations.) The incentive fund is to depend on disposable profit (*SHN*, 1987, nos. 5, 13).

No change is envisaged in the treatment of the wage tariff system except that it is to be revised more often.

From the foregoing it is clear that the planners are engaged in a quest for an effective wage system, and this is the reason why its structure often changes, a phenomenon which introduces uncertainty into the system and therefore is not very helpful to the implementation of the objectives of the planners.

The adoption of adjusted net output as presently applied, though it is not a strict sales indicator (it includes depreciation and changes in inventories), and even more net output which will be in the next five-year plan (it will not include depreciation), is an advance on what was used before. The future linkage of wage-bill growth to achieved net output is even an improvement over what exists now, particularly if the normative could be uniform and long-term, which is doubtful.

Still, the effectiveness of wage-bill regulation is reduced by the distorted price system which makes net output as well as profit inobjective quantities and as a result introduces inequities in remuneration which have nothing to do with performance. I have also doubts as to whether the transition to an incremental normative will be helpful and sustainable. Such a linkage benefits the enterprises with reserves and enterprises which turned a deaf ear to calls for more demanding plans. On the other hand, enterprises which responded to such calls will be penalised.

Managers and workers as well must be interested in higher economic efficiency if the drive towards it is to have any chance of success. Under existing conditions, when nominal wages grow slowly and real wages stagnate or even decline for some groups, there cannot be great enthusiasm for the planners' objectives. It is generally accepted that greater differentiation in wages is needed, and the authorities concur; however, the new wage rates are less differentiated than before[6] (Baštýř, 1984). True, the authorities have mainly relied on differentiation in bonuses to do the trick. However, evaluations of the campaign for wage effectiveness[7] show that no noticeable progress has been achieved in this respect. Because there is little for distribution, managers are reluctant to engage in fights against strong resistance to differentiation (V. Hájek, 1985; Kozár, 1986).

Regulation of Employment

Employment regulation in the 1980s has changed several times. In the beginning, employment limits were maintained, primarily for white collar workers. Soon they were abolished for the rest of the five-year plan. At the same time, enterprises were allowed to use all the savings from work force reduction for wage increases in the hope that this would be a strong stimulus to labour economy (Stařecký, 1982; Pick, 1982; Ujházi, 1982).

The expectations of the planners did not materialise; on the contrary, many enterprises tried and try to increase their work force. Among the reasons for this development one can mention the expectation of enterprises that economic growth will be accelerated and therefore they wanted to have reserves (see Jirava, 1984). Probably another factor was the very small wage increases in 1981–85 which could be achieved without labour economy. The psychological inhibition of managers against revealing reserves which they tried to hide from the planners and the fear that the rules of the game might be changed surely played a role.

It seems that employment limits are again in force (*SHN*, 1984, no. 42). The 'Principles' promise to apply employment limits only exceptionally and for a short period. Apparently they hope that labour economy will be promoted by the incentives built into the wage regulation and by increased taxes on wages which will enhance labour costs. However, there are no reasons to expect that incentives will work this time if they have not up to now, since no great systemic changes are contemplated. They also promise to limit recruitment of workers for priority sectors and suggest that reallocation of labour be motivated by wage differentials.

Investment Decisions and Financing

The 1980 document introduced (and the 1984 document confirmed with some modifications) two categories for investment in fixed assets from the viewpoint of decision making and financing. The first group comprises so-called binding and centralised investment projects which are included in the national plan. Binding investment projects which have a claim for preferential treatment are approved by the central government, whereas centralised investments require only the approval of the republican governments (Vančik, 1985). This first group of investment projects was financed up to 1986 from the construction fund which every PEU and enterprise had. Apart from unproductive investments, certain important investments in the field of science and technology, exports, etc, which are beyond the financial ability of PEUs, are financed directly from the state budget (Řechtáčková, 1985). The second group includes the rest of the investment projects and was financed up to 1986 from the development fund, a fund which was an integral part of the stimulation fund.[8] Starting with the current five-year plan, both categories of investment are to be financed from a single investment fund (*SHN*, 1984, no. 42).

The two funds used for financing investment were formed differently. The construction fund was in fact assigned to enterprises depending on the estimated costs of the approved investment projects. The development fund was formed on the basis of a normative set by the authorities. In the financing of the first category of investment, government subsidies are obtainable if criteria of efficiency are met. No subsidies are available for the second category of investment (Řechtáčková, 1985). Bank credit is available for both categories of investment (for the second, primarily for modernisation). Extension of credit is not supposed to be automatic. The bank has the right to screen the projects for their effectiveness. Projects promising better returns can be provided with more credit. For projects with a shorter gestation period and/or geared to modernisation of existing capacities the interest can be lower than average. Differentiation in the interest rate is also used to accelerate the construction work (Kûrka, 1981; 1983).[9]

The transition to a single investment fund in PEUs and enterprises aims at bringing its size more in tune with the performance of economic units and in this way making them more interested in the returns on investment. The fund consists of allocations from profit and the amortisation fund, both on the basis of normatives differentiated by the investment plans of economic units, and from the sale of assets (*SHN*, 1985, no. 50). The switch to the investment fund is also supposed to be an integral part of the efforts to give economic units greater leeway in decision making about investment. The only change the 'Principles' promise in investment regulation is to eliminate some less important binding targets, and this will presumably not have a great effect on the system of management.

The changes in the regulation of investment activities, which have been discussed, are far from reaching the roots of the tendency to overinvest with all its negative effects especially low returns on investment. Financing of investment from the enterprises' 'own resources', as applied after 1980, is more or less a formality. And it will remain so as long as the financial situation of enterprises is not really dependent on their performance (the transition to a single investment fund does not make a great difference) and as long as they are not allowed to use their resources according to their own considerations, a measure which is unviable in a centralised system. For this reason, the application of Bank credit and a differentiated rate of interest as instruments of investment regulation cannot have an important effect on the behaviour of economic units.

That this is so is confirmed by the circumstance that all the negative phenomena are reproducing themselves. Dispersal of funds for investment projects in 1983 was 25 per cent above the optimum according to some views, and 35 per cent according to others, and the amount of unfinished projects was 40 per cent above the optimum (*HN*, 1983, no. 8; Vančik, 1985). Despite efforts, budgeted costs for unfinished projects increased in 1981–85, though not dramatically. The average completion time increased substantially over the plan estimates (it was approximately five years; housing construction is not included). Endeavours to improve the structure of investment at the expense of construction work were achieved, but are still at a high level (in 1981–85 construction work in the material sphere made up 48.1 per cent) at a time when the stress is on reconstruction and modernisation. At the same time capital productivity declined (Vašák, 1986; Věrtelář, 1986; Svoboda, 1986).

Foreign Trade

With the return to the old centralised system in 1969, the changes to make economic units feel increasingly the effects of foreign trade and to give an increasing number of producing organisations the right to enter into direct trade relations with foreign firms were reversed. Neither the 1980 document nor the 1984 document brought important systemic changes to foreign trade regulations; the state monopoly and assignment of targets (though their number was slightly reduced) in foreign trade, and separation of domestic and foreign markets have been maintained (Hlavatý, 1985). Both documents, however, brought some changes to export stimulation.

In the 1980s the main incentive for exports promotion has been the fund for material stimulation of exports applied in PEUs (for motivating enterprises involved in exports) as well as in foreign trade corporations. The allocated funds which can be transferred to other enterprise funds depend on the level of the so-called *differential indicator*, which measures the difference between achieved prices on foreign markets and domestic wholesale prices, and on the set priorities in the structure of exports. If the differential indicator falls below a minimum, set flexibly, no further allocation of funds are forthcoming (*SHN*, 1980, no. 11).

Another incentive recently reintroduced is the right of enterprises to use a portion of foreign exchange produced by exports to finance imports. In addition, under certain conditions, a small portion of the retained foreign exchange can be used for the improvement of working conditions and the health care of the workers (*SHN*, 1985, no. 46; *SHN*, 1986, no. 14).

The 'Principles' do not devote much time to foreign trade, perhaps because there was a special decision on foreign trade (*Rudé právo*, 1987, 13 January). They promise to introduce in the future a more realistic uniform exchange rate for the crown. The special decision on foreign trade produces some minor changes in the stimulation of exports and extends cooperation between producing enterprises and FTC. The ministry of heavy industry has taken over the management of a limited number of FTCs and a very few other FTCs have been subordinated to producing enterprises. It is necessary to wait and see whether the promise of the law proposal on enterprises to ease the state monopoly in foreign trade will really bring about further progress in this area. The law proposal also promises joint ventures with foreign firms.

Despite being very dependent on foreign trade, the Czechoslovak leaders are reluctant to liberalise its management very much. They still hope that some minor organisational and motivational changes may bring about improvement in foreign trade. They therefore stick to the state monopoly in foreign trade. There is also a reluctance to put domestic production under increased pressure from foreign markets because of fear of imported inflation. The mentioned stimuli are by themselves not strong enough (the Fund for material stimulation of exports is a small fund)[10] to bring about a change in the declining efficiency of foreign trade. Attempts to bring about improvements in the technological parameters of products, especially in engineering branches, have not been successful despite large investment.[11] Most of the machinery is exported to heavily indebted developing countries on long-term credit, at a time when Czechoslovakia is determined to reduce its own indebtedness (K. Hájek, 1985).

11.4 ORGANISATIONAL SYSTEM

With the abandonment of the reform in 1969 the pressure to dismantle the hierarchical build-up ceased. On the contrary, a trend to more industrial concentration prevailed. In the 1980s PEUs have been made the basic unit of management in the economic sphere, and the role of enterprises within PEUs has become dependent to a great degree on the top managers of PEUs. In the course of time, the directorates in PEUs have centralised in their hands primarily the disaggregation of plan targets, finances and technical and economic development of the sub-branch, entrusted to them (Chmela and Kodým, 1983). According to one source, there is a tendency to make combines, which are the most centralised, the principal form: it is mainly the trusts, the loosest form, which are to be reorganised into combines (Remeš *et al.*, 1985, p. 122).

One could argue that the industrial concentration is in line with the existing centralised system and expect that the promised reform will also bring a deconcentration in industry, all the more because concentration in Czechoslovakia is too high. Without it, a weakening of the monopolistic position of suppliers is inconceivable. However, the 'Principles' make it clear that no great changes can be expected; at most, some specialised enterprises incorporated in PEUs for purely administrative reasons will be allowed to become independent. The law proposal on enterprises contains conflicting rules: on one hand, mergers are supposed to be in the domain of the founder, and, on the other, enterprises are allowed to enter into voluntary associations for a certain purpose. Probably the voluntary association will require the approval of the founder.

11.5 CONCLUDING REMARKS

Judging the Czechoslovak sources themselves, the provisions of the 1980s have not had a great effect on the economy. Some aspects of the provisions were instituted with delay and others contrary to the adopted principles. The fact that the five-year plan for 1981–85 was approved after great delay (1983), as a result of worsening external equilibrium, undercut the intention of the planners of making the five-year plan the main instrument of planning (Dvořák, 1985, p. 119; Beneš, 1986). There was also a delay in the start of the current five-year plan.

The transition to 'continuous updating' of wholesale prices, instead of the traditional price revision made once in a long period, has introduced some flexibility in pricing. However, this has not eliminated the known shortcomings of a price system set from above and insulated from world market influences.

The wage regulation system applied in 1981–85 turned out to be, as could be expected, too complicated and demanding on administration. The normatives have often been set arbitrarily and frequently changed, and, as a result, incentives, in as far as they acted at all, had primarily a short-term impact. As a result, it did not really serve as an instrument for regulating wages; it was, rather, used for the subsequent evaluation of wage evolution. Under such conditions, the desired objective to link wages more closely to performance, has not been achieved (Bezděkova and Papežová, 1986; Beneš, 1986).

Changes in foreign trade regulation have been too small to have a real effect on enterprises. Exporting enterprises have been little exposed to the effects of world market prices; subsidies drawn from the state budget have guaranteed enterprises prices almost equal to those in domestic markets. The exchange rate of the crown is passive and has little effect on the structure of exports (Šafaříková, 1984; Dvořák, 1985, p. 127; K. Tardos, 1986).

The provisions of the 1980s have not brought about a turnaround in the slow progress in technology; the central planners have relied too much on exogenous factors (as incentives) at a time when innovations should result to a great extent from grappling with problems arising in the process of production. The two-level prices alone are not a sufficiently strong stimulus in the face of the many known factors which discourage enterprises from innovating.

Concentration in industry combined with uncertainties about the position of many enterprises in associations has also been a disturbing element in the working of the system.

Taking all these together, it is clear that the provisions had little effect on the performance of the economy. In a critical appraisal, two economists wrote that the impact of the provisions was reflected in 'the activisation of lightly mobilisable reserves, and rationalisation provisions and innovations of short-term character' (Bezděková and Papežová, 1986).

It is no accident that the 1980s in Czechoslovakia have not brought about a genuine reform. The last thing the Czechoslovak leaders want is to experiment with reforms since they may endanger their positions. A reform, mainly if it is designed along the lines of the reform of the 1960s, means an admission that the reformers of the 1960s, who were sharply criticised, purged and ridiculed, were correct after all. Probably this is also the reason why the 'Principles' do not include any direct indication about market forces and their application. Therefore the leaders have followed a policy of preserving the *status quo* (Kusin, 1982) which has also been reflected in minimal changes in the structure of the Politbureau. This policy is also in the interest of a great many middle cadres who gained positions of responsibility during the purges in the beginning of the 1970s.

Does this mean that the recent promise of a far-reaching reform is only a lip service? There are good reasons for the suspicion that this is so. On the other hand, it seems that the best policy for depriving the opposition of ammunition is to have some 'reform'. In my opinion the outcome of the promise of a reform will depend very much on what happens in the USSR.

The promised provisions in the 'Principles' are mostly steps in the right direction, but they alone cannot cure the ills of the economy. No doubt, the promised improvements in the drafting of state plans, by giving a greater role to financial flows and by applying the rule of economic efficiency, are desirable and topical. One can, however, doubt whether the adoption of the economic efficiency rule will have any great effect on the restructuring of the economy since this is the area where power relations play a paramount role.

Giving enterprises more leeway in decision making about drafting plans, wages (by introducing normatives), incentives and investment, is progress over the past. However, these changes will not create an environment in which enterprises will be forced to produce products efficiently in a structure and quality required by the market. Formally, enterprises have a right to a certain extent to choose their suppliers; however, under the existing monopolisation, it is a right without great value. True, the 'Principles' promise to protect the buyer, but the protection they offer is in the enforcement of supply contracts, and this is not really much protection. First, the supplier, due to his monopolistic position, can influence the contract according to his best interests, and there is no reason why contracts should now be enforced if they have not been hitherto (Dvořák, 1987).

The great stress on self-financing which has to induce enterprises to behave efficiently is in principle correct. However, it can work only under certain conditions: it can in no way work if enterprises are assigned targets which they have no right to reject, even if they could more efficiently use their capacity to fill other orders, and if the tax burden is too high so that little profit remains at their disposal. It does not seem that the reform is going to meet these preconditions (see also p. 188).

The fact that the Czechoslovak leaders are not interested in giving large room for market forces, combined with lack of change in the great concentration of industry, seems to indicate that they intend to follow partly the East German route in the system of management, all the more because the Soviets do apparently the same.

Appendix: Recent Changes in the System of Management in the German Democratic Republic

by Horst Betz

INTRODUCTION

In 1963 the German Democratic Republic (GDR) became the first of the Comecon countries to introduce significant modifications to the management system of its economy. The New Economic System of Planning and Management (NES) featured not only organisational and functional changes in the cumbersome central planning apparatus but also, most significantly, a system of economic levers to supplement the central plan and replace many of the administrative directives issued to the enterprises. Profit, in a new enhanced role, was to serve both as an enterprise performance indicator and a source of investment funds over and above the state loans, which were to supplant, at least partially, outright grants. Capital stock was revalued at replacement cost, complemented by a new set of depreciation rates and followed by a comprehensive industrial price revision and an interest charge on capital.

As early as 1965, however, there began a gradual trend towards recentralisation and the closing of what had been originally termed an 'open reform'. By 1971, the NES already renamed the Economic System of Socialism (ESS) in 1967 was essentially defunct. Under the impact of events in the CSSR and serious domestic economic difficulties, such as supply shortages and disproportionalities, the ideologically more comfortable and practically more convenient administrative predominance over the economy, stressing 'plan authority' and 'plan discipline', had been restored. More specifically, a further promising price reform had been stopped, the role of profit downgraded, investment decisions recentralised, the number of quantitative control coefficients increased again and enterprise plans broken down by the month.

DEVELOPMENT OF ECONOMIC AND SOCIAL POLICY OBJECTIVES SINCE 1971

When Honecker presided over his first party congress in 1971 he also announced a new long-run objective termed the 'primary task' (*Hauptaufgabe*) which was to lay the groundwork for what came to be called the Advanced System of Socialism (ASS) (Direktive, 1971). Even though the primary task, in the form of the 'inseparable unity' of economic and social policies, represents but a reaffirmation of Stalin's basic economic law of socialism it was accorded special prominence by incorporating it into the amended constitution of 1974 and the new party programme of 1976.

During the early years of the primary task little was offered by way of programmatic or operational details beyond an increasing emphasis on intensification in the productive process on the basis of the scientific-technological revolution. The one major change, as will be seen, was the reorganisation of industry on the basis of combines in 1979 which laid the structural and organisational groundwork for the multitude of measures designed to improve economic management, planning and stimulation.

It was also in the second half of the 1970s that the economic situation of the GDR worsened markedly. Its reserves for further extensive growth had been exhausted and the terms of trade deteriorated to a crisis level mainly due to the rapid price increases of energy sources and other industrial raw materials. Indebtedness to Western countries had reached its limits and, in addition, deficits were incurred in trade with the Soviet Union.

With the pronouncements of the 'Economic Strategy for the 1980s' and the 'Economic Strategy with a View to the Year 2000' at the 1981 and 1986 party congresses respectively, the primary task as 'the major battleground of the SED (Socialist Unity Party)' became not only programmatically more specific but also operationally more concrete as reflected in the multitude of economic measures discussed below. The specific points of the two economic strategies are quite similar. They stress 'socialist rationalisation' to promote increased labour productivity, enhanced product quality in the interest of international competitiveness, modernisation of plant and equipment, more efficient utilisation of material and energy resources and a larger supply of consumer durables.

There is, however, a difference in emphasis. During the last few years efforts for renewed economic growth and a reduction of foreign indebtedness have been concentrated on so-called 'key industries' and product refinement. The former, somewhat reminiscent of the structure determining branches responsible for many of the disproportionalities under the ESS, are so named because they 'open the doors to novel sources of efficiency . . . [and] economy in the use of labour, energy, materials and capital funds' (Nick, 1986). Included are microelectronics, new industrial processes, CAD/CAM, robot technology, nuclear energy, biotechnology and laser techniques. They represent the forefront of the combination of science with production, also called 'socialisation of knowledge'. Closely connected is product refinement, i.e. the production of higher quality products by means of advanced technology as well as recycling and the increasing use and processing of domestic energy and raw materials.

Before looking in some detail at the numerous changes in industrial organisation, planning, balancing, financing and stimulation designed to give effect to the primary task two important points need to be made. First, unlike the directive for the NES there is no one document presenting an integrated programme of economic reform. Closest to it comes a far-reaching speech by the party's major economic spokesman, G. Mittag, delivered at the 1983 Economic Conference of the GDR to which reference will be made below (Mittag, 1984).

This lack of a single comprehensive reform document is related to the second point, namely that the word 'reform' is no longer part of the official vocabulary in the GDR. Instead, all measures affecting the system of management are subsumed under the expression of 'perfecting the system of management, planning and economic accountability'. This may be so for a number of reasons. First, perfecting a system is to convey a more positive picture, an important consideration for the legitimacy of the regime. Second, being an on-going process, perfecting does not require the presentation of a comprehensive set of specific details and time horizons which, as experience has taught, may have to be changed or abandoned; the pressure of success is not as immediate. Third, the term reform may raise undesirable expectations such as decentralisation, enterprise autonomy, or political relaxation. Overall then, perfecting the system is ideologically safer than reforming it.

INDUSTRIAL REORGANISATION: THE COMBINES

The 1979 decree on the establishment of combines (*Gesetzblatt*

[GBL], 1979, no. 38) was the single most important step towards reorganising the system of management and planning; this change in the industrial structure became the major point of reference for all subsequent reform measures. The establishment of combines was to represent the major organisational basis for socialist rationalisation. Combines had existed as early as the 1960s, but within the overall system of management and planning they always stood in the shadow of the Associations of State Enterprises (VVBs) as the top management organs for their respective industrial branches. These were, however, mere 'administrative units of management without any organic relation to the productive process' (Mittag, 1984).[1]

At present there exist, under the jurisdiction of eleven industrial ministries, 175 centrally managed combines in industry and construction which consist of between twenty and forty member enterprises, employ on average 25 000 people and are responsible for some 90 per cent of industrial production. They represent horizontal, vertical and lateral combinations for all phases of production from the supply of raw materials to the sales of the final product including their own research and development divisions.

The hoped for advantages which can be gleaned from the above-mentioned decree and various GDR commentaries are as follows. First, to make the recentralised planning and balancing process both more flexible and transparent. With the elimination of the VVBs and establishment of the combines as 'the basic economic units' one step in the information flow and decision-making processes was done away with. Management decisions were now taken in immediate proximity to the actual productive process. Second, to take advantage of economies to scale not only in production through specialisation and division of labour as well as a more efficient use of energy and raw materials but also in administration and organisation of the combine to promote improved coordination between the various member enterprises. Third, to internalise external economies by establishing scientific and marketing facilities more closely related to the productive process. Fourth, vertical integration and/or establishment of new units were designed to overcome long-standing supply problems regarding raw materials, semi-finished and highly specialised products as well as providing the needed capacities to produce special and replacement parts for the modernisation of plant and equipment, i.e. combines were to manufacture their own means of rationalisation. Integrating into the combines units to produce means of rationalisation and carry out repairs does not, of course, only undermine efficiency and enhance the monopoly position of the combine, but also raises serious questions regarding the pace of technological progress and innovation if great emphasis is placed on the reconstruction or modernisation of essentially old equipment. Fifth, the very size of combines was considered most conducive to the implementation of retraining and redeployment of labour. Finally, in the interest of meeting the challenges in the strategic area of international trade, most of the foreign trade enterprises were integrated into the combines in order to do away with the rigid organisational separation of trade from production. This allows combines with foreign trade enterprises a greater role in international economic relations both through their marketing organisations and by participating in the negotiations of foreign trade contracts. The foreign trade monopoly of the state, however, remains intact since the foreign trade enterprises also have to answer to the Ministry of Foreign Trade which, together with the respective industrial ministries, issues foreign exchange plan targets to the directors-general of the combines. Also, unlike the funds earned by other combine enterprises those earned by foreign trade enterprises cannot be integrated into those of the combine as a whole.

The chief executive officer of the combine is the director general who performs the dual functions of an entrepreneur and 'above all [that of a] political functionary' (Koziolek, 1985) or as one commentator put it, 'using the metaphor of the Kantean categorical imperative he must think and act as if he were responsible for the whole economy' (Krömke, 1980). In his actions on behalf of the combine he enjoys much greater latitude than his counterpart in the old VVBs. He actively participates in both plan preparation and execution. He not only provides the ministry with information on the combine's productive, innovative and marketing potentials in the preparatory stage of the planning process but also, once the plan has been set he disaggregates the targets and assigns them to the individual enterprises.

The decrees on combines and balancing (*GBL*, 1980, no. 1) for example, also delegate to the director-general the responsibility for preparing equipment and consumer goods balances as well as ratification of combine and enterprise balances in general with the exception of those concerning raw materials, imports and exports and the continued provision for the needs of the population in which cases the minister ratifies. Internally, the director-general has considerable authority to effect organisational changes such as the consolidation and relocation of enterprises and, above all, to decide on the use of funds earned by the combine enterprises. This particular aspect represents a potential source of conflict between the combine and its individual enterprises who are supposedly 'economically and legally independent units'. This independence, however, is modified by the phrase 'in the framework of the production and management process of the combine'. Thus the director-general has in practice considerable latitude, the exact extent of which is still subject to considerable debate, especially since his actions in the redistribution of net profits as well as amortisation and performance funds earned by individual enterprises do affect the latters' motivation.

Another problem discussed in the literature concerns the size of combines. While it is conceded that gross production was greatly stimulated by large-scale enterprises cautions are issued against the 'illusion' that size alone could lead to increased labour productivity. Small and medium-sized enterprises with greater flexibility in their assortment and responsiveness to special user and consumer needs (e.g. services and repairs), it is argued, should be made more equal partners in industrial production (Hensel and Kuciak, 1984). On the other hand, the leading authority on combines, G. Friedrich, maintains that there is no economic law which says large enterprises are less responsive and flexible than small and medium-sized ones (Eilenberger, 1984).

Once the combines had been established as 'the backbone of socialist economic planning' and their functions and responsibilities more clearly delineated 'it became necessary to decide, within the context of the economy as a whole, on new measures for the continued perfection of management, planning and economic accountability' (Mittag, 1984). Beginning in 1981, a veritable flood of decrees and directives was introduced over the next several years in pursuit of four major operational goals: (1) the continued improvement of economic management according to the principles of democratic centralism; (2) the perfection of state planning and balancing as the primary foundations for socialist management to ensure proportional economic development; (3) more effective utilisation of performance indicators for combines and enterprises to promote growth through more efficient production; and (4) to enhance enterprise self-reliance and economic stimulation by means of perfecting economic accountability on the basis of the plan. As can be seen the centralist elements continue to be accorded the most prominent place.

CHANGES IN THE SYSTEM OF PLANNING AND BALANCING

Having established central planning and balancing as the major management instruments, considerable efforts have been made in the GDR, as in the other socialist countries, since the late 1960s to make the five-year plan an economic steering device of major operational importance, so far, however, without much success. Its major impact still is not so much as a firm and reliable guide to enterprise production but rather as a political and ideological document. The operational shortcomings of the five-year plan and the reasons why the enterprises are almost exclusively guided by the annual plan can be seen in the frequent changes made to and supplements published for the 1976–80 and 1981–85 planning outlines and targets. These modifications are to no small degree a reflection of a certain amount of experimentation, changing economic circumstances, increasing emphasis on product refinement and key technologies and, above all, to accommodate the combine reforms and measures affecting the accountability of enterprises.

The most important change in planning methodology, next to the problems raised by changing performance indicators discussed below, is the closer integration of the combines into the planning process. After the plan targets in the form of indicators have been established by the State Planning Commission disaggregation proceeds in two stages, by the industrial ministries for the combines under their jurisdiction and by the combines, in turn, for their constituent enterprises. Also, manpower, financial and material inputs are, once firmed up by the balancing system, allocated in the same sequence to combines and enterprises on the basis of binding branch-wide normatives. Mittag argues that the new planning methodology makes for a more complete integration of the basic economic units into the central plan and, as a consequence, a better synchronisation of the planning process with the qualitative performance indicators (Mittag, 1984).

At present some 100 binding plan indicators exist for centrally administered combines and represent the basis for balancing, materially and financially, the economic process as a whole for the purpose of promoting efficiency as well as to stimulate and control productive efforts. Like other socialist countries, the GDR has been continually in search of a single synthetic indicator setting targets and evaluating results. While there has been agreement on the performance components to be evaluated, i.e. the volume of 'demand-satisfying' production, quality of production and efficiency of production, finding an appropriate synthetic indicator has proven elusive. Instead, groups of three or four indicators have been designated as 'major' or 'basic' ones. From 1980 through 1983 industrial commodity production, net production and basic materials cost per 100 marks of commodity production were in use as 'basic performance indicators'. In 1983 (*GBL*, 1983, SDr. 1122) a new group of 'main performance indicators' were introduced: net production, net profit, products and services for the population, and exports. For the first time industrial commodity production lost its prominent rank because of the ever more apparent disadvantages associated with it – waste of materials and a neglect of quality requirements and assortment considerations – at a time when the call had gone out for increased labour productivity, efficient use of resources and quality improvement according to world standards. It was pointed out, however, that industrial commodity production would continue to play a role in the planning process. After all, it could not be dropped altogether as long as material balances in commodity production continue to be maintained. In addition, it has the operational advantage of being easily calculated and can, therefore, perform at least a preliminary control function. As for the indicator 'basic materials cost per 100 Mark of commodity production', it proved to be too complicated; its calculation was time-consuming, it conflicted with contractually fixed technical specifications and was generally regarded to be too closely tied to industrial commodity production.

The promotion of net production (commodity production minus use of materials and productive services and depreciation) and net profit (simplified: gross profit minus capital levy) was designed to enhance economy in use of energy and raw materials, labour productivity, and generally, improve the cost-yield ratio. However, any financial performance indicator will have its limitations circumscribed by the as yet prevailing inflexibilities of the price system. The indicator 'products and services for the population' reflects the renewed emphasis on that part of the primary task calling for an improvement of the material and cultural standard of living while the attention to exports underscores the significance of international trade which, according to Mittag influences some 40 per cent of national income.

As part of the concern for improvement (the official word is *Qualifizierung*) of the central planning mechanism the leadership has also issued a call for higher standards in central balancing, the 'core of socialist planning'. At every stage of the productive process balances, both material and financial, come into play to avoid disproportionalities and bottlenecks. In 1982 the balancing authority for strategically important resources such as energy and raw materials was centralised with the Council of Ministers and the State Planning Commission. According to the State Planning Commission there were in 1984, 2136 centrally determined balanced deciding on 76 per cent of total production (Rost, 1984). All efforts to improve the effectiveness of balancing as an 'operational management instrument' go in the direction of devising fully or partially integrated balances by way of input-output tables. These show the material relationships not only between the branches of production but also between production and its use for consumption, investment and international trade respectively.

To reinforce the effectiveness of balancing and assure compliance with centrally determined priorities a considerable number of additional measures of 'direct steering' have been introduced. Most prominent among them were the so-called *Staatsauftraege* (direct production orders from the State) and a directive establishing economy-wide normatives for the use and inventories of materials (*GBL*, 1982, no. 28). The latter established quota allotments and upper limits for the use of material inputs subject also to a strict control mechanism; it was designed to prevent the waste of energy and other raw materials. While the combine director-general was accorded limited authority on establishing internal enterprise norms for the use of inputs and maintenance of inventory he has to conform to centrally determined normatives in the form of binding plan indicators. As to the *Staatsauftraege*, they were designed, on the basis of legally sanctioned special orders of the highest priority, to promote product innovation on the basis of scientific-technological progress. They were abolished, without comment, in 1986 and not replaced (*GBL*, 1986, no. 24). Commentaries in *Wirtschaftswissenschaft* had, however, already expressed criticisms and advocated a greater delegation of authority in this matter to combines and more reliance on inter-combine contractual relations.

PARAMETRIC MEASURES TO PROMOTE ECONOMIC ACCOUNTABILITY AND STIMULATION

For the express purpose of integrating the interests of the combines with those of society as a whole, a number of changes and innovations have been introduced to the arsenal of indirect steering mechanisms. In the search for a more balanced approach to commodity-money relationships greater attention was paid again, beginning in the early 1980s, to steering instruments of a monetary nature such as profit, credit, enterprise funds and various taxes and levies. In considering the various measures and their impact one must remember how profits are used and various enterprise funds financed. Gross profit over and above costs of production is subject to the capital levy with net profit as the residual. After payment of the net profit tax (in the form of binding absolute amounts and by branch) the remaining net profit is used to finance fully the premium and performance funds and, partially (the rest being financed out of costs), the investment, risk and circulating capital funds. Other combine and enterprise funds such as the wage fund, cultural and social fund as well as those for maintenance and science and technology are part of the planned cost structure. The wage fund is part of the system of central plan indicators assigned to enterprises as an absolute sum and it use is subject to central control. It is to cover the planned gross wages of all employees. The actual size of the fund depends on the fulfilment of quantitative and qualitative indicators (e.g. net production, product quality). Given the size of the wage fund and the efforts to increase productivity by means of labour saving devices, this particular fund, as will be seen, became subject of one of the most significant parametric changes.

A first basic step was the 1982 directive on 'Economic Accountability on the Basis of the Plan' (*GBL*, 1982, no. 3). It was also the first major document designed to give effect to the economic strategy pronounced at the 1981 party congress. Of major importance was the intention to enhance cost effectiveness and discipline. Towards that end rigid cost limits were established which, if exceeded, led to an automatic blocking of certain enterprise funds. Other provisions demanded strict cost-yield considerations of certain enterprise funds. These considerations were even extended to the area of science and technology.

Also combines and enterprises were required to meet their state profit deductions even in cases where planned net profits could not be met. They would then have to honour their obligations either by drawing on their own internal funds or apply for credit with the state bank. Should excess profits be realised due to successful cost saving measures additional contributions to the premium and performance funds were permitted. Enterprise rewards or penalties were also made a function of the degree of product refinement achieved and the performance in export markets. Finally, by way of preserving greater central control, the watchdog role of the chief auditor was strengthened to ensure proper compliance by combines and enterprises with the new regulations.

The one common theme permeating the multitude of directives touching on economic accountability has been the increasing significance accorded to profit (*GBL*, 1983, no. 11). Until the early 1980s its major function had been to ensure that the planned financial needs of productive units were met. Now, in the context of the priority assigned to cost-yield considerations it is, similar to the NES, also to encourage resource saving methods of production by means of allowable contributions to combines or enterprise funds. Of major importance for the stimulative function of net profit are the performance and premium funds, both wholly financed out of net profit.

The performance fund is designed to stimulate the achievement of excess profits through increased productivity, improved quality of production and better working and living conditions for employees. However, no personal financial rewards in the form of premiums or wages are allowed. As to its use, measures of internal financing for the purposes of rationalisation (including the repayment of investment credits) were given priority over those affecting workers' welfare. At least 25 per cent of the fund were to be used for centrally planned rationalisation investment, while no more than 150 marks per full-time equivalent employee could be spend on improvement of working and living conditions. With the introduction of a new investment fund in 1987 a new directive on the performance fund became necessary limiting its planning, formation and use exclusively to the improvement of working and living conditions (*GBL*, 1987, no. 3).[2]

Premium funds serve to stimulate workers' efforts by way of year-end bonuses for meeting and exceeding quality, assortment, export and productivity targets. According to the latest directive (*GBL*, 1986, no. 19) it is financed through a basic amount of at least 820 marks per full-time equivalent employee plus additional funds for exceeding at least two performance indicators selected according to the particular sector of the economy.

Attempts to influence enterprise behaviour are confined not only to the uses of net profit but also its determinants in the first place. It is in this connection that the capital or production funds levy and the wage-bill tax are of considerable importance. The capital levy was first introduced in 1966 under the NES. It represents, in essence, an interest charge on capital but is not considered a cost, rather it is the difference between gross and net profit and is to promote improved utilisation of existing capacities and discourage idle equipment and excessive inventories commonly used as a hedge against changing plan obligations. During the 1980s the provisions governing the operations of the capital levy underwent a number of significant changes. According to the latest version (*GBL*, 1985, no. 13) the uniformly applicable rate of 6 per cent was retained only for working capital; for other funds the change is levied at a rate to be announced in the annual plan and, in line with the latest revaluation of capital equipment, applied against the net value of plant, equipment and unfinished investment projects. In this way the older equipment is less heavily taxed and, in connection with other investment regulations discussed below, provides a greater incentive for the modernisation of existing plants. There is also a penalty of an additional 6 per cent charged on excess inventories and all investment projects finished late.

The most prominent and perhaps even radical attempt at reducing the wage bill and improving labour productivity (by discouraging the hoarding of labour and encourage greater capital intensity) was the introduction, in 1983, of a so-called 'contribution to social funds' (*GBL*, 1983, no. 11). The name itself seems to suggest an increased revenue source to finance the rising expenditures associated with financing the 'second paycheck' or social consumption in the form of subsidy for such things as basic food items, housing and medical services which according to the party programme, is to increase faster than remuneration by way of wages and salaries. In effect it is a tax of a uniform normative of 70 per cent on the planned wage funds of enterprises and combines. While it does represent a new revenue source for the state its primary purpose was to raise labour productivity by means of indirect rather than direct steering. This wage-bill tax, unlike the capital charge, is to be 'part of enterprise costs, industrial prices and, therefore of net production', though only the prices for new products may reflect the tax. Also, it must not affect 'prices of products and services for the population'. To ameliorate the difficulties which the absorption of this charge would bring to some enterprises provisions were made for temporary state subsidies.

The net effect on the state budget appears to be insignificant since there have been counterbalancing effects through the reduction in other revenues from and an increase in subsidies to combines and enterprises. By and large, the introduction of this new 'economic lever' has not only made labour relatively more expensive, but also cut into profits which should encourage greater cost consciousness. Interestingly enough, however, commentaries on this measure in the GDR literature are almost non-existent.

In light of the enhanced responsibilities of combines and as a counter-balance to the various monetary steering instruments a more elaborate state control mechanism became unavoidable, a point also stressed by Mittag. In addition to productivity increases a major concern during the rationalisation process over the last few years has been product quality, especially in view of the preoccupation with meeting international standards in highly competitive export markets and as import substitutes. As a result directives on quality control and appropriate sanctions were adopted with the responsibility for the achievement and promotion of appropriate quality in production assigned to the ministries.

Banks, too, were given increasing control authority such as overseeing the use of combine wage funds, checking on and making suggestions regarding the proper use of factor reserves and issuing requests for intervention by central authorities if their proposals are not met.

CHANGES IN THE PRICE SYSTEM

It has generally been recognised in the GDR that a realistic valuation of cost-yield results by means of the new performance indicators makes considerale demands on the price system. It has undergone a number of revisions without, however, achieving a proper reflection of relative scarcities; it is still centrally planned and administered.

In 1968 so-called fund-related prices had been introduced for about one-third of industrial production. In addition to the standard cost components they included capital cost and were to assist capital intensive enterprises who had to pay their capital charges out of profit. But like other changes in the price system begun under the NES and ESS this development was not continued in the 1970s. In 1976 prices according to the 'price-performance ratio' were established for new products in an attempt to stimulate innovation. In essence, enterprises were granted additional profits based on how their new products 'performed' (in terms of use value) in relation to comparable ones. The attempts to measure and compare use values of new products proved rather impractical. The efforts to manipulate the determination of comparable use values by enterprises exceeded those devoted to the intended innovative activities.

In 1983 a new directive on the calculation of prices established some new ground rules (*GBL*, 1983, no. 35). First of all, it abolished the experiment of price formation on the basis of the 'price-performance ratio'; in essence industrial prices remain based on cost. It should be pointed out, however, that regular upward wholesale price revisions have taken place to reflect rising international energy and raw material prices. For example, between 1981 and 1985 price changes came into effect for some 85 per cent of total industrial production. The average price increase lay between 15 and 20 per cent. Subsequent price revisions will also apply to 'products already in production' which, until then, had to absorb the wage bill levy without the benefit of higher prices. This would allow the authorities time to evaluate the effectiveness of the wage-bill levy. Second, prices for new products could reflect the wage bill levy in cost calculations. In addition, to promote the manufacturing of new and innovative products, higher mark-ups for a period of three years may be granted for enhanced product refinement, reduced material inputs and greater export profitability. Penalties are assessed for outmoded and low quality products. Considerations of use value, while subject to a number of strict limitations, have, of course, still not completely eliminated. As one Western commentary puts it: 'Enterprises still have . . . considerable leeway [in determining] the properties of use value. As a result of these measurement problems . . . gross production will be overvalued and even more so net production . . . [and since] net production is less than gross production the numerically equal price effect is of relatively greater weight' (*Wochenbericht*, 1987, no. 5). This has, of course, serious implications for the reliability of net product as one of the major performance indicators.

Whatever changes in industrial prices have taken place, however, the prices for basic consumer items have been, as a matter of ideological commitment, kept stable, a markedly different practice from most other East European countries. Prices of luxury or 'Exquisit' goods, though, have been raised considerably. By and large, then, while there have been changes in prices there has been no change in the system of price formation. 'Prices will continue to remain firmly in the hands of the socialist state' (*GBL*, 1983, no. 35).

INVESTMENT DECISIONS AND FINANCING

In the last several years investment activities in the GDR have been basically oriented towards a better integration of scientific-technological progress into the productive process with particular emphasis on key industries, product refinement and the expansion of domestic energy and raw material sources. Time-consuming investment projects of an extensive nature do not enjoy much favour anymore. Instead preference is accorded to the maintenance, replacement, expansion and repair of existing capital stock, modernisation of plant and equipment as well as internal (to combines) production of so-called means of rationalisation. The major non-industrial investment activity is housing construction, the dominant social policy component of the 'primary task', in pursuit of the often stated objective to eliminate the housing problem by the year 1991.

Basically investment decisions are made as part of the central planning process and projects are financed out of the state budget, enterprise funds and bank credits. As can be gleaned from the various new directives on investment, the right of combines to make their own investment decisions has become rather more constrained. At present it is largely restricted to manufacturing their own means of rationalisation. Even here the use of their own financial resources is governed by binding plan indicators. On the other hand, since the construction of means of rationalisation is becoming ever more important the prospect at least exists that combines may be given a greater say on investments.

Of eminent significance in the planning, assessment and control process of investment projects are the provisions of the directive on investment preparation (*GBL*, 1985, no. 17) which clearly tightens central control over all phases of the investment process at the expense of the combines. For example, all projects of more than five million marks in value (even if self-financed) are subject to assessment by state authorities to ensure that the following stipulated requirements are met; improvement of cost-yield relations with prompt recovery of financial means invested, an increase of labour productivity faster than of capital stock, a net savings of jobs, meeting or improving on centrally determined time-normatives for completion (usually within two years) and use of investments for continued improvement of working and living conditions of employees. This directive was supplemented last year by one of the formation of industrial prices for investment goods including the modernisation of existing stock. Its purpose was to safeguard price calculations on the basis of the 1983 price directive, to improve on the reliability of the price component in contractual relation between suppliers and producers and preclude any effects on consumer prices (*GBL*, 1986, no. 39).

By way of direct intervention into the investment decisions and activities of enterprises a decree was issued in 1983 which extended 'on the basis of effective and economical maintenance', the normative period of utilisation of most capital stock by 30 per cent in order to economise on funds (*GBL*, 1983, no. 23). It also caused a reduction in depreciation rates and contribution to the amortisation fund and, of course, an increased dependence on old equipment which makes it more difficult to meet plan requirements.

For the financing of investment projects enterprises have to rely heavily on their own resources such as net profits in excess of the plan and, until this year, the performance fund as regulated by the 1983 financial guidelines mentioned above. The other major source is bank credit with the use of differential interest rates (the basic rate is 5 per cent) as stimuli for meeting or exceeding output and completion date targets as well as sanctions for less successful performances. The latest 'stimulative' measure governing investment financing delegates somewhat greater responsibilities to the combines in 'earning and using financial resources for the purposes of modernisation of reconstruction of capital stock' (Mittag, 1986; *GBL*, 1987, no. 3). For this purpose an investment fund is to be established fed, on the basis of normatives, from net profit and amortisation and can also be used for extra-plan investments.

Finally, mention must be made of the long overdue revaluation of capital stock (in excess of a value of 2000 marks) on the basis of industrial prices in effect on 1 January 1986 (*GBL*, 1984, no. 37). This produced a more realistic picture of capital costs and together with increased material input prices and wage costs should make both for a more efficient use of plan and equipment and a more reliable indication of the effects of intensification efforts in general.

CONCLUSION

There is no question that the numerous changes in the GDR economy over the last several years have produced signs of success in the areas of productivity increases (even though changing price bases made comparisons difficult) and foreign debt reduction. The efforts to improve on the economic performance in the late 1970s and early 1980s have been characterised by attempts to find just the right mixture (dialectic unity?) of administrative and parametric measures. The one glaring shortcoming, of course, is that despite all the changes in the level and improvements in the calculation of prices, the system of price formation as such has remained the same, firmly in the hands of the central authorities. As to the organisation of industry, the leadership continues to express its unwavering commitment to the combine structure as the means to synchronise the interests of the basic economic units with those of society as a whole particularly in their pursuit of the continued development of key industries in an age of rapid technological change. It remains to be seen, however, what will happen once the initial efficiency gains through concentration and intensification cannot be readily continued and even some disadvantages of large size begin to show.

It is also evident that, whatever new methods of indirect steering (with concomitantly tighter controls, though) have been introduced, there are no indications whatsoever that the system would tend towards greater decentralisation of the decision-making process similar to that in Hungary. A comparison of average annual national income growth rates (4.5 per cent in the GDR as against 1.4 per cent in Hungary over the period of the 1981–85 five-year plan) and Gorbachev's reference to the GDR as a model for the Soviet economy would certainly help to confirm the present course of action with its continued call for 'further strengthening of the principle of democratic centralism through a higher quality of central management and planning'. As a matter of fact, in numerous recent articles in *Wirtschaftswissenschaft* and *Einheit* prominent authors (Friedrich, Hager, Koziolek, Mittag, Nick, Reinhold) have presented elaborate defences of the centralist domination over the economy against 'suggestions' for decentralisation in the form of enterprise autonomy and market socialism. Such developments would not only undermine the 'creative' role of the party and state but also destroy the organic unity between the economy and society as a whole. They would also deprive socialist ownership of the means of production of its essence by promoting group property. Finally, in pursuing a continued policy of *Abgrenzung* (demarcation) against the Federal Republic of Germany (also part of the 1974 constitutional changes) there is a need for a clearly defined separate political and economic identity and every effort is made to stress the difference between the two systems. Decentralising the economic decision-making and control apparatus would detract from this identity. After all, the population in the GDR already enjoys the highest standard of living in Eastern Europe plus the realistic prospects for further improvements in economic and social conditions.

Conclusion

In this conclusion I will concentrate on two points: (1) recording the most important systemic achievements in reforming the systems of management in the last two decades and, primarily, (2) discussing some of the problems the reformers still face, especially in an indirect system (such as the Hungarian) in their drive to deepen the reform of the system of management. I believe that the USSR and Czechoslovakia will face more or less similar problems once they decide to fully abandon the traditional management system. In discussing this second point I assume that the countries under review are committed to the essentials of the socialist economic system: collective ownership of means of production in key sectors of the economy, macro-planning, full employment, more equal distribution of income, and social programmes.

First, even the pessimists must acknowledge that progress has been achieved in reforming the systems of management. The extent of this progress varies considerably by countries. Taking into consideration the reforms announced in 1987 in the USSR and CSSR, the reforms of the 1980s go beyond the reforms of the 1960s, with the exception of Czechoslovakia.

In Hungary (and to a much lesser extent in Poland, considered on a general level) the autonomy of enterprise has been substantially extended; the assignment of targets and rationing of inputs – the two most characteristic features of centralised systems – have been eliminated. (In Poland the rationing of inputs survives, but this is more a result of shortages.) Market forces influence significantly the activities of industrial enterprises in the competitive sphere. Some progress has been achieved in subjecting price movements to market forces. Taxes play an increasing role as regulators; they have fully or partly replaced normatives, which were linked to the achieved level of performance. The role of credit and the interest rate have increased and will probably increase even more (in Hungary) with the ongoing disintegration of the mono-banking system. In the introduction of capital markets some progress has been accomplished. The private sector has been considerably expanded. Hierarchical relations have been weakened, and the management of enterprises has been to some extent democratised by giving employees the right to participate in decision making through their representatives. Hungary has probably abandoned the centralised system for good.

Despite all these changes, many shortcomings characteristic of the traditional management system survive. An environment which would force enterprises to pursue economic efficiency in the first place, is far from being in place. No doubt, the shortcomings in the management system are to blame for this, though by no means entirely; economic policy must take its share too. For example, shortages which impede economic efficiency have much to do with economic policy. To use a hyperbole, if the 'steel eaters' still have their way, shortages must persist. As long as the socialist economies are unable to adjust to the rapid changes in demand in domestic and world markets, their economies must suffer from shortages.

In the USSR and Czechoslovakia the changes achieved in the 1980s are modest and do not change the essence of the traditional system. In both countries, the authority of economic units has been extended somewhat in wage regulation, employment and investment. Indirect methods play a greater role in the management of the economy; the assignment of targets in absolute amounts has been replaced in some areas by normatives. On the other hand, concentration in industry has continued.

Gorbachev's reform will surely make more important systemic changes, though it will not be radical (compared to the Hungarian). In my opinion, Gorbachev's reform is the beginning of a series of reforms. As soon as it turns out that the current reform has not produced the expected results – which is more than probable – the Soviets will push for more substantial changes. The possibility that the Soviets will return to a neo-Stalinist regime, to a reactionary model, as J. Berliner (1983) calls it, is minute. A growing part of the ruling elite is becoming increasingly aware that the widening gap in technology between the USSR and the West, which threatens the Soviet Union's position as a superpower in the long run, cannot be plugged without a reform. In addition, Gorbachev's policy of 'openness' has accelerated the process of destruction of many illusions about the 'advantages of socialism' and has provided a great part of the intellectual community with the courage needed to take a stand for reform.

The present Czechoslovak leaders would rather prefer not to make substantive systemic changes. They are more afraid of the political consequences of such changes than they are of the economic consequences in the event of no systemic changes, since, at the moment, the economic situation is not critical in Czechoslovakia. Developments in Czechoslovakia will depend very much on what happens in the USSR.

Second, the thirty years from the first wave of reforms and the twenty from the second show that the process of reforming the systems is complicated, will require great efforts and will stretch out over a long period. With some qualification it is possible to argue that nowadays the focus of the reforms is to find a proper combination of planning and the market mechanism for the sake of promoting economic efficiency and democratisation of the political system. This in itself is great progress since, for some time, the view prevailed that planning and the market mechanism were not reconcilable. On both sides of the aisle (socialist and capitalist) the tendency was to view planning and the market mechanism as linked exclusively to a certain system, the former to socialism and the latter to capitalism.

Of course, there is a great difference between individual countries – primarily between the USSR, for the time being the representative of the traditional system, and Hungary – in views about where the line between coordinating mechanisms should be drawn. In the USSR and Czechoslovakia the fight is going on, to put it on a general level, to convince the political leaders to leave to the market the tasks which planning cannot perform well. Yet there is no agreement about what planning can or cannot do well. The changes themselves are in the initial stage. In Hungary most reformers would like to see the central authorities reserve to planning only what cannot be carried out satisfactorily by the market. Needless to say, there is again disagreement about the market's capabilities. Some believe that the market is the panacea for all the ills of the economy. It is only natural that people have a tendency to overvalue the goods they offer for sale. The systemic changes which have been made hitherto are still far behind what most reformers would like to see.

To carve out manoeuvering space for the market requires carrying out systemic changes in several key building blocks of the management system, in pricing, the incentive system, wage regulation, investment activity regulation and also introduction of a capital market and a genuine labour market, expansion of the private sector, elimination of excessive monopolisation, etc. But, at the same time, some building blocks (wage and incentives determination) cannot properly promote economic efficiency without giving greater room to the working of market forces. The economies of the countries are in a vicious circle from which it is not easy to escape.

The bringing about of rational prices may be the toughest nut to crack. It is so difficult because in the traditional system prices were and are used for many purposes other than for measuring social costs, utility and scarcity, and this treatment of prices was and is compounded by the fact that domestic prices were and are fully separated from the effects of foreign markets. Since prices have ceased to be a socially neutral parameter, any attempt to adjust them to their fundamental economic role clashes with vested interests and certain political committments and imperatives. Unlike the Polish central planners who tried unsuccessfully to solve the problem with great leaps, the Hungarian planners for almost twenty years have tried to come to grips with the problem by annual adjustments in consumer prices, the area of greatest difficulty. It is not disparaging to say that they are still far from the objective. The reason for this is simple: the adjustments must primarily solve specific acute problems at the expense of the general problem.

Another alternative, to allow prices to find their proper level, is an unthinkable solution under the current political and economic system. In the existing monopolistic position of suppliers and because of shortages, such a step would lead to rampant inflation which would affect mostly the segment of the population forming the mainstay of the regime. The legitimacy of the regime would be undermined.

It is no less difficult to create a powerful incentive system which would interest managers and workers alike in promoting economic efficiency and innovations. The very principles which distinguish a socialist system from a capitalist one (collective ownership, commitment to more equal distribution of income, full employment) hamper the unfolding of a powerful incentive system. Yet a socialist system in theory could allow wide wage differentials resulting from productive services, but probably could not tolerate for long a wide variety of unearned incomes which do not enrich the economy, but are perhaps needed in a market economy in order to create plenty of room for private initiative. I use the word 'theory' intentionally because in practice it will be politically more than difficult to reverse substantially the present state of narrow wage differentials, at least in a short time (cf. Abalkin, 1986). Due to unending propaganda, workers in socialist countries associate socialism with narrow wage differentials, and attempts to change the situation are deeply resented. Political leaders are reluctant to engage in a fight against workers on whose goodwill the stability of the regime is very dependent.

The existing incentive systems are geared rather to short-term interests, which is not surprising considering the nature of the management system and the psychology of managers and workers alike. However, a permanent improvement in economic efficiency is not achievable unless managers are made interested in the long-term development of the enterprises they manage. To this end, all the countries vowed to guide their economies by five-year plans based on long-term prognoses. In addition, in the USSR and Czechoslovakia, the stress is going to be on long-term normatives. In Hungary, many economists press for measures to stimulate the long-term expansion of enterprise assets (Szabó, 1987).

This is not to say that the effectiveness of the incentive system in socialist countries cannot be improved. However, it will probably never be as powerful as in a capitalist system. This in itself may not be an insurmountable disadvantage for socialist countries, provided they are able to offset it with a permanent increase in real wages (thus closing the gap which exists between advanced capitalist and socialist systems with regard to the level of real wages compared to national income per capita), with a smooth supply of goods which will respond readily to changes in demand for products, quality and design, with full employment and with the gradual expansion of human rights. Full employment can act as the strongest offsetting factor as long as high rates of unemployment persist in capitalist countries.

Let me dwell for a moment on the proposition to increase real wages, all the more because this figures little in the plans of the reformers. In my opinion, one of the reasons for the critical economic situation in socialist countries is the policy of low wages, the reasons for which I explained in my other book (Adam, 1984). If strong incentives to better performance and innovations are to be created, it is necessary, among other provisions, to reverse the policy of low wages. Of course, this cannot be accomplished in a short period; however, it must be part of the economic policy to heal the ills of the economy. The expansion of the private sector, where real wages are much higher, could be instrumental in the solution of the problem. An exodus from the state sector, brought about by better employment conditions in the private sector, will help liquidate overemployment and increase average wages there. Increases in wages will stimulate substitution of capital for labour and will also create preconditions for widening wage differentials.

A permanent improvement in economic efficiency cannot be expected without creating an environment in which enterprise financial conditions will depend on their performance alone, or, to use Kornai's terminology, unless enterprises are exposed to a 'hard budget constraint'. This is a problem which all the countries under review are faced with, but it is more urgent in countries where enterprises have gained a great degree of autonomy, as in Hungary and Poland. As experience shows, this is not a problem which can be easily solved. On the one hand, the authorities in Hungary and Poland are afraid that enterprises may gain access to excessive funds by abusing the system through taking advantage of various loopholes – which has often been true – and generating inflationary pressures, and therefore have often resorted to withdrawing a portion of enterprise funds even at the cost of violating their own rules. On the other hand, enterprises in financial trouble (or even if they are not) will not hesitate to ask for subsidies, tax relief, etc., often with success, and enterprises with 'excessive' funds try to get rid of them by investing them (without due regard to economic efficiency) or by paying higher wages.

To reverse such a situation requires: putting enterprises under the pressure of market forces. This, in turn, requires a rational price system, an intensive demonopolisation of the economy, expansion of the private sector, and also less frequent bailing out of enterprises, which the governments are at present reluctant to do for political and employment reasons. It also requires leaving enterprises the funds they are 'entitled' to. Some control mechanism is desirable for wages without which there is serious danger of inflation which, in turn, may undermine the working of market forces. I have serious doubts whether, under a socialist system, enterprises which have a free hand in determining wages and in which workers' representatives have a great say in decision making can limit wage increases to productivity growth.

Market forces may also contribute to a better use of resources, including human, and thus to improvement in economic efficiency. All four countries (Hungary to a lesser extent) find themselves in a paradoxical situation: they suffer from labour shortages, but at the same time, in some sectors of the economy (sometimes even in the same branch or enterprise where labour shortages exist) overemployment occurs. There are many reasons for this situation: apart from the fact that labour is cheap and therefore there is a tendency to hoard it since enterprises are not exposed to a 'hard budget constraint', the central planners are reluctant to act decisively because of, *inter alia*, fear of unemployment. If the socialist countries want to improve economic efficiency, they will have to find a solution to the problem of overemployment without compromising the principle of full employment. Needless to say, this will not be easy. Any success in this regard will also help to bring wages more closely in line with performance.

One of the greatest shortcomings of the traditional system of management was and is that it is not sufficiently conducive to innovations and that, as a result, a widening technological gap has developed between East and West in civilian industries. This gap is not only due to economico-systemic factors, but is also, to a great extent, a consequence of the authoritarian system.

This is not to say that in Hungary, with the abandonment of the centralised system, an environment fully favourable to innovations has been created. As is known, innovations come about to a great extent under the pressure of competition, domestic and foreign alike. To create competitive conditions, which are also crucial for the working of market forces, is not easy, especially when foreign markets are to be involved. This is not only because of vested interests, but also because a large exposure of the domestic economy to the effects of foreign markets is fraught with many dangers under existing conditions.

For political and, to a lesser extent for economic reasons, workers' participation in decision making is becoming an integral part of systems of management. No doubt, socialism without industrial democracy is a hollow system. For the time being, self-management has not made a noticeable dent in the system of management in Hungary and Poland, where it already exists. Sooner or later the reformers will be faced with a difficult problem: to make workers' participation meaningful and at the same time prevent excessive wage increases and wage differentials.

Finally, economico-systemic changes alone are not sufficient to bring about a turn-around in the economy. They need to be combined with changes in the political system, mainly in countries which have abandoned or are in the process of abandoning the centralised system. Changes in the political system in the direction of its democratisation are also justified for several economic reasons: they have to create greater room for market forces, limit the planning system to certain important macro-proportions and democratise it, make the reform irreversible, etc.

Let me examine briefly the second reason. As already mentioned, centralised planning has been discredited in the traditional system by the inability of the planners to ensure market equilibria, to subject sufficiently investment to efficiency criteria and to make sure that the structure of the economy adjusts to the ongoing technological revolution, to mention the most important shortcomings. The indirect system of management deserves a better mark, though far from a good one. The call for democratisation of the political system and planning, in the form already indicated above, aims at reducing the influence of the bureaucracy and special interests on the distribution of funds for investment, one of the main reasons for slow progress in restructuring the economy and for the low returns on investment. If the call is heeded, this will be at the same time a test of the extent to which democratisation can restore planning to its original objective, which is to steer consciously macro-proportions important for the long-term development of the economy towards certain aims warranted on economic grounds, and desired by a majority. Such a test, which must, of course, consist of several experiments for understandable reasons, will prove whether socialism is a viable system.

Notes

1 The Centralised System of Management

1. Some economists use the terms economic system, economic mechanism, and system of management interchangeably.
2. For practical reasons I will often use a shorter term for system of management of the economy, such as management system or system of management.
3. If private plots in agriculture are classified as the first economy, and objections can be raised to such a classification, then they are an exception.
4. Only in the 1960s and especially in the 1980s did fully-fledged normatives become an integral part of the system.
5. Apart from money incentives, moral incentives are used. In a sense, in the campaigns for the fulfilment of the plans, stress is primarily put on moral incentives. They are used a great deal in order to spur workers to participate in so-called socialist competition.
6. The introduction of the branch ministerial system meant the end of the Supreme Council of the National Economy which was in charge of industry as a whole. As a result, the role of Gosplan as coordinator of industrial activities increased (see Nove, 1982, p. 215).
7. More recently, they are well discussed in A. Nove's book (1983, pp. 68–117).
8. One of the purposes of the 1965 Soviet economic reform and the more recent experiments is just to make enterprises attentive to the requirements of the market and in such a way to correct the negative effect of the centralised system in this respect.

2 Common and Contrasting Features of the Reforms of the 1960s

1. I use this term for Poland, Czechoslovakia and Hungary.
2. According to E. Zaleski, the real motivating power of the debate was dissatisfaction with the reduction in bonuses for managers, technicians and administrative workers (Zaleski, 1966, pp. 67–8; *Istoriia . . .*, 1980, vol. 6, p. 282).
3. For information on the reform of 1970 see Kierczyński, 1984; Mieszankowski, 1984; Flakierski, 1973.
4. The economic reform of 1958 is of importance for the history of reforms primarily because it introduced two novelties to the management system. It reorganised industrial and construction enterprises into associations (productive economic units – PEUs) and instituted them as basic units of management. The rationale behind this move was to bring the directive activity, which before was exercised by ministerial administration departments, closer to enterprises and thus allow the ministries to devote themselves fully to strategic planning and economic policy. The PEUs

survived the economic reform of the 1960s and are still in force. Introduction of long-term normatives – an idea which popped up for the first time in a Soviet debate (Vergner, 1957) – was the second novelty. The purpose of the long-term normatives – to give enterprises a feeling of certainty – was correct, but it was unrealisable, as will be shown later.

5. The proposal in a modified form was published in Bokor, *et al.*, 1957.
6. At that time the Soviet leaders might also have been afraid of the consequences which a far-reaching reform might have on the philosophical premises on which the centralised system is based. The introduction of the market mechanism, or even greater stress on profit, means admitting that the interests of society and enterprises are not identical. And this contradicts what the leaders used to maintain.
7. There were debates in the countries about what should go first, the reforms or these substantive changes. Some favoured the latter, very often in the hope that the reforms would thus be prevented.
8. For more see Adam, 1979, pp. 92–100. The debate about gross income versus profit was also influenced by political considerations. At that time, gross income was used by the Yugoslavs, and mainly Hungary was afraid that this might cast a shadow on its reform.
9. The Polish authorities preferred to try to solve this problem by a one-shot action.
10. In Czechoslovakia and Hungary, the number of turnover tax rates was reduced from 10 000 to 1000.

3 The Soviet Economic Reform of 1965

1. This is probably surprising news for economists who are not very familiar with the Soviet system.
2. Sales were used primarily in enterprises whose products were in short supply, while profit was applied in enterprises where an increase in output was not planned (Liberman, 1965; Veselkov and Mymrina, 1971).
3. The bonus fund may be expressed mathematically as

$$F = Nq \cdot W \cdot Q + Np \cdot W \cdot P, \text{ where}$$

F is incentive fund; Nq is normative for one per cent of increase in sales over the previous year, expressed in per cent (in some enterprises sales were replaced by profit); W is basic wage bill (i.e. without incentive fund); Q is rate of increase in sales; Np is normative for 1 per cent of rate of profit, expressed in per cent; and P is rate of profit.
4. 'There can be no question that retail prices can be revised only along the lines of reducing', stated Kosygin in his report at the Central Committee (Sharpe, 1966, p. 30).
5. The price reform was also intended to reduce the wide variation in profitability in relation to cost for individual products. The rationale for this move was to discourage enterprises from deviating from the set product mix.

6. The Russian Federal Republic was short of 1.5 million workers (Sielunin, 1971, p. 151).
7. The investment financed by long-term credit was part of centralised investment.

4 The Economic Reform in Czechoslovakia, 1966–69

1. In the resolution it was stated that there was to be an endeavour to integrate social planning with the utilisation of commodity – money relations. But even the Action Programme of the Party did not bring a dramatic change; it called for a 'renewal of the positive functions of the market as a necessary mechanism for the functioning of the socialist economy and verification of whether the work of enterprises was expanded purposefully. We do not have in mind a capitalist market but a socialist market and not its spontaneous but regulated utilisation' (*Rok* . . ., 1969, p. 130).
2. Again using their monopoly position, the branch directorates in the role of suppliers tried to determine which of their enterprises would fulfil certain orders; this was clearly in conflict with government regulations (*PH*, 1966, no. 6, p. 93).
3. Gross income was defined as the sum which remains with the enterprise after the deduction of material costs, depreciation and the turnover tax from receipts resulting from sales of goods and services. In addition, gross income usually included the value of changes in inventories and in the value of unfinished products; thus it was not a sales concept.
4. In mining wholesale prices increased by 50 per cent whereas in the consumer goods industry which belonged to the low-wage industries the increase amounted to only 20 per cent (*Statistické přehledy*, 1968, no. 3).
5. The 1958 reform brought into existence three kinds of productive economic units (PEUs): (1) branch enterprise (*oborový podnik*) – usually vertically integrated enterprises which consist of one leading and one or more associated enterprises. The manager of the leading enterprise is at the same time the manager of the associated enterprises and is directly subordinated to the branch ministry; (2) in a concern enterprises have only rights which are delegated to them by the concern; (3) a trust is the loosest organisation of the three; the management of the trust is separate from the management of enterprises. The management of the trust is a link between the branch ministry and enterprises (Remeš, *et al.*, 1985, pp. 120–2).
6. There was quite a passionate debate about the role of enterprises, including the distintegration of compulsory associations. Some expressed concern that opening the gate wide for the disintegration of some associations might get rid of weaker enterprises (e.g. Šik, see Golan, 1973, p. 29); others feared that by giving enterprises the full right to disintegration, Czechoslovakia might end up in a position contrary to the existing trend in the West (Kraus, 1968; Šupka and Srba, 1968). Some argued that in the first stage enterprises should be freely allowed to associate and only in the next stage should they be led with the help of economic levers to integration. At the same time, enterprises with varying

organisation and exercise of property rights should exist side by side (Horálek, *et al.*, 1968).

5 The Hungarian Economic Reform of 1968

1. The architects of the reform were not united in their views about its direction. Even the three-member committee which prepared the final version of the initial guidelines could not agree, and, as a result, two versions were submitted for a decision. The version which was defeated called for keeping the assignment of targets, though with fewer indicators (see Szamuely, 1984).

2. The formulas were:

$$P_w = \alpha W/(\alpha W + K) \cdot P,$$
$$P_d = P - P_w, \text{ or}$$
$$P_d = K(\alpha W + K) \cdot P$$

It follows that

$$P_w/P = \alpha W/(\alpha W + K) \text{ and}$$
$$P_d/P = K/(\alpha W + K),$$

where P_w is the sharing fund (subject to taxation), P_d is the part earmarked for development (subject to taxation), P is profit, α is the multiplier, W is the wage bill, K is the fixed and working capital.

The part of profit earmarked for the sharing fund had thus been set as a ratio of the wage bill to the amount of the wage bill plus fixed and working capital, multiplied by profit. Because the denominator thus set is much greater than the numerator, the part accruing to the sharing fund would be relatively small. Therefore a wage multiplier was introduced and fixed at two on the average.

3. At first glance it seems that the Hungarians who invented the two-channel price-type formula did not really apply it in their producer price revision, though Czechoslovakia and Poland did. In reality the Hungarians did so also, but in a modified form. The new prices had to incorporate a surplus for the state in the form of taxes (a tax of 5 per cent on fixed assets and a 25 per cent tax on wages) includable in the cost of production, and a profit for enterprises which amounted on the average to 6.5 per cent of fixed assets.

4. For information on the linkage of producer and consumer prices and reconstruction of the turnover tax see Chapter 2.

5. As a result of these pressures, the institution of unjustified profits came into being. Profits resulting from misuse of enterprises' monopoly position in setting prices above the competitive level were regarded as unjustified, and enterprises could be penalised because of them (Hare, 1976).

6. Apart from this indirect wage regulation, direct regulation, which was quite extended in 1976, existed.

7. The formula for the distribution of profit itself was a disincentive – though a weak one – to labour economy. The size of the sharing fund was directly dependent on the wage-bill.

8. The conversion ratio was 40 Ft for one rouble and 60 Ft for one dollar.

6 The Polish Economic Reform of 1973

1. The reform introduced a new element to central planning, the so-called problematic programmes (*programy problemowy*). These were selected problems of strategic importance for the whole economy; they could be of a purely economic nature (the solution of the fuel economy) or of a social nature (housing). These programmes were priority plans and could be assigned to organisations as binding targets for several years; they were included in long-term plans as well as in five-year plans (see Kubiczek and Bazgier, 1975, pp. 250–3; Porwit, 1978, pp. 141–66; Golinowski, 1974, pp. 50–1).
2. For information about the linkage of producer and consumer prices see Chapter 2.
3. As to write-offs for depreciation, only those of fixed assets which came about as a result of investment credit and were put into operation after the conversion to the new rules of the reform could remain to organisations (Topiński, 1975, p. 181).
4. For increases in the fund up to 2 per cent above the normative, the organisation had to pay 50 per cent of the increment in the fund in taxes. For increases above 8 per cent, the marginal tax was 90 per cent.
5. The reform retained the year-end rewards which were introduced in 1956 for the first time. Originally, the size of the fund was linked to the fulfilment of success indicators (for more see Zieliński, 1973, pp. 236–7; Fick, 1967, pp. 235–8), an arrangement which was abolished in units converted to the new system. The size of the so-called enterprise fund for rewards was determined, as before, as a percentage of the wage bill, and was to grow on the basis of a long-term normative to a maximum of 8½ per cent of the wage bill which amounts to an additional month's wage for enterprise personnel (for more see Adam, 1979, p. 143).
6. The reform introduced a whole series of incentives in order to stimulate investors and construction organisations to complete investment projects on time and, where possible, accelerate their completion, and reduce costs. The bonuses came from a fund for rewards included in the investment costs. Interestingly enough, 70 per cent of the bonuses had to be distributed among manual workers (Gliński, Kierczyński and Topiński, 1975, p. 126).
7. The conversion was not done directly, but through the so-called gold zloty.
8. Korsak's (1978) study gives a comprehensive insight into the working of the WOGs in various areas.
9. In the modified WOG system introduced in 1977 output added was defined uniformly for all units (Golinowski, 1977).

7 Common and Contrasting Features of the Reforms of the 1980s

1. In Czechoslovakia there was tremendous pressure for change in the political system, but this was motivated primarily by political considerations.

2. The document was written by a collective from various research institutes and edited by well-known economists.

3. The ongoing technological revolution offered an opportunity to the socialist countries to demonstrate the advantages of planning. In the West the revolution proceeds rapidly, but is accompanied by much pain and hardship produced by unemployment. Had the socialist countries been able to do the same without pain, this would have been a triumph. Yet the socialist countries have failed miserably; the gap in technological progress has increased.

4. More recently, many people in Poland (including Trade Union members) have been outraged by the government's decision to continue the expansion of the energy sector, though the same amount of energy could be produced through modernisation which would have cost much less.

    In Hungary, the complaint is that the authorities have indulged in huge, inefficient investment projects (e.g. the building of a water power station on the Danube in cooperation with Czechoslovakia, the joint investment with the Soviets to open new gas fields in Jamburg) and have been very slow in restructuring the economy.

5. The term 'Provisions of the 1980s' always means provisions introduced before the reforms initiated in 1987 in the USSR and/or Czechoslovakia.

6. Better balanced plans are to be achieved by an extension of the method of balancing (in both countries, material balances for 1981–85 were increased) (Ler, 1980; Bornstein, 1985a).

7. Full *khozraschet* is, according to P. Bunich (1986), a broader term than self-financing. It also includes among others self-financing of the functional staff, participation of workers in decision making, and legal autonomy. I use the terms interchangeably and in the sense of self-financing.

8 The Hungarian Economic Reform in the 1980s

1. In Hungary there is disagreement about how to evaluate the 1985 provisions. Some reject calling the provisions a reform because this could be interpreted as a reform of the 1968 reform, and they prefer rather to talk about the modernisation of the management system which is the official approach. Others reject calling the 1985 provisions a reform because they believe that they do not go far enough. The resolution was published in *Társadalmi Szemle*, 1984, No. 5.

2. The Hungarians by no means intend to introduce a self-management system *a la* Yugoslav. On the whole the view prevails in Hungary that the Yugoslavs have gone too far in their decentralisation, and for this reason the coordination of economic activities has become very difficult.

3. According to O. Gadó's computations it was approximately 80 per cent in 1985. In his report the minister of finance put the figure for 1987 at 90 per cent (*Nsz*, 1987, September 19).

4. Income tax will affect especially many scientists and university professors whose standard of living (because of low earnings from their main jobs) depends primarily, or to a great extent, on publications and lectures. On the other hand, incomes from moonlighting and illegal activities will not be much affected by the income tax. Thus income tax will not contribute much or at all to a more proper earnings differentiation.

5. Many first meetings of the enterprise councils ended in hefty salary increases for the managers, often in the hope that managers would reciprocate.
6. Starting with 1987 enterprises can no longer choose the regulation form; they must apply the one which is handed down to the branch or sub-branch in question. Tax rates have been increased and are no longer applied to average earnings but to total earnings in the case of REL (before, the tax was meted out on the average earnings earned at a certain date each year), and to the total increment in earnings in the case of REI. Instead of the promised elimination of the surtax, the rules for its avoidance have become more stringent. Now output added must grow twice as fast as earnings to be exempt from the hefty surtax (Pongrácz, 1986).
7. The dismissal of ten workers at once is contingent on the approval of regional authorities. If approval is given, the dismissal notice must be extended to six months. During this period, workers are entitled to their average wages without really working. If, within the six months, they cannot find jobs, they are entitled to reduced benefits for another six months (*Magyar Közlöny*, 1986, no. 28).
8. The number of unemployed is to increase by the end of 1987 to 10 000 and in 1988 to 30 000–40 000. It is predicted that in 1989–90 the situation will become even worse, because stronger age cohorts will enter the labour market (J. Timár, 1987).
9. I am obliged to F. Vissi for information on pricing.
10. For more see *Turnover Tax-System in Hungary*, published by the Hungarian Ministry of Finance 1985, no. 24, edited by O. Gadó.
11. They are also under pressure by IMF to do so.
12. Some believe that agreements replaced in many cases 'competitive prices'.
13. In cases where enterprises are short of funds and cannot get bank credit, but are involved in an important investment project, they may turn to the state.
14. This statement requires a qualification. It is true when the differentiated subsidies the exporters receive are disregarded.
15. A bankruptcy law was finally enacted in 1986. Its importance is that the procedure for liquidation is no longer solely in the hands of the authorities: the courts play an important role. Some 55 enterprises, mainly small ones, have been subjected to bankruptcy procedures; in 1987 none of them was liquidated (Harsányi and Szőcs, 1987).

9 The Polish Economic Reform of 1982

1. In his press conference, F. Kubiczek (first deputy of the Planning Commission) mentioned that three large enterprises are to be liquidated (*Rzeczpospolita*, 1986, 5–6 April). In 1986 the number of enterprises which got on the list of possible candidates for bankruptcy increased. Greater pressure is exerted on enterprises, usually smaller ones, to improve their financial record (*TL*, 1987, March 5).
2. In 1983, 45 per cent of consumer goods in terms of sales were priced at fixed prices, 15 per cent at regulated and 40 per cent at contractual prices.

In the case of producer goods the grouping was the following: 32 per cent, 13 per cent and 55 per cent respectively (Baka, 1984b, p. 6).

3. According to Fedorowicz (1983) the official price increases brought about equilibrium only in some foodstuffs.

4. The new Trade Unions are quite militant and take different positions from the government on many questions. In Poland many believe that this is not a ploy to attract more workers to the unions.

5. Increases in the number of employees and/or increases in wages reduce profitability and the need to pay higher taxes. Profitability could be defined, as for example in Hungary, as profit over fixed capital plus wages. In such a case the role of wages is substantially reduced. The architects of the reform objected that this could be done only after reevaluation of capital, which was supposed to be carried out by the end of 1983.

6. The allocation to the reserve fund need not be smaller than 10 per cent of the profit; however, if the total fund exceeds 4 per cent of all the costs of production of the enterprise in a certain year, allocation to the fund is not needed.

7. Criticism was levelled at high tax progressivity, not only on wage increases but also, on the employee fund. Some saw it as a disregard for promises – given in the past – that bonuses would total the amount of a thirteen month's wage (Szczepanski, 1984).

8. The number of job vacancies is continuing to grow; in 1981 it was 119 000 (against 26 000 job seekers) and in march 1987, it was 423 000 (against 4000). The greatest shortage, were in construction and the textile industry, probably because of prolonged maternity leave. Interestingly enough, labour shortages have been felt the least in the coal industry. High wages and various privileges must be given credit for this situation (*Report* . . . , 1984).

9. I have heard the same argument separately from Professors U. Wojciechowska and K. Ryč.

10. I am obliged to Professor W. Trzeciakowski for this information.

11. National income produced increased by 15 per cent (against the planned 10–12 per cent); it was still twelve points short of the pre-crisis level (1978).

10 Gorbachev's Economic Reform

1. They were applied for the first time in the Czechoslovak reform of 1958, and later in the Soviet 1965 reform and, of course, in the Hungarian 1968 reform.

2. It is worth mentioning that the Soviet Union is the only country among the four countries I usually research which, up to now, has taken planned profit as a basis for distribution of profit.

3. The wage bill for the rest of the personnel was formed as in the past. Thus the wage bill of enterprises applying the wage normative was a sum of both the wage bill of production personnel and that of non-production personnel.

4. For more about the system before 1981, see Adam 1980.

5. It is also noteworthy that, historically, new methods of management of the economy have first been applied to the regulation of the bonus fund. Here

we have a deviation from this rule; new methods are applied to wage regulation first.

6. In order to discourage construction enterprises from starting too many investment projects, the 1979 decree extended the measures applied experimentally in the 1965 reform. The investor (starting in 1981) was not to pay until the construction work was fully completed and accepted. The funds needed for financing the construction work were to be borrowed by construction enterprises from the bank. It was hoped that this would encourage construction enterprises to accelerate the completion of projects, all the more because the 1979 provision also contained incentives (*SEG*, 1979, no. 32). According to L. Abalkin (1986), the mentioned measure has never been put into effect and does not appear in the new resolution on construction(*EG*, 1986, no. 40). The construction industry, which wields great influence, probably killed it.

7. New production associations may consist of structural units performing industrial, constructional, transportational, marketing and research activities. These units have minimal rights. PAs may also include independent enterprises whose status depends on the law and decisions of the association in question. Associations, which fulfil for such enterprises the function of a superior authority, are allowed to centralise many of the functions to which an independent enterprise is entitled, according to the new law on enterprises.

8. To mention the most important: State Committee for Construction, Bureau of Machine Building, Bureau for Fuel and Power Complex and Foreign Economic Commission.

9. Optimistic expectations that state orders will take up only part of production capacity have turned out to be a fallacy. There are promises that the role of state orders will decline in 1989 and that many of them will be placed through competitive tenders.

10. The transfer of quality control in many enterprises to officials outside the jurisdiction of enterprises may also have a favourable effect on the quality of products (*EG*, 1986, no. 50). First reports show that the new controllers mean business (Csaba,1987).

11 The Czechoslovak Attempts to Improve the System of Management in the 1980s

1. Some indication about the direction of the changes can be obtained from several ongoing experiments. However, far-reaching conclusions cannot be drawn since very often the changes applied to the whole economy are different from those in the experiments.

2. The financial resources of economic units include apart from profit, a portion of the amortisation fund (since 1986, 60 per cent) and a possible subsidy to exports.

3. These price increases were a reaction to increased prices in foreign markets, but also to increasing costs of coal extraction at home.

4. In the period 1981–84 consumer prices increased by 7.9 per cent which was substantial considering that the CSSR followed a policy of rigid price stability; it is not clear to what extent other factors played a role in this increase.

5. Adjusted net output is, in Czech, *úpravené vlastní výkony*, which translated exactly means 'adjusted own achievements'. It is defined as a sum of sales, plus changes in the value of unfinished products and inventories, all this reduced by costs of materials, energy and penalties. In other words adjusted net output includes depreciation, so the term 'adjusted' is warranted since it is not a pure net-income indicator.

6. The authorities have introduced two novelties into the wage-rate system. One is to expand the remuneration of workers on the basis of their personal classification (not according to the classification of the job they perform) and the second is to make the wage rates more flexible, more dependent on the development of average earnings (Baštýř, 1984; *SHN*, 1984, no. 42). Both measures, if well handled, may have some favourable effect on the quality of work.

7. In connection with the publication of the 1980 document a great campaign for the enhancement of wage effectiveness was launched. Its purpose is to base the size of wages strictly on work results, that is merit. To this end all the work norms, technical coefficients and applied stimuli had to be verified from the viewpoint of their effectiveness and measures taken for their improvement. The campaign is still in progress.

8. The second group was included in the plan in the form of a limited total.

9. In 1980, investment was financed from the following sources: own (52.2 per cent; of it 25.8 per cent from the amortisation fund), subsidies from the state, 4.7 per cent, and bank credit (31.0 per cent). In 1984, the figures were 65.8 (37.1), 1.7 and (31.8) per cent respectively (Beneš, 1986).

10. Many economists are critical of the way the differential indicator is determined. They argue that its level depends too much on factors beyond the control of enterprises and, in addition, it is not an objective indicator (Matějka, Matouš and Vrba, 1986; Šafáříková and Novák, 1983).

11. In the beginning of the 1980s Czechoslovak machinery products were sold on foreign markets at US$2.70 per kilogramme whereas West European were sold at US$7.70.

Appendix: Recent Changes in the System of Management in the German Democratic Republic

1. The Associations of State Enterprises (VVBs) were responsible for the productive process of their enterprises as well as the administration of the new economic levers. Towards this end they were granted greater legal and financial independence. With the abolition of the National Economic Council under which the VVBS had operated, the industrial ministries again became their immediate bosses. The VVBs list financial (auditing) control over their branches which reverted to the Ministry of Finance and their directors-general were again transformed into mere subordinates to their minister. The 1979 decree on combines brought the formal abolition of the VVBs.

2. If planned net profits are met, 100 marks per full-time equivalent employee can be channelled into the fund and more, up to a maximum of 150 marks, in cases of overfulfilment. If net profits plans are not met these amounts are reduced correspondingly.

Bibliography

For space reasons only full references to books, regardless of the language in which they are published, are listed. References to periodical and newspaper articles are listed without titles unless they are published in English . Papers, journals and statistical yearbooks indicated in an abbreviated form in the text are not listed in the bibliography. If, from an edited volume of studies, several studies are used, besides the author, the editor(s) of the volume as well as the first word of the title are indicated. The full reference to the volume is listed under the name of the editor(s).

ABALKIN, L. (1981) *PKh*, no. 3.

ABALKIN, L. (1986) *Znanie*, nos. 43–4.

ACTION PROGRAMME OF THE COMMUNIST PARTY OF CZECHOSLOVAKIA (1969), in *Rok šedesátý osmý*. Prague.

ADAM, J. (1973) 'The incentive system in the USSR: the abortive reform of 1965', *Industrial and Labor Relations Review*, no. 1, October.

ADAM, J. (1974a) *Wage, Price and Taxation Policy in Czechoslovakia 1948–1970*. Berlin: Duncker & Humblot.

ADAM, J. (1974b) 'The System of Wage Regulation in Hungary', *The Canadian Journal of Economics*, no. 4.

ADAM, J. (1979; 1980) *Wage Control and Inflation in the Soviet Bloc Countries*. London: Macmillan; New York: Praeger.

ADAM, J. (1980) 'The Present Soviet Incentive System', *Soviet Studies*, no. 3.

ADAM, J. (1984) *Employment and Wage Policies in Poland, Czechoslovakia and Hungary since 1950*. London: Macmillan; New York: St Martin's Press.

ADAM, J. (1987) 'The Hungarian economic reform of the 1980s', *Soviet Studies*, no. 4.

AGANBEGIAN, A. G. (1983) *EKO*, no. 8.

ANTAL, L. (1981) 'Development of economic control and management', *Acta Oeconomica*, no. 3–4.

ANTAL, L. (1983) 'Carrying on with Economic Reform', *The New Hungarian Quarterly*, no. 91, Autumn.

ANTAL, L. (1985a) *Gazdaságirányitási és pénzügyi rendszerünk a reform útján*, Budapest.

ANTAL, L. (1985b) 'About the Prosperity Incentive', *Acta Oeconomica*, no. 3–4.

ANTAL, L. (1987) *F*, no. 32.

A gazdasági mechanizmus reformja (1966) materials of the meeting of Central Committee, May 1966, Budapest.

A Magyar Szocialista Munkáspárt határozatai és dokumentumai 1963–66 (1978), Budapest.

A szocialista országok gazdasági mechanismusa (1984) a collective work of authors from several socialist countries, Budapest.

BAJCURA, A. (1969) *Hmotná zainteresovanosť v priemysle*, Bratislava.

BAKA, W. (1978) in *Wzrost . . .* J. Lewandowski and W. Siwiński (eds). Warsaw.

243

BAKA, W. (1983a) *Polska Reforma Gospodarcza* 2nd edn, Warsaw. This book also includes the text of the 'Directions'.
BAKA, W. (1983b) interview, Supplement to *Rzeczpospolita*, 15 December.
BAKA, W. (1984a) *HN*, nos. 51–52.
BAKA, W. (1984b) *Polish Economic Reform*. Warsaw.
BALASSA, A. (1979) *A magyar népgazdaság tervezésének alapjai*. Budapest.
BALASSA, A. (1984), in *Gazdaság* . . . M. Pulai and F. Vissi (eds). Budapest.
BALASSA, B. (1970) 'The economic reform in Hungary', *Economica*, February.
BALASSA, B. (1978) *Valóság*, no. 7.
BALÁZS, A. (1984) *F*, no. 45.
BALÁZSY, S. (1987) *KSz*, no. 10.
BALOGH, F. (1971) *F*, no. 51.
BÁNKI, P. (1973) *KSz*, no. 2.
BARTOSZEWSKI, S. (1986) *BK*, nos. 7–8.
BAŠTÝŘ, I. (1984) *SHN*, no. 17.
BAUER, T. (1983) 'The Hungarian alternative to Soviet type planning', *Journal of Comparative Economics*, vol. 7.
BAUER, T. (1987) *KSz*, no. 5.
BAZAROVOVÁ, G. (1985) *FaU*, no. 4.
BENEŠ, L. (1986) *FaU*, no. 4.
BEREND, T. I. (1981) 'Reflections on the Sixth Hungarian Five-Year Plan (1981–1985)', *Acta Oeconomica*, nos. 1–2.
BEREND, T. I. (1983) *Gazdasági útkeresés 1956–65*. Budapest.
BERÉNYI, J. (1974) *Lohnsystem und Lohnstruktur in Osterreich und Ungarn*. Vienna:
BERLINER, J. (1983) 'Planning and management', in *The Soviet Economy: Toward the Year 2000*. A. Bergson and H. S. Levine (eds). London: Allen & Unwin.
BERNÁŠEK, M. (1969) 'The Czechoslovak Economic Recession 1962–5', *Soviet Studies*, no. 4.
BEZDĚKOVÁ, M. and PAPEŽOVÁ, V. (1986) *PH*, no. 6.
BIALECKI, K. (1986), in *Organizacja i Technika Handlu Zagranicznego*, K. Bialecki, Z. Kaminski and H. Wojciechowski (eds). Warsaw.
BIELASIAK, J. (1983) 'The Party: permanent crisis', in *Poland, Genesis of a Revolution*, A. Brumberg (ed.). New York: Vintage Books.
BOBROWSKI, Cz. (1985) *ZG*, nos. 51–2.
BÓDY, L. (1984), in *Gazdaság* . . . M. Pulai and F. Vissi (eds). Budapest.
BOKOR, J. et al. (1957) *KSz*, no. 4.
BORLÓI, R. (1984) *Munkaügyi Szemle*, no. 11.
BORNSTEIN, M. (1974) 'Soviet price theory and policy', in *The Soviet Economy*, 4th edn, M. Bornstein and D. R. Fusfeld (eds). Homewood, R. Irvin.
BORNSTEIN, M. (1976) 'Soviet Price Policy in the 1970s', in *Soviet Economy in a New Perspective*, US Congress, Washington.
BORNSTEIN, M. (1985a) 'Improving the Soviet Economic mechanism', *Soviet Studies*, no. 1.
BORNSTEIN, M. (1985b) 'The Soviet industrial price revision', in *Socialist*

Economy and Economic Policy, Essays in honour of Friedrich Levcik, G. Fink (ed). Vienna: Springer.

BÖRŐCZY, F. (1984), in *Az európai KGST-országok gazdasága* (edited by a collective). Budapest.

BOSSÁNYI, K. (1984) *NSz*, 6 November.

BOSSÁNYI, K. (1986) *Gazdaság*, no. 2.

BOTH, F., POKORNÝ, J. and VOJÁK, J. (1966) *Odbory a hmotná zainteresovanosť v novej sústave riadenia*. Bratislava.

BOURA, V. (1984) *HN*, no. 28.

BROWN, A. A. and MARER, P. (1973) 'Foreign trade in the East European reforms', in *Plan and Market*, M. Bornstein (ed.). New Haven: Yale University Press.

BRUS, W. (1964) *Modely socialistického hospodářství*, trans. from Polish. Prague.

BRUS, W. (1979) 'The East European reforms: what happened to them?' *Soviet Studies*, no. 2.

BRUS, W. (1983) 'Economics and politics: the fatal link', in *Poland, Genesis of a Revolution*, A. Brumberg (ed.). New York: Vintage Books.

BRUS, W. (1985a) 'Economic history of communist Eastern Europe', in *The Economic History of Eastern Europe 1919–1975*, vol. III, M. C. Kaser (ed.). Oxford: Oxford University Press.

BRUS, W. (1985b) 'Socialism – feasible or viable?' *New Left Review*, September–October.

BUDA, I. and PONGRÁCZ, L. (1968) *Személyi jövedelmek, anyagi érdekeltség, munkaerő-gazdálkodás*. Budapest.

BUNIČ, P. (1987) *HN*, no. 39.

BUNICH, P. (1980) *VE*, no. 2.

BUNICH, P. (1986) *EG*, no. 24.

BURY, J., KARWANSKI, B. and MIGDAL, T. (1976) *Place i premie*. Warsaw.

BUSH, K. (1970) 'The Implementation of the Soviet Economic Reform', *Osteuropa Wirtschaft*, no. 2.

CAMPBELL, R. (1968) 'The Economic Reform in the USSR', *American Economic Review*, no. 2, May.

CHEBLAKOV, A. A. (1984) *Proizvodstvenniie obedineniia v systeme upravleniia otrasliiu*. Minski.

CHMELA, V. and KODÝM, M. (1983) *HN*, no. 10.

CHOLEWICKA-GOZDZIK, K. (1974) in *Nowy system ekonomiczno-finansowy w organizacjach przemyslowych*, J. Sliwa (ed.). Warsaw.

CIAS, B. (1983) *Finanse*, no. 12.

CICHOWSKI, E. (1973) *Finanse*, no. 8.

CICHOWSKI, E. (1985) *Finanse*, no. 2.

CIEPIELEWSKI, J. (1977), in *Kraje socjalistyczne po drugiej wojnie swiatowe 1944–1974*, J. Ciepielewski (ed.). Warsaw.

CLEMENT, J. (1986) *Osteuropa: Zeitschrift für Gegenwartsfragen*, nos. 8–9.

CSABA, L. (1987) *Külkereskedelmi Szemle*, no. 10.

CSIKÓS-NAGY, B. (1965) 'New Aspects of the Profit Incentive', *The New Hungarian Quarterly*, no. 20, Winter.

CSIKÓS-NAGY, B. (1968) *Általános és szocialista árelmélet*, Budapest.

CSIKÓS-NAGY, B. (1969) 'The new Hungarian price system', in *Reform* . . ., I. Friss (ed.). Budapest.

CSIKÓS-NAGY, B. (1980) *A magyar árpolitika*. Budapest.

CZEITLER, S. (1972) 'Regulators in foreign trade', in *Reform* . . ., O. Gadó (ed.). Budapest.

DENTON, G. R. (1971) *A New Economic Mechanism? Economic Reform in Hungary*. PEP London, Broadsheet 526.

DERIPASOV, A. (1986) *PKh*, no. 7.

'Directions of Economic Reform', in *Polska Reforma Gospodarcza*, W. Baka (1983a). Warsaw.

'Directions in changes in the system of functioning of the economy 1986–90' (1986) *GP*, no. 2.

DIREKTIVE DES VIII. Parteitags der SED zum Fünfjahrplan für die Entwicklung der Volkswirtschaft der DDR 1971–1975 (1971).

Discussions with directors of enterprises (1968), *HN*, no. 38.

DRUCKER, P. (1986) 'The Changed World Economy', *Foreign Affairs*, Spring.

DVOŘÁK, J. (1985), in *Soustava plánovitého řízení, efektivnost a intenzifikace československé ekonomiky*, J. Dvořák et al., Prague.

DVOŘÁK, J. (1987) *Nová mysl*, no. 4.

DYKER, D. A. (1985) *The Future of the Soviet Economic Planning System*. London: Croom Helm.

EGIAZARIAN, G. A. (1976) *Materialnoe stimulirovanie rosta efektivnosti promyshlennovo proizvodstva*. Moscow.

EILENBERGER, R. (1984), *WW*, no. 9.

ERNST, P. (1968) *HN*, no. 40.

FALLENBUCHL, Z. (1986) 'The economic crisis in Poland', in *East European Economies: Slow Growth in the 1980s*, US Congress, Washington.

FALUVÉGI, L. (1984) *Valóság*, no. 9.

FEDOROWICZ, Z. (1977) *Finanse organizacji gospodarczych*. Warsaw.

FEDOROWICZ, Z. (1978) *Mechanizm ekonomiczno-finansowy sterowania jednostkami gospodarczymi*. Warsaw.

FEDOROWICZ, Z. (1983) *Finanse*, no. 3.

FEIWEL, G. R. (1968) *New Economic Patterns in Czechoslovakia*. New York: Praeger.

FEIWEL, G. R. (1972) *Soviet Quest for Economic Efficiency*. New York: Praeger.

FELKER, J. L. (1966) *Soviet Economic Controversies*. MIT Press. Cambridge, Mass.

FICK, B. (1967) *Fundusz zakladowy*. Warsaw.

FLAKIERSKI, H. (1973) 'The Polish economic reforms of 1970', *Canadian Journal of Economics*, no. 1.

FLÓR, F. and HORVÁTH, S. (1972) *Iparvállalatok jövedelem – és munkaerö-gazdálkodása*. Budapest.

FORMÁNEK, K. and PICK, M. (1965) *PH*, nos. 7–8.

FRISS, I. (1969) (ed.) *Reform of the Economic Mechanism in Hungary*. Budapest: Akadémia.

FRISS, I. (1969) 'Principal features of the new system of planning, economic control and management in Hungary', in *Reform* . . ., I. Friss (ed.). Budapest.

FRISS, I. (1978) *Valóság*, no. 7.

GADÓ, O. (1969) 'The new system of trade in production goods', in *Reform* . . ., I. Friss (ed.). Budapest.

GADÓ, O. (1972) (ed.) *Reform of the Economic Mechanism in Hungary, Development 1968–71*. Budapest: Akadémia.

GADÓ, O. (1985) (ed.) *Turnover Tax-System in Hungary*. Publication of the Hungarian ministry of finance, no. 24, Budapest.

GARBUZOV, V. (1965) *EG*, no. 43.

Gesetzblatt der Deutschen Demokratischen Republik, Collection of Laws of the German Democratic Republic.

GINZBURG, S. (1965) *EG*, no. 43.

GLADKII, I. I. (1986) *EG*, no. 43.

GLIŃSKI, B. (1975) (ed.) *Zarys systemu funkcjonowania przemyslowych jednostek inicjujacych*. Warsaw.

GLIŃSKI, B., KIERCZYNSKI, T. and TOPIŃSKI, A. (1975) *Zmiany w systemie zarzadzania przemyslem*. Warsaw.

GLIŃSKI, B. (1977) *System funkcjonowania gospodarki. Logika zmian*. Warsaw.

GOLAN, G. (1971) *The Czechoslovak Reform Movement, Communism in Crisis*. Cambridge: Cambridge University Press.

GOLAN, G. (1973) *Reform Rule in Czechoslovakia, The Dubček Era 1968–1969*. Cambridge: Cambridge University Press.

GOLDMAN, J. and KOUBA, K. (1967) *Hospodářský růst v ČSSR*. Prague.

GOLEBIOWSKI, J. W. (1977), in *Kraje socjalistyczne po drugej wojnie swiatowej, 1944–1974*. Warsaw.

GOLINOWSKI, K. (1974), in *Nowy system* . . ., J. Sliwa (ed.). Warsaw.

GOLINOWSKI, K. (1977) *GP*, no. 9.

GOLINOWSKI, K. (1982) *GP*, no. 9.

GOMULKA, S. and ROSTOWSKI, J. (1983) 'The reformed Polish economic system 1982–1983', *Soviet Studies*, no. 3, July.

GORBACHEV, M. S. (1986a) Speech on the XXVII Congress of the Party, February 1986, *EG*, no. 10.

GORBACHEV, M. S. (1986b) *EG*, no. 33.

GORBACHEV, M. S. (1987) *EG*, no. 27.

Government economic guidelines for 1969 (1968) *HN*, no. 32.

GROSSMAN, G. (1977) 'Price control, incentives and innovation in the Soviet economy', in *The Socialist Price Mechanism*, A. Abouchar (ed.). Durham: Duke University Press.

GRÜNWALD, R. (1984) *FaU*, no. 1.

GUSAROV, S. A. (1973), in *Teoretické základy a praxe hospodářské reformy v SSSR*, trans. Russian. Prague.

GVISHIANI, D. M. (1986) *EG*, no. 18.

GYURÁK, K. (1984) *F*, no. 32.

HÁJEK, K. (1985) *FaU*, no. 4.

HÁJEK, V. (1985) *Práce a mzda*, no. 3.

HALUŠKA, I. (1987) *HN*, no. 16.

HANSON, P. (1983) 'Success indicators revisited: the July 1979 Soviet Decree on planning and management', *Soviet Studies*, no. 1.

HANSON, P. (1986) 'The shape of Gorbachev's economic reform', *Soviet Economy*, no. 4.

HARE, P. G. (1976) 'Industrial Prices in Hungary', Part II, *Soviet Studies*, July.

HARSÁNYI, E. and SZŐCS, Gy. (1987) *F*, no. 49.

HAUS, B. (1983) *Evolucja struktur organizacyjnych przemyslu.* Warsaw.

HAVASI, F. (1984) *TSz*, no. 5.

HAVASI, F. (1985) *Gazdaságpolitika – gazdaságirányitás* (selected speeches and articles) Budapest.

HAZARD, J. N. (1967) 'The politics of Soviet economic reform', in *Planning and the Market in the USSR: The 1960s*, A. Balinky, (ed.). New Jersey: Rutgers University Press.

HEJKAL, J. (1965) *PE*, no. 4.

HENSEL, D. and KUCIAK, G. (1984) *WW*, no. 3.

HETÉNYI, I. (1969) 'National economic planning in the new system of economic control and management', in *Reform...*, I. Friss (ed.). Budapest.

HEWETT, E. A. (1987) 'General Overview of the Reform', *Soviet Economy*, January–March.

Historická statistická ročenka ČSSR (1985) Prague.

HLAVATÝ, E. (1985) *Ekonomický časopis*, no. 9.

HÖHMANN, H. H. (1985) *Osteuropa Zeitschrift für Gegenwartsfragen des Osten*, no. 1.

HÖHMANN, H. H. (1983), in *Sowjetunion 1984/3*. Cologne: Hanser.

HOLUBICKI, B. (1977a) *GP*, no. 6.

HOLUBICKI, B. (1977b) *GP*, no. 9.

HORÁLEK, M. (1966) 'Problems of the wage system in Czechoslovakia', *Czechoslovak Economic Papers*, no. 7.

HORÁLEK, M., SOKOL, M., KOŽUŠNÍK, C. and TUREK, O. (1968) *SHN*, no. 14.

HORVÁTH, L. (1980), in *Gazdasági szabályozók*, L. Horváth (ed.). Budapest.

HŮLA, V. (1976) *HN*, no. 17.

IGNATUSHKIN, V. P. and FILATOV, V. T. (1984) *Finansy SSSR*, no. 8.

Istoriia sotsialisticheskoi ekonomiki SSSR (1976–80), collective work vols 1–7, Moscow.

JAKUBOWICZ, S. (1973) *GP*, no. 8.

JAKUBOWICZ, S. (1975) in *Zarys...*, B. Glinski (ed.). Warsaw.

JĘDRYCHOWSKI, S. (1973) *Finanse*, no. 4.

JĘDRYCHOWSKI, S. (1982) *Zadluzenie Polski w krajach kapitalistycznych.* Warsaw.

JĘDRYCHOWSKI, S. (1984) *Finanse*, nos. 7–8.

JEZDÍK, V. (1987) *PH*, no. 3.

JIRAVA, M. (1984) *HN*, no. 11.

JÓZEFIAK, C. (1986) 'The Polish reform: an attempted evaluation', Research Report no. 116, Vienna Institute for Comparative Economic Studies.

JUCHNOWICZ, M. (1985) *Ekonomika i Organizacja Pracy*, no. 12.

KABAJ, M. (1977), in *Ekonomika pracy*, A. Sajkiewicz (ed.). Warsaw.
KABAJ, M. (1984) *Ekonomika i Organizacja Pracy*, nos. 4 and 5.
KADLEC, V., KOUBA, K. and KOUDELKA, M. (1969) Panel discussion, *Nová mysl*, no. 7.
KALINOWSKI, W. and KARPIŃSKI, P. (1984) *GP*, no. 3.
KAPUSTIN, E. I. (ed. in chief) (1984) *Ekonomicheskoi stroi sotsialisma*, vol. 3. Moscow.
KARDOS, I. (1984) *F*, no. 46.
KARPIŃSKI, A. (1985) *ZG*, no. 1.
KATZ, A. (1974) *The Politics of Economic Reform in the Soviet Union*, 2nd printing. New York: Praeger.
Khoziaistvennaia reforma v SSSR (1969). Moscow: Pravda.
KIERCZYŃSKI, T. (1984) *GP*, no. 9.
KIERCZYŃSKI, T. (1985) *Finanse*, no. 2.
KISIEL, H. (1984) *Finanse*, nos. 7–8.
KLETSKII, V. and RISINA, G. (1970) *PKh*, no. 8.
KOCANDA, R. (1967) *PH*, no. 10.
KODET, Z. (1966) *PE*, no. 4.
KOLARIK, I. (1984), in *Gazdaság . . .*, M. Pulai and F. Vissi (eds). Budapest.
KOLDOMASOV, Ju. (1965) *VE*, no. 11.
KÓNYA, I. (1971) 'Further improvement of the system of the enterprise income and wage regulation', *Acta Oeconomica*, no. 1.
KORNAI, J. (1983) *Contradictions and Dilemmas, Studies on the Socialist Economy and Society*. Budapest: Akadémia.
KORNAI, J. (1986) 'The Hungarian reform process: visions, hopes and reality', *Journal of Economic Literature*, December.
KORSAK, R. (1978), in *Studia . . .*, U. Wojciechowska (ed.). Warsaw.
KOSTA, J. (1973) 'The Main Features of the Czechoslovak Economic Reform', in *The Czechoslovak Reform Movement 1968*, V. V. Kusin (ed.). Santa Barbara; Oxford.
KOSTA, J. (1984) *Wirtschaftssysteme des realen Sozialismus*. Cologne: Bund Verlag.
KOSYGIN, A. N. (1966) 'On Improving Industrial Management, Perfecting Planning and Enhancing Incentives in Industrial Production', in *Reform of Soviet Economic Management*, M. E. Sharpe (ed.). New York.
KOUBA, K. (1968), in *Úvahy o socialistické ekonomice*, K. Kouba et al., (eds). Prague.
KOUBA, K. (1969) *Nová mysl*, no. 3.
KOUDELKA, M., LIBNAR, D. and HAVEL, M. (1968) *SHN*, no. 47.
KOVALEV, A. (1986) *ST*, no. 1.
KŐVÁRI, Gy. (1981), in *Munkagazdaságtan*, J. Timár (ed.). Budapest.
KOWALIK, T. (1986) 'On crucial reform of real socialism', *Forschungsberichte* no. 122, The Vienna Institute for Comparative Economic Studies, Vienna.
KOZÁR, A. (1986) *HN*, no. 5.
KOZIŃSKI, W. (1984) *BK*, nos. 10–11.
KOZIOLEK, H. (1985) *WW*, no. 9.
KOZMA, J. (1987) *Nsz*, 12 March.

KRAUS, O. (1968) *PH*, no. 2.
KRÖMKE, C. (1980) *Einheit*, no. 6.
KROTOV, Ju. (1970) *PKh*, no. 7.
KRYLOV, R., ROTHSTEIN, L. and TSAREV, D. (1966) *PKh*, no. 4.
KUBICZEK, F. and BAZGIER, J. (1975), in *Spoleczno – gospodarczy rozwój Polski w latach 1971–1975*, F. Kubiczek (ed.). Warsaw.
KUBICZEK, F. (1986) Press conference, *Rzeczpospolita*, 5–6 April.
KUDEŘIKOVÁ, H. (1985) *HN*, no. 28.
KUDRNA, A. (1967) *Práce a mzda*, no. 10.
KUDRNA, A. (1968) *Práce a mzda*, no. 10.
KULICH, M., MARKVART, V. (1965) *PH*, nos. 7–8.
KŮRKA, V. (1981) *Investični výstavba*, no. 2.
KŮRKA, V. (1983) *Investični výstavba*, no. 6.
KUSHNIRSKY, F. I. (1982) *Soviet Economic Planning, 1965–1980*. Boulder: Westview.
KUSIN, V. V. (1982) 'Husak's Czechoslovakia and economic stagnation', *Problems of Communism*, May–June.
KUTÁLEK, Z. (1966) *PH*, no. 8–9.
KÝN, O. (1975) 'Czechoslovakia', in *The New Economic Systems of Eastern Europe*, H. H. Höhmann, M. Kaser and K. C. Thalheim (eds). Berkeley: University of California Press.
LAKI, M. (1983) *Vállalatok megszünése és összevonása*. Budapest.
LAPTEV, V. V. (1973) *Sovetskoe gosudarstvo i pravo*, no. 8.
LÁZÁR, Gy. (1982) *KSz*, no. 12.
LEDWOROWSKI, D. (1986), in *Procesy* . . ., Warsaw.
LÉR, L. (1980) *HN*, no. 11.
LEVCIK, F. (1981) *Europaische Rundschau*, no. 2.
LEWANDOWSKI, J., SIWINSKI, W. (1978) (eds) *Wzrost a funkcjonowanie gospodarki socjalistycznej*. Warsaw.
LIBERMAN, E. (1962) *Pravda*, September 2.
LIBERMAN, E. (1965) *EG*, no. 5.
LIPIŃSKI, J. and WOJCIECHOWSKA, U. (1975) *GP*, no. 3.
LIPOWSKI, A. (1975), in *Zarys* . . ., B. Glinski (ed.). Warsaw.
Magyar Közlöny, Collection of Laws of Hungary.
MARER, P. (1986) 'Economic reform in Hungary: from central planning to regulated market', in *East European Economies: Slow Growth in the 1980s*, US Congress, vol. 3, Washington.
MARGULIS, Ju. (1976) *Finansy SSSR*, no. 3.
MARZEC, J. (1974), in *Nowy system* . . ., J. Sliwa (ed.). Warsaw.
MATĚJKA, M., MATOUŠ, J. and VRBA, J. (1986) *HN*, no. 28.
MATITS, A. and TEMESE, J. (1986) *Tervgazdasági Fórum*, no. 4.
MATULIAVICHUS, A. (1984) *Pkh*, no. 10.
MELLER, J. (1977) *Place a planowanie gospodarcze w Polsce 1950–1975*. Warsaw.
MIESZCZANKOWSKI, M. (1984) *ZG*, no. 29.
MIESZCZANKOWSKI, M. (1985) *ZG*, no. 38.
MITTAG, G. (1984) *WW*, no. 1.
MITTAG, G. (1986) *Einheit*, no. 10.
MLÝNÁŘ, Z. (1983) *Krize v sovětských systémech 1953–1981*. Cologne.

MORAVEC, E. (1967) *Práce a mzda*, no. 6.
MORAVEC, E. and HOFFMAN, J. (1985) *Práce a mzda*, nos. 12–13.
MORVA, T. (1969) 'Interrelations between national and enterprise planning' in *Reform* . . ., I. Friss (ed.). Budapest.
MOSKALENKO, V. (1971) *PKh*, no. 8.
MOSÓCZY, R. (1979) *A KGST-országok gazdaságpolitikája 1976–80*. Budapest.
Műszaki Élet, Hungarian monthly.
NAGY, S. (1987) *F*, no. 2.
NASILOWSKI, M. (1985) *ZG*, no. 20.
NICK, H. (1986) *WW*, no. 9.
NOVE, A. (1982) *An Economic History of the USSR*. Harmondsworth: Penguin Books.
NOVE, A. (1983) *The Economics of Feasible Socialism*. London: Allen & Unwin.
NOVIKOV, K. (1969) *Kommunist*, September.
NYERS, R. (1966), in *A gazdasági mechanizmus reformja*. Budapest.
NYERS, R. and TARDOS, M. (1978) 'Enterprises in Hungary Before and After the Economic Reform', *Acta Oeconomica*, nos. 1–2.
PAJESTKA, J. (1973) *ZG*, no. 27.
PAJESTKA, J. (1975), in *Zarys* . . ., B. Glinski (ed.). Warsaw.
PAJESTKA, J. (1985) *ZG*, no. 37.
PANCER, A. (1984) *Praca i Zabezpieczenie Spoleczne*, nos 8–9.
PÉCSI, K. (1984), in *Az európai KGST-országok gazdasága*, collective work, Budapest.
PENC, J. (1983) *Praca i Zabezpeiczenie Spoleczne*, no. 3.
PETŐ, M. (1986) *TSz*, nos. 8–9.
PICK, M., (1982) *Práce a mzda*, no. 10.
PLEVA, J. (1966) *PH*, no. 6.
PODSHIVALENKO, P. D. (1969), in *Khoziaistvennaia reforma*. Moscow.
POHL, O. (1966) *F*, no. 8.
Polityka, Polish weekly.
PONGRÁCZ, L. (1984), in *Gazdaság* . . ., M. Pulai and F. Vissi (eds). Budapest.
PONGRÁCZ, L. (1986) *Munkaügyi Szemle*, no. 12.
PORTES, R. D. (1970) 'Economic reforms in Hungary', *American Economic Review*, May.
PORTES, R. D. (1972) 'The Strategy and Tactics of Economic Decentralization', *Soviet Studies*, vol. 23.
PORWIT, K. (1978), in *Kompleksowe programy rozwoju w krajach RWPG*, R. N. Jevstignieva (ed.). trans: Russian, Warsaw.
Práce a mzda, Czechoslovak journal.
'Procesy realne i problemy systemowe handlu zagranicznego Polski', 1982–1986 (1986), in *Studia i Materialy, Polska Akademia Nauk*, Warsaw.
PULAI, G. (1987) *Munkaügyi Szemle*, no. 11.
PULAI, M. and VISSI, F. (1984) (eds) *Gazdaságirányitás 1985*. Budapest.
PYSZ, P. (1983) *Österreichische Osthefte*, no. 3.
RÁCZ, A. (1984a) *F*, no. 27.
RÁCZ, A. (1984b) *Munkaügyi Szemle*, no. 9.

RADNÓTZI, J. (1986) *F*, no. 50.
RAKOTI, V. (1984a) *Finansy SSSR*, no. 6.
RAKOTI, V. (1984b) *PKh*, no. 5.
ŘECHTÁČKOVÁ, O. (1985) *PH*, no. 1.
Reforma Gospodarcza (1983) Collection of Acts and Instructions about their Implementation, Warsaw.
REH, M. (1968) *FaU*, no. 6.
REMEŠ, A., ŠAFÁŘ, J., KLEIBL, J. and KOPP, K. (1985) *Základy ekonomiky socialistického průmyslu a průmyslových podniků*. Prague.
Report of the Consultative Economic Council (1984) *ZG*, no. 45.
Report of the Consultative Economic Council for 1981–85 (1986) *ZG*, nos. 14 and 15.
Report of the Consultative Economic Council for 1986 (1987) *ZG*, nos. 7 and 8.
RÉVÉSZ, G. (1986) *KSz*, July–August.
Rok šedesátý osmý (1969), Prague.
ROST, H. (1984), *Die Wirtschaft*, no. 4.
ROTSTEIN, L. (1985) *EG*, no. 41.
Rudé právo, Czechoslovak daily paper.
RUDOLPH, F. (1986) *WW*, no. 7.
RUMER, B. (1985), in *Sowjetunion 1984/5*. Cologne: Hanser.
RUMIANTSEV, A. and FILIPPOV, V. (1969), in *Khoziaistvennaia reforma v SSSR*, Moscow.
RYDKO-SILIVANOV, V. V. (1984) *Dengi i kredit*, no. 4.
RYZHKOV, N. (1987) Pravda, 30 June.
Rzeczpospolita, Polish daily paper.
RZHESHEVSKII, V. (1971) *PKh*, no. 9.
RZHESHEVSKII, V. (1973) *PKh*, no. 3.
RZHESHEVSKII, V. (1984) *ST*, no. 5.
SABOLČÍK, M. (1984) *PH*, no. 4.
SADOWNIK, H. (1984), in *Reforma po Starcie*, H. Krol (ed.). Warsaw.
ŠAFAŘÍKOVÁ, V. and NOVÁK, S. (1983) *HN*, no. 33.
ŠAFAŘÍKOVÁ, V. (1984) *FaU*, no. 4.
SÁRKÖZY, T. (1985) *Egy gazdasági szervezeti reform* (manuscript).
Sbírka zákonů, Collection of Laws of the CSSR.
SCHROEDER, G. (1968) 'Soviet economic reforms: a study in contradictions', *Soviet Studies*, July.
SCHROEDER, G. (1969) 'The 1966–67 Soviet industrial price reform: A study in complications', *Soviet Studies*, no. 4.
SCHROEDER, G. (1971) 'Soviet Economic Reform at an Impasse', *Problem of Communism*, July–August.
SCHROEDER, G. (1982) 'Soviet economic "Reform" decrees: more steps on the trademill', in *Soviet Economy in the 1980s: Problems and Prospects*, Part I, US Congress, Washington.
SCHWEITZER, I. (1982) *A vállalat-nagyság*. Budapest.
SEBESTYÉN, J. (1985) *F*, no. 45.
ŠEDIVÝ, Z. (1968) *HN*, no. 46.
SELUCKÝ, R. (1970) *Czechoslovakia: The Plan that Failed*, London: T. Nelson.

SEROV, V. and BORODIN, V. (1986) *EG*, no. 34.
SHARPE, M. E. (1966) (ed.) *Reform of Soviet Economic Management*, White Plains, New York: International Arts and Science Press.
SHKURKO, S. (1975) *ST*, no. 1.
SHOR, A. I. (1973), in *Teoretické základy a praxe hospodářské reformy v SSSR*, trans. Russian. Prague.
SIBIREV, A. I. (1984), in *Problemi sovershenstvovaniia sotsialisticheskovo khoziaistvennovo mekhanizma*. Leningrad.
SIELUNIN, W. (1971) *Reforma gospodarcza w ZSSR*, trans. Russian. Warsaw.
ŠIK, O. (1964) *Nová mysl*, no. 10.
ŠIK, O. (1966) *Rudé právo*, 18, 22 and 23 February.
ŠIK, O. (1967) *Nová mysl*, no. 8.
ŠIMON, B. and ŘÍHA, L. (1968) *Život strany*, no. 10.
SITARIAN, S. (1987) *Pravda*, 28 December.
SLIWA, J. (1974) (ed.) *Nowy system ekonomiczno-finansowy w organizacjach przemyslowych*. Warsaw.
SOBOTA, J. (1985) *ZG*, no. 30.
SOJÁK, Z. (1987) *HN*, no. 13.
SOKOL, M. (1965) *Nová mysl*, no. 2.
SOKOL, M. (1966) *PH*, nos. 8–9.
SOKOL, M. (1968) *PH*, no. 2.
ŠOUREK, S. (1981) *PH*, no. 4.
ŠOUREK, S. (1983) *HN*, no. 6.
ŠOUREK, S. (1985) *HN*, no. 50.
STANIEK, A. (1984) *BK*, no. 8.
STAŘECKÝ, V. (1982) *Práce a mzda*, no. 8.
Statistické přehledy, Czechoslovak statistical monthly.
STOLAREK, B. (1978), in *Studia . . .*, U. Wojciechowska (ed.). Warsaw.
SUBOCKII, Ju. V. and SIGINEVICH, A. E. (1985), in *Rol khoziaistvennovo mekhanizma v soverschenstovovanii ekonomiki razvitovo sotsialisma*, V. M. Ivanchenko (ed.). Moscow.
SUCHAREVSKII, B. M. (1975), in *Trud i zarabotnaia plata v SSSR*. Moscow.
SULYOK, B. (1969) 'Major financial regulators in the new system of economic control and management', in *Reform . . .*, I. Friss (ed.). Budapest.
Summary on the debate on foreign trade (1967) *PH*, no. 3.
ŠUPKA, L. and SRBA, J. (1968) *HN*, no. 47.
SVOBODA, F. and KUBELKA, V. (1965) *PH*, nos. 7–8.
SVOBODA, J. (1986) *HN*, no. 5.
SZABÓ, K. (1987) (ed.) *Vagyonérdekeltség – reform*. Budapest.
SZALAI, E. (1982) 'The new stage of the reform process in Hungary and the large enterprises', *Acta Oeconomica*, nos. 1–2.
SZAMUELY, L. (1984) 'The second wave of the economic mechanism debate and the 1968 reform in Hungary', *Acta Oeconomica*, nos. 1–2.
SZCZEPANSKI, J. (1984) *Finanse*, no. 9.
SZCZEPANSKI, J. (1985) *Finanse*, nos. 2 and 4.
SZIKSZAY, B. (1985) *TSz*, no. 1.

SZTYBER, W. B. (1978) *System cen w gospodarcze socjalistycznej*. Warsaw.
SZYDLAK, J. (1972) *GP*, no. 8.
TARDOS, K. (1986) *PSz*, no. 6.
TARDOS, M. (1982) 'Development program for economic control and organization in Hungary', *Acta Oeconomica*, nos. 3–4.
TARDOS, M. (1986) 'The Conditions of developing a regulated market', *Acta Oeconomica*, nos. 1–2.
TARDOS, M. (1987) 'The Role of Money in Hungary', *European Economic Revue*, vol. 31.
TESÁŘ, J. (1965) *PH*, nos. 7–8.
TESÁŘ, J. (1966) *PH*, nos. 8–9.
TESÁŘ, J. and PETERA, B. (1968) *PH*, no. 2.
TIMÁR, J. (1987) *TSz*, no. 11.
TIMÁR, M. (1973) *Gazdaságpolitika Magyarországon 1967–1973*. Budapest.
TIMÁR, M. (1986) *F*, nos. 51–2.
TOMÁŠEK, P. (1967) *Odměňování v nových podmínkách řízení*. Prague.
TOPIŃSKI, A. (1975), in *Zarys* . . ., B. Glinski (ed.). Warsaw.
TROJAN, J. and VACOVSKÝ, V. (1969) *Nová mysl*, no. 2.
'Turning Point and Reform' (*Fordulat és reform*) (1987), Collective works. (Budapest). In a modified version published in *KSz*, no. 6.
TYMIŃSKI, A. (1977) 'Change in the Price System for Producer Goods in Poland 1971–76', *Soviet Studies*, July.
TYPOLT, J. and NOVÁK, O. (1966) *PH*, no. 2.
TYPOLT, J. (1968) *PH*, no. 2.
UJHÁZI, K. (1982) *PH*, no. 8.
URBAN, L. and LÉR, O. (1982) *PE*, no. 11.
URBAN L. and LÉR, O. (1986) *HN*, no. 7.
URBAN, L. (1987) *PE*, no. 6.
VALEŠ, V. (1968) *HN*, no. 44.
VANČIK, M. (1985) *PH*, no. 4.
VARGA, G. (1987) *F*, no. 44.
VARGA, I. (1957) *KSz*, nos. 10 and 12.
VAŠÁK, D. (1986) *PH*, no. 4.
VERGNER, Z. (1957) *PH*, no. 3.
VĚRTELÁŘ, V. (1986) *PH*, no. 1.
VESELKOV, F. and MYMRINA, L. (1971) *VE*, no. 2.
VINTROVÁ, R. (1984), in *Reprodukční proces v ČSSR v 80. letech*, R. Vintrová, (ed.). Prague.
Vita a népgazdasági tervezés feladatairól az 1980as évek Magyarországán (1984) Budapest.
VOLKOV, M. I. (1985) *Dengi i kredit*, no. 4.
WALTER, S. (1974), in *Nowy system* . . ., J. Sliwa (ed.). Warsaw.
Warunki Dzialania Przedsiebiorstva (1984) Collective work. Warsaw.
WASS VON CZEGE, A. (1985) *Berichte des Bundesinstituts für Ostwissenschaftliche und Internationale Studien*, no. 10, Cologne.
WIESEL, J. (1974) *Gazdaság*, no. 2.
WILCSEK, J. (1969) 'The place and functions of state-owned enterprises in the new system of economic control and management', in *Reform* . . ., I. Friss (ed.). Budapest.

Wochenbericht, Research reports of the German Economic Institute in Berlin.

WOJCIECHOWSKA, U. (1978) (ed.) *Studia nad systemem wielkich organizacji gospodarczych 1973–1975*. Warsaw.

WOJCIECHOWSKA, U. (1978), in *Studia* . . .., U. Wojciechowska (ed.). Warsaw.

WOJCIECHOWSKA, U. (1984) Paper on the Polish reform presented at a conference in Frankfurt.

WOJCIECHOWSKI, B. (1986) in *Procesy* . . . Warsaw.

WOJCIECHOWSKI, H. (1986), in *Organizacja i technika handlu zagranicznego*, K. Bialecki, Z. Kaminski and H. Wojciechowski (eds). Warsaw.

ZAKHAROV, V. S. (1986) *Dengi i kredit*, no. 1.

ZALESKI, E. (1966) *Planning Reforms in the Soviet Union 1962–1966*. Chapell Hill.

ZAWISLAK, A. (1973) *GP*, no. 8.

ZDYB, Z. (1985) *Finanse*, no. 3.

ZDYB, Z. (1986) *Finanse*, nos. 7–8.

ŽIDLICKÝ, M. (1967) *FU*, no. 1.

ZIELINSKI, J. G. (1973) *Economic Reforms in Polish Industry*. Oxford.

ZIELINSKI, J. G. (1978) 'On system remodelling in Poland: a pragmatic approach', *Soviet Studies*, January.

Život strany, Czechoslovak weekly.

Index

Please note that some common items are not indexed at all (e.g. USSR, Poland, Czechoslovakia, Hungary), and some selectively (e.g. economic reform, prices, economic efficiency, economic growth); 'd' stands for 'definition'.